The Core of Christian Faith

American University Studies

Series VII
Theology and Religion

Vol. 38

PETER LANG
New York · Bern · Frankfurt am Main · Paris

William Madges

The Core
of Christian Faith

D. F. Strauss and His
Catholic Critics

PETER LANG
New York · Bern · Frankfurt am Main · Paris

Library of Congress Cataloging-in-Publication Data

Madges, William
    The core of Christian faith : D. F. Strauss and his Catholic
critics / William Madges.
    p. cm.—(American university studies. Series VII, Theology
and religion ; vol. 38)
    Bibliography: p.
    Includes index.
    ISBN 0-8204-0521-3
    1. Jesus Christ—Historicity—History of doctrines—19th century.
2. Strauss, David Friedrich, 1808-1874. Leben Jesu.   3. Jesus
Christ—Biography.   4. Bible. N.T. Gospels—Criticism,
interpretation, etc.—History—19th century.   5. Catholic Church—
Germany—Doctrines—History—19th century.   6. Jesus Christ
—History of doctrines—19th century. I. Title. II. Series:
American university studies. Series VII, Theology and religion ; v.
38.
BT303.2.M35   1988
232.9'08—dc19   87-18936
ISSN 0740-0446   CIP

CIP-Kurztitelaufnahme der Deutschen Bibliothek

Madges, William:
The core of Christian faith : D.F. Strauss and his
cath. critics / William Madges. – New York; Bern;
Frankfurt am Main; Paris: Lang 1987.
    (American University Studies: Ser. 7,
    Theology and Religion; Vol. 38)
    ISBN 0-8204-0521-3

NE: American University Studies / 07

Printed by Weihert-Druck GmbH, Darmstadt, West Germany

FOR

Marsha, Mary, and Anna,
dear companions in life

CONTENTS

PREFACE

Several people have contributed in a special way to the creation of this book. I wish to express my thanks to all of them.

The cogent criticism of Brian Gerrish, Langdon Gilkey, and David Tracy helped greatly to improve this manuscript. I also wish to acknowledge Douglas McGaughey and Patrick J. Nugent, Jr., who read all or part of the text. Their careful evaluation of it and the warmth of their friendship greatly assisted the completion of this project.

Kenneth R. Overberg, S. J., by releasing me from some of my teaching responsibilities, gave me needed time to work on the book. He also assisted the project through his unfailing personal encouragement. Robert J. Murray provided additional institutional support. To them and to the Garry Faculty Development Fund, which aided the publication of this book, I extend my sincere thanks.

Finally mention must be made of those to whom I dedicate this book: my wife Marsha, my mother Mary, and my aunt Anna. Their unceasing support and love have sustained me in my work. I am profoundly grateful for the ways in which they have enriched my life.

INTRODUCTION

The publication of D. F. Strauss's Life of Jesus in 1835 simultaneously made Strauss a theological celebrity and ushered in a period of intense historical research into the life of Jesus of Nazareth. The extensive Protestant reaction to Strauss's book has been noted and studied. Little attention, however, has been paid to the response Strauss's work evoked from his Roman Catholic contemporaries. The literature that does make mention of the Catholic response tends either to treat the topic superficially or to misrepresent the Catholic reaction.[1] Even Albert Schweitzer's The Quest of the Historical Jesus (1910), which provides the most adequate general statement on the Catholic reaction, is sorely inadequate. Except for a brief, appreciative comment concerning Kuhn's Life of Jesus, it too is devoid of any critical exposition of the Roman Catholic responses. Schweitzer admits that Strauss's work "caused a great sensation" in Catholic theology, but he fails to sketch the contours of that reaction in general or to analyze the individual replies in particular.[2]

One of the fundamental aims of the present work, therefore, is to provide a careful exposition of the "great sensation" Strauss's Life of Jesus caused among his Catholic contemporaries. This study focuses on the four major books written in the 1830s and 1840s as Catholic responses to Strauss. It also includes a sketch of the various journal articles published by Catholic respondents during this time. The premise of this exposition is that the ultimate motivation and significance of both Strauss's Life of Jesus and the major Catholic responses is theological rather than historical. More specifically, the respective gospel interpretations of Strauss and his critics are shaped by and reflective of their particular construals of Christian faith.

For this reason, the debate between Strauss and his Catholic critics has a value that transcends its historical context. Contemporary readers of their exchange can learn in an exemplary way of the serious pitfalls that result if the historical person of Jesus is considered either inconsequential or absolutely essential for the core of Christian faith. In the former case, exemplified by Strauss, Christian faith risks losing both its historical grounding and its distinctiveness vis-à-vis other religions. In the latter case, exemplified by Strauss's Catholic critics, Christian faith tends to fal-

sify historical judgments about the Bible and risks losing its decisive existential character. The final chapter of this book highlights the attempt of
some contemporary Catholics and Protestants to overcome the impasse of
the original Strauss-Catholic debate. The theological urgency of such an
endeavor becomes patent after an historical exposition of Strauss's and his
Catholic critics' interpretation of the gospels and their underlying convictions about the nature of faith.

Chapter 1 describes the genesis of Strauss's The Life of Jesus
Critically Examined. The chapter intends to demonstrate 1) that historical-critical tools and Hegelian ideas were the two sources that decisively
influenced Strauss's mythological interpretation of the gospels, and 2) that
the construction of an idealized christology was the theological goal behind
that type of interpretation.

Chapter 2 analyzes the response of the important Tübingen theologian,
Johannes Evangelist von Kuhn. By examining his essays on hermeneutics
and his incomplete Life of Jesus (1838), the chapter discloses that Kuhn
recognized the confessional nature of the gospels and even admitted the
possibility of intentional distortion by the evangelists, without acceding,
however, to Strauss's formulation of contemporary faith. The chapter
suggests that, although he was not sufficiently circumspect in his historical
judgments, Kuhn offered a generally perceptive critique of The Life of
Jesus Critically Examined and pressed a valid theological objection to
Strauss's construal of faith.

Chapter 3 examines the replies of Martin Joseph Mack, the co-editor of
the Tübingen Theological Quarterly, and Maurus Hagel, a staunch critic of
rationalism. The chapter shows that both scholars concurred in rejecting
Strauss's denigration of the importance of historical knowledge about Jesus
without being able effectively to pierce the armor of Strauss's historical-
critical case.

Johann Leonhard Hug, one of the premier Catholic exegetes of the
nineteenth century, is the subject of Chapter 4. The aim here is to disclose
the tension between Hug's understanding of faith and his desire to examine Scripture critically. The exposition demonstrates that his moral and
historical construal of faith finally subverted his critical assessment of the
gospels.

Chapter 5 surveys the shorter Catholic replies to Strauss which appeared in journals such as <u>The</u> <u>Catholic</u>, the <u>Historical-political</u> <u>Newspaper</u> <u>for</u> <u>Catholic</u> <u>Germany</u>, and the <u>Candid</u> <u>Press</u> <u>Concerning</u> <u>Theology</u> <u>and</u> <u>Church</u>. These essays reveal a striking diversity of tone, ranging from strident anti-Protestantism to commendatory assessment. Although these essays establish that the journal literature added little to the theological aspect of the debate between Strauss and his Catholic critics, they nonetheless define the wide parameters in which the Catholic critiques of Strauss operated and they further describe the character of Catholic theology in the nineteenth century.

The final chapter shows how the theological debate at issue between Strauss and his contemporary critics continues today, albeit at an advanced stage and in a more nuanced form. The progress consists not merely in hermeneutical advances and refined exegesis, but also, and more importantly, in the recognition that there is a third alternative to the opposing theological viewpoints of Strauss and his nineteenth-century Catholic critics. This new alternative suggests that the "Jesus" who is essential to faith is neither the idea represented by the actual Jesus of Nazareth (Strauss's view) nor the historical Jesus himself (view of the Catholic critics), but rather the existential-historical Jesus.[3] This concluding chapter demonstrates that support for this new alternative has come from both Protestant and Catholic theologians, even though both groups retain some of the characteristic theological emphases of their nineteenth-century predecessors. To substantiate this claim, brief reference is made to the christological proposals of Hans Küng and Edward Schillebeeckx, on the one hand, and to those of Van Harvey and Schubert Ogden, on the other. The book concludes with the observation that attention to the nineteenth-century Strauss-Catholic debate serves theology today by showing that the partial validity of the rival claims made then has called for a third, alternative construal of Christian faith.

NOTES

[1]Müller is an example of the former tendency. Gotthold Müller, _Identität und Immanenz: Zur Genese der Theologie von David Friedrich Strauß_ (Zurich: EVZ-Verlag, 1968), p. 12, note 30. Ziegler and Harris are examples of the latter tendency. Ziegler misrepresents the Catholic reaction by highlighting Franz von Baader, while passing over the much more substantial and important contributions of Hug and Kuhn. Theobald Ziegler, _David Friedrich Strauß_, 2 vols. (Strassburg: K. J. Trübner, 1908), 1:207. Harris, on the other hand, leaves the impression that the Catholic responses were inspired by the pope and that Hug was in the vanguard, whereas, in fact, Kuhn and Mack had already responded independently to Strauss. Horton Harris, _David Friedrich Strauss and His Theology_ (Cambridge: Cambridge University Press, 1973), p. 71.

[2]Albert Schweitzer, _The Quest of the Historical Jesus_, trans. W. Montgomery with a Preface by F. C. Burkitt (London: A. and C. Black, 1910), p. 107. Franz Courth's book, _Das Leben Jesu von David Friedrich Strauss in der Kritik Johann Evangelist Kuhns: Ein Beitrag zur Auseinandersetzung der Katholischen Tübinger Schule mit dem Deutschen Idealismus_ (Göttingen: Vandenhoeck & Ruprecht, 1975), is valuable in that it is the only work up to the present that provides a careful study of any of the Catholic critics of Strauss.

[3]The term "existential-historical Jesus" is drawn from Schubert Ogden's _The Point of Christlogy_ (San Francisco: Harper and Row, 1982). By this term Ogden means to specify "Jesus in his meaning for us." See pp. 55-62. "Historical Jesus," by contrast, refers to the image of Jesus that can be drawn on the basis of historical criticism and retrieval. Cf. Van A. Harvey, _The Historian and the Believer_ (New York: Macmillan, 1966), pp. 265-68.

CHAPTER 1

DAVID FRIEDRICH STRAUSS'S LIFE OF JESUS

David Friedrich Strauss raised a storm of controversy when he published the first volume of The Life of Jesus Critically Examined on June 1, 1835. The appearance four months later of the second volume, which culminated in Strauss's endeavor to re-establish dogmatically that which he had destroyed critically in the preceding sections of his work, did little to still the uproar.[1] From all orthodox quarters--ministers, theologians, and lay persons alike--came a resounding "no" to Strauss's position. Theologians condemned Strauss's view as philosophically skewed and theologically unsound; lay persons cried out against the author's lack of religious feeling and the book's unabashed assault upon the traditional faith.

Although the young theologian had expected a negative response to his ideas, he appears to have been scarcely prepared for the size, swiftness, and ad hominem character of much of that reaction.[2] C. A. Eschenmayer (1770-1852) portrayed Strauss as the most recent Judas in the church, and he used Strauss's book as evidence of the existence of Satan.[3] The Evangelical Church Newspaper, one of the most influential Protestant newspapers of the day, labelled Strauss's book "a triumph of Satan and pronounced its author and all who shared his point of view to be the vile products of carnal unions between unclean spirits and whores."[4] Other people went so far as to believe that Strauss was the anti-Christ and that the world would actually end in 1836.[5]

What did in fact result from the publication of Strauss's book was not the end of the world, but the end of Strauss's academic career. Two months after the first volume of The Life of Jesus had appeared on bookstore shelves, Strauss was removed from his post as instructor at the Protestant seminary in Tübingen. He was reassigned to a lyceum in Ludwigsburg, where he was to teach classical languages. A year later he gave up his position there and moved to Stuttgart. At the age of twenty-seven, Strauss stood at the zenith of public attention. But the price he paid for his meteoric rise was considerable: Never again would he hold an academic post in theology.

The critical response to Strauss's book was prodigious. More than two score reviews were written in the years immediately following its publication. The vast number of replies is not surprising for three interrelated reasons.

First, Strauss radically called into question the historical basis of Christian faith. He took the initial step made by rationalistic criticism of the gospels to its logical conclusion. Rationalism had discarded the supernaturalistic reading of the gospels, yet retained the conviction that the gospels still reported history. Strauss insisted that this presupposition be discarded as well and that the critical inquiry finally be made "whether and to what extent at all we stand upon historical ground in the gospels."[6] Strauss's inquiry subjected the two major modes of biblical interpretation current in his day, supernaturalism and rationalism, to a scathing critique. He challenged their common presupposition that the gospels contain reports from eyewitnesses and that, therefore, real historical events lie behind all the supernatural happenings recorded in them. The result of Strauss's inquiry was a view of the gospels in which history was extensively replaced by myth. Although the application of the category of myth to the study of the Bible was not new, Strauss's consistent application of it to the entire range of the gospel narrative was.[7] The extension of the boundaries of the mythical to embrace the widest possible area struck most of Strauss's contemporaries as an attack on Christianity at its very core.

Second, Strauss's book threatened to destroy the respectability of Hegelianism. Hegel's thought had provided theoretical support both for the maintenance of Christianity as the absolute religion and for the re-establishment of monarchy as the most appropriate form of government. Strauss's Life of Jesus, which appeared to be firmly established upon Hegelian principles, explicitly raised the question whether religion and philosophy could be harmoniously reconciled on Hegelian terms, and it implicitly subverted the assumption that Hegelianism offered unambiguous support for the traditional political system.[8] Just as Strauss's attack on the popular methods of biblical interpretation roused their proponents to defend them, so too did his critique of the christological conclusions drawn by some from Hegel's speculative principles provoke a heated response.

Third, Strauss's book quickly acquired the status of a litmus test for theological orthodoxy. It heightened the struggle between the orthodox and liberal lines of thought by bringing down the wrath of the former upon not only Strauss, but all those who attempted a mediating line between the claims of orthodoxy and the claims of the modern world.[9] To demonstrate one's orthodoxy, it was advantageous to denounce Strauss. Failing that, it was desirable at least to avoid any public connection or sympathy with Strauss's position. For this reason, some of Strauss's friends asked him not to review their own books favorably because that would jeopardize their jobs. Writing a refutation of Strauss's views became one of the best ways of attaining public or ecclesial promotions after 1835.[10]

The Original Plan and the First Edition

Strauss developed the plans for his future <u>Life of Jesus</u> while he was in Berlin during the latter part of 1831 and the first few months of 1832. Strauss had gone to the university there in order to hear the master, Hegel, in person. He was crushed to learn of Hegel's death soon after he arrived in Berlin. But he stayed on in the city, filling his time by attending the lectures of Schleiermacher, Marheineke, and others and by studying the notes from Hegel's lectures. The latter stimulated Strauss's plan for the lectures he hoped to conduct upon his return to Tübingen.[11]

The lectures were conceived according to an Hegelian scheme. They were to fall into three dialectically related parts. The traditional part was to present the life of Jesus as it perdures in the traditional consciousness of the Church; the critical part was to undermine the naive conception of the gospels and partially to destroy the traditional faith; the dogmatic part was to reestablish the truth of Jesus' life in a higher fashion. Although Strauss never held the lectures, he did commit his ideas to paper.

Strauss's book of 1835 remained true to the theological intention, if not the structure of the lecture plans of 1832.[12] That intention was to force Strauss's audience to follow him in freeing themselves and their Christian faith from a stultifying fixation on the historical person of Jesus. Of his intent in 1832, Strauss said:

> I could, therefore, even at once and in detail, restore
> something dogmatically as soon as it is critically de-
> stroyed, whereby the matter would lose much of its rigor
> and its offensiveness. But I don't want that. Rather, I
> want to present the contraries in all their sharpness and
> purity. Thus there would arise at the end of this second
> part . . . indignation over the devastation of the sanctu-
> ary. Therefrom would arise the aspiration to reestablish
> that which had been destroyed. And this would be the
> transition into the third, dogmatic part.[13]

Strauss was so successful in destroying both the supernaturalist and
rationalist portrayals of Jesus' life that most of his critics forgot, or never
realized, that his intent was a positive and constructive one. Destruction of
the traditional picture of Jesus held by believers was necessary to make
possible a speculative christology that would better serve the needs of the
modern world. Strauss envisioned his critical work as the preliminary step
in the construction of a modern Christian dogmatics.[14] Moreover, he was
convinced that his speculative christology was not only more credible, but
also was as existentially and religiously satisfying as belief in the mythical
christology of orthodoxy.[15]

Strauss's christology conceived of the gospel portrait of Jesus' life as
the graphic presentation of the idea that the human spirit is united with
infinite Spirit and is, in fact, its self-expression. Strauss found intimations
of this christology in Hegel. But he went beyond the Berlin philosopher by
asking what Hegel's general speculative premises might mean in the concrete case of the historical figure of Jesus. At this point, the work of
Friedrich Schleiermacher, although not entirely adequate, was suggestive.
It forcefully made the case that only an historical investigation of the biblical texts could ground the affirmation that the perfect union of the divine
and the human had occurred in Jesus. Having obtained notes of Schleiermacher's lectures on Jesus' life, Strauss concluded that Schleiermacher had
not fully heeded his own call for an examination free from dogmatic presuppositions.[16] He thus returned to Tübingen in May, 1832 with the resolve to construct a christology that neither rejected an historical analysis

of the gospels (orthodoxy) nor floundered at the halfway mark between orthodoxy and truly consistent historical criticism (Schleiermacher).[17]

Above all else Strauss wanted to write a "scientific" life of Jesus. This meant that two principal requirements had to be satisfied. First, his work had to be guided by "a lack of prejudice and a scientific indifference toward results and consequences."[18] In other words, the biblical texts had to be examined according to the same hermeneutical principles applied to other historical documents. Strauss would allow no special pleading for the historical veracity of events recorded in the Bible simply because Christians believed the book to be inspired by God. Second, Strauss's exposition of Jesus' life had to conform to the chief tool of historical criticism, namely, the principle of the similarity of all events.[19] This principle required Strauss to doubt the miracle stories of the gospels on the premise that nature miracles and the like do not occur today.[20] Here Strauss was following the lead of Thomas Woolston (1670-1733) and Hermann Samuel Reimarus (1694-1768), who had already cast doubt upon the historical reality of the miraculous events described in Scripture.

Such a "scientific" approach to the gospels was bound to upset orthodox believers. But Strauss insisted that scientific rigor and theological work had to go hand in hand if Christian faith were to survive in the modern world. Strauss's insistence rested upon the conviction that the core of Christian faith still remains after a scientific critique of the gospels because the truth of faith is separable from the historical facts of Jesus' life. Scientific method may destroy the form in which Christian truth is believed to be present in the gospels, but it will not destroy the essential content of the gospels.[21] Hence, Strauss subjected the gospel narratives to a scathing critique, fully confident that

> Christ's supernatural birth, his miracles, his resurrection and ascension remain eternal truths regardless of how much their reality as historical facts may be doubted.[22]

To express the eternal truth of the Christian faith in an acceptable form for modern people, Strauss first had to clear the path of encumbrances. The two greatest were the current modes of biblical exegesis. The supernaturalist position was scientifically unacceptable because it presupposed the divine verbal inspiration of the Bible and, correlatively, maintained the facticity of Jesus' miracles. Strauss found the former presupposition hermeneutically invalid and the latter conviction metaphysically untenable.

> This conviction has become so very much the consciousness of the modern world that, in real life, the opinion or claim that a supernatural cause, a divine potency, has intervened somewhere in a direct way is regarded as ignorance or deceit.[23]

The rationalist position, by contrast, sought to conform to the modern worldview. It did not insist upon literal biblical inspiration or scriptural inerrancy. And it explained the presence of the miraculous in the gospels either as the fictitious and deceitful production of the authors, the innocent exaggeration of historical events characteristic of ancient heroic literature, or the result of mistaken reporting by eyewitnesses who did not clearly perceive the events they witnessed.[24] Strauss criticized this type of interpretation for beguiling educated Christians with its transformation of supernatural occurrences into natural events, without requiring them to relinquish the belief in an underlying historical core behind the demystified supernatural events.

As an alternative to the defects of the supernaturalistic and rationalistic methods, Strauss offered a consistently mythical interpretation of the gospels. This approach, Strauss argued, was superior for three reasons. First, it was the most scientific type of exegesis. The mythical interpretation required neither the <u>sacrificium</u> <u>intellectus</u> of the supernaturalists nor the forced and convoluted interpretations of the rationalists. Rather, it maintained a scientific view of the world without succumbing to an incredible interpretation of the gospel narratives.[25] Second, the mythical interpretation brought the most satisfying theological results. It sacrificed the unimportant historical reality of narrated events in order to preserve the truth of the ideas embedded in those stories.[26] For Strauss, the intellectual content of the Christian vision, not the form of its presentation, was the crucial element in Christianity. Third, the mythical interpretation provided the most appropriate understanding of the formation of the gospels.

It viewed the gospel authors neither as lifeless channels through which God's words flowed nor as frauds or fools, who either sought to deceive their audience about Jesus for their own personal gain or failed to recognize the real causes of Jesus' miracles.[27]

In using myth as a tool in biblical interpretation, Strauss was building upon the foundation Christian Gottlob Heyne (1729–1812) had laid when he applied the myth category to classical literature. Heyne's conception of myth as the characteristic form of expression in the "childhood" of the human race and his division of myths into historical and philosophical myths contributed not only to a new appreciation of the character of ancient literature, but also to the formation of a "mythical school" of biblical exegesis.[28]

Strauss sought to extend to the New Testament the gains this school had made in its interpretation of the Old Testament. Strauss perceived that most of his colleagues were hesitant to apply the concept of myth to the New Testament because they thought that myth was confined to pre-literate societies.[29] Even those few scholars who did not share this presumption, but rather permitted limited application of the myth category to the New Testament, failed to use the category clearly and consistently. On the one hand, some did not employ a pure concept of myth. Such a pure conception would dispense with the need for an historical basis to stories about supernatural events, and it would explain how the mythical story was generated. Strauss summarized his criticism of these interpreters:

> The inability purely to conceive the concept of myth in reference to the biblical story was shown, on the one hand, in the preponderant proclivity for the assumption of historical myths. This is nothing other than a lack of trust in the Spirit and in the Idea, as if these were not able to produce stories entirely on their own, but rather absolutely needed an external--even if a most accidental--inducement for it. On the other hand, [this inability was shown] in a mixing together of the historical—mythical standpoint with the natural explanation, in that . . . the individual traits of a report were treated as if it had been picked up from the mouth of eyewitnesses.[30]

On the other hand, Strauss reproved others for not applying the concept of myth in a consistent and comprehensive fashion. Although these scholars admitted that the beginning and/or the end of the gospel story of Jesus' life was mythical, they nevertheless could not surrender the historical character of the story from Jesus' baptism to his resurrection. Strauss accused these mediating theologians of arbitrarily deciding which parts of the gospels belonged to the category of history and which parts to the category of myth.[31]

Strauss sought to overcome the weaknesses of all previous forms of the mythical interpretation by applying a clearly conceived concept of myth to the entire gospel narrative. He defined the myths of the New Testament as nothing other than the "dressing up in historical form of primitive Christian ideas, fashioned in legends that are unintentionally inventive."[32] And he argued that logical consistency had to label as artificial the restriction of the locus of myth to the infancy narratives or the account of Jesus' ascension. To the rebuttal that the evangelists were dishonest if they fabricated a story simply in order to convey certain religious or philosophical ideas, Strauss replied that they were absolved from the charge of intentional deception because the production of myths and legends was "never the work of an individual." Rather, the entire early Christian community was involved in their production through the process of oral tradition. The gradual transformation of the community's ideas about its founder into apparently historical events was "neither conscious nor intentional," but it was certainly natural.[33] Once the oral process behind the gospels is acknowledged and the character of the early Christians understood, the disagreement in chronology as well as the lack of harmony in the content of the gospels is immediately comprehensible. Both are the result of the subtle and gradual process of mythicization. Thus, the mythical interpretation of the gospels is the only appropriate one; it removes "the countless difficulties" that neither the supernaturalist nor the rationalist interpretation could dislodge.[34]

Despite the cogency of Strauss's argument from the perspective of twentieth-century historical criticism, his predilection for the mythological approach to the New Testament was not simply the result of scientific, historical analysis. Strauss was _predisposed_ to find myth in the gospels. This predisposition was entailed by his conviction that all religions, by their very nature, required the use of pictorial images and myths to express their ideas.

> ...the Hebrew and Christian religions, like all others, have their mythi. And this result is confirmed, if we consider the inherent nature of religion ...If religion be defined as the perception of truth, not in the form of an idea, which is the philosophic perception, but invested with imagery; it is easy to see that the mythical element can be wanting only when religion either falls short of, or goes beyond, its peculiar province, and that in the proper religious sphere it must necessarily exist.[35]

With such a conception of religion, Strauss could defend his mythical approach against orthodox critics on the grounds that it preserved "the absolute content" of the gospels, i.e., the idea inherent in them, while shedding the pictorial form in which it was presented.

Strauss's predisposition to find myths is indicated by his failure to establish in the first edition of his work the criteria by which he intended to distinguish the mythical from the historical in the gospels. Although he sought to justify his omission, Strauss was not much disturbed by his inability to give a cogent presentation of his historical criteria prior to interpreting individual parts of the gospel narratives.[36] This was so because Strauss was not ultimately interested in giving a historical portrayal of Jesus' life. His intent, rather, was to cause the traditional conception of Christian faith to totter by undermining the historical reading of the gospels.[37] The dialectical procedure of opposing contrary interpretative methods (supernaturalistic versus rationalistic) and contrary gospel accounts (playing one evangelist off against the other) was ideally suited to this end.[38] The inability to isolate authentic historical material in the gospels resulted in excessive historical skepticism, which, in turn, disclosed the pervasive presence of myth throughout the gospels and supported Strauss's christological project.

There is little doubt that Strauss's revolutionary reading of the gospels was influenced by a number of sources. The two most decisive influences were historical criticism and an Hegelian philosophy of religion Strauss's originality consisted in his construction of a non-supernatural, non-exclusivist christology with the aid of these two tools. To disclose the precise proportion in which Strauss mixed these two components of his work, we turn to examine his relation first to F. C. Baur (1792–1860), one of the most creative proponents of historical criticism of the New Testament in the nineteenth century, and then to G. W. F. Hegel (1770–1831).

Strauss's Relation to F. C. Baur

Although Strauss and Baur are often mentioned in the same breath as the path-breakers of the historical–critical conception of the church's early history, there are divergences in their understanding and application of historical–critical method. Strauss used historical–critical method primarily to negate the historical truth of most of the gospel stories in order to clear the way for his speculative christology. Baur, on the other hand, used it primarily to construct a historically reliable picture of the evangelical history, even though he shared Strauss's speculative, and even Hegelian, interest in the history of Christianity.[39] Consequently, it is misleading to characterize (as Baur sometimes did) Strauss's historical work as negative and Baur's as positive. The work of both scholars had a corrosive effect upon the traditional view of the gospels' historical content. Nonetheless, the degree of interest each had in the history of earliest Christianity for its own sake varied.

That Baur had a formative effect upon Strauss is to be expected. He was one of Strauss's teachers at Blaubeuren during the years 1821–1825, and he continued to have academic and personal contact with Strauss in Tübingen after his transfer there in 1826.[40] Although Baur's conception of myth as "the pictorial representation of a concept or an idea" had little effect upon Strauss's understanding of Christianity in the 1820s, it later occurred to Strauss that what was true in Baur's presentation of pagan religions might also be true of Christianity.[41] By exposing Strauss to psychological and allegorical interpretations of religious phenomena, Baur prepared Strauss for reception of the mythological approach to Scripture.[42] Moreover, Strauss came away from Baur's lectures at Tübingen with the conviction--common to Baur, Schelling, and Hegel--that philosophy and theology have the same content, i.e., the Absolute in its self-disclosure in history.[43]

Despite considerable congruence in their views of God's relation to the world and of their understanding of ancient religions, tension surfaced between Strauss and Baur after the publication of The Life of Jesus Critically Examined. The major reason for this was Strauss's pique that Baur soon began to distance himself from his former student. Strauss rightly felt that this maneuver masked their propinquity on major issues. In the earliest phase of the uproar over Strauss's book, Baur was Strauss's defender.[44] But when the Evangelical Church Newspaper alleged in May, 1836 that Baur's "impudent criticism" of the pastoral epistles bore the sign of Strauss's influence, Baur felt constrained to state publicly his relation to Strauss's views. His reply to the newspaper, the "Extorted Explanation" of 1836, marked the beginning of strained relations with Strauss.[45] Baur's delineation of his divergence from Strauss is of interest to us insofar as it identifies certain salient features of Strauss's historical-critical work.

The chief difference between Baur and Strauss was the amount of unhistorical material they found in their respective analyses of the New Testament documents. Baur claimed that he sought to preserve as much as possible of what is historical, whereas Strauss aimed at destroying as much as possible. Baur, moreover, identified two deficiencies of Strauss's Life of Jesus that promoted its excess of negative judgments concerning the historical content of the gospels: the use of the mythical point of view as a monolithic tool of interpretation, and the misuse of "internal criticism" in the presentation of the gospels' history.[46] The Catholic Johannes Kuhn would lodge the same criticism against Strauss. And Strauss himself later admitted the partial validity of Baur's (and, by extension, Kuhn's) observation.

Strauss confessed to Baur in 1846 that the purpose of his Life of Jesus had been achieved when he had proven a story to be unhistorical. He saw the difference between his own and Baur's approach to the gospels to be that the latter made the determination of how an unhistorical story had been formed the main emphasis of his study, whereas Strauss attempted such a reconstruction only to strengthen his case for the story's lack of an historical basis.[47] Strauss admitted that the guiding force behind his book was dogmatic, not historical:

> ...I am no historian. With me everything has proceeded
> from a dogmatic (respectively, anti-dogmatic) interest
> and he [i.e., Baur] may rightly disapprove of that from his
> historical-critical point of view.[48]

Nonetheless, Strauss continued to believe that it was misleading for Baur to characterize his own historical criticism as positive and Strauss's as negative.[49] Strauss's Life of Jesus was indeed negative, but in a restricted sense: only insofar as it was primarily interested not in understanding why and how the gospels came to be formed, but in discovering whether what the gospels had reported was historically true.

The second area of notable divergence between Strauss and Baur was in the importance accorded to an examination of the gospel sources. Whereas Baur spent considerable energy in seeking to identify them, Strauss neglected to examine these sources.[50] Baur was right, therefore, to accuse Strauss of executing a critique of the gospel history without a critique of the gospels themselves.[51] Strauss' failure to determine how the evangelists intended to use their stories meant that he interpreted the story of Jesus' life in abstraction from its literary and theological context. That Strauss was little interested in the literary character of the gospels is revealed by the scant attention he paid to the interrelationship of the gospels and to the external testimony concerning their origin and authorship. This neglect increased the negativity of the results of Strauss's study.

Strauss and Baur also differed in their interpretation of the nature of the fourth gospel. Baur felt that Strauss's mythical theory was least applicable to John's gospel. As Baur saw it, the gospel is more properly understood as the conscious creation of its author rather than as the unintentional product of the consciousness of a Christian community.[52] As on some other points, here too Strauss reluctantly agreed that Baur's criticism was partially justified.[53]

In sum, Strauss and Baur shared an enriching, if troubled relationship. On the one hand, Strauss was justified in feeling that his former teacher had not properly acknowledged his positive contribution to the study of the New Testament. On the other, Baur was correct to point out the ways in which Strauss's dogmatic concerns sometimes subverted his use of historical-critical method. The delineation of the aims of their respective studies and the explication of the divergences in their critical results underline, however, the theological intent of Strauss's approach to the gospel presentation of Jesus' life. They also demonstrate his relative lack of interest in historical knowledge about Jesus for Christian faith. The accomplishment of The Life of Jesus Critically Examined was to employ a radical form of historical criticism of Scripture in order to construct a consistently mythical interpretation of the gospels and thereby to clear the way for a strikingly modern reformulation of the essence of Christian faith. The philosophical presuppositions that fed Strauss's project are further highlighted by Strauss's relation to the thought of Hegel.

Strauss's Relation to G. W. F. Hegel

Of all the philosophers Strauss read, Hegel had the greatest influence. This does not mean, however, that Strauss was a slavish disciple of the Berlin philosopher. In fact, many of Hegel's admirers accused Strauss of misrepresenting or misusing Hegel's views concerning the relationship between religion and philosophy, on the one hand, and between history and idea, on the other. As the ensuing presentation shall make clear, Strauss did adopt a number of Hegelian ideas, but his integration of those ideas with the tools of historical criticism led him to confront questions that Hegel did not answer and to interpret some aspects of Hegelian philosophy in a manner different from that of the Hegelian theologians of the right and of the center.[54]

The clearest convergence between Hegel's philosophy and the presuppositions of Strauss's Life of Jesus occurs at three points: the conception of God, the view of the relation of religion to philosophy, and the identification of the essential idea of religion.

Strauss shared Hegel's conception of God as the infinite spirit which manifests itself in the finite forms of the natural world and the human spirit.[55] He did not conceive of God's relation to the world in terms of a personal creator beyond and external to the universe, but in terms of the incarnational principle of an eternal reconciliation. Following Hegel, Strauss held that God's activity in history is self-diremptive and self-reconciling. God was believed to become truly self-conscious in the activity of human consciousness. Strauss thought that Hegel's central idea concerning the divine-human relationship was that "when God is expressed as spirit, it immediately follows--since the human person is also spirit--that both are not different in themselves."[56] Strauss supported this Hegelian conception. Although the "panpersonal," immanent conception of God is worked out more fully in Strauss's Christian Faith of 1840, it is already present in the 1835 Life of Jesus as one of its major implicit presuppositions.[57] Some of Strauss's critics saw a direct correlation between this non-traditional conception of God and Strauss's elevation of the human species as the subject of christological predicates.[58]

Strauss also adopted Hegel's distinction between religion and philosophy on the basis of their respective methods. Hegel believed that although both have the same content, namely, the self-diremptive and self-reconciling activity of Absolute Spirit, each expresses it in a different way. Religion uses sensible representations and images (Vorstellungen), while philosophy employs concepts (Begriffe). Although philosophy is thereby formally superior to religion, Hegel maintained that the latter is the material condition of the former. In the case of the final philosophy (Hegel's), the absolute religion (Christianity) is the presupposed requisite.[59] This was so because Christianity expressed the incarnation, the central activity in Spirit's coming to consciousness of itself in an exemplary way. Christian faith in its religious form was a deficient type of knowledge because it spoke of this truth in a pictorial--and therefore, limited--way. Hegelian philosophy, by contrast, was a higher expression of it because it spoke of the religious content in a conceptually appropriate way.[60]

Although he appears to have moved away from this Hegelian position in the 1840s, Strauss integrated it into the structure of his Lives of Jesus in the 1830s.[61] In the process of molding the "true content" of the gospels into the appropriate philosophical form, he transformed the literal content of the gospels and transvalued their meaning. Strauss undertook this transformation in order to make Christian theology fit the demands of Hegel's philosophy and to raise Christian faith to the highest form of knowledge. In defense of his predominantly negative evaluation of the apparent historical sense of the gospels, Strauss appealed to Hegel's Phenomenology of Spirit:

> Just as sense certainty . . . is the starting point for knowledge in general, believing certainty and its object, the religious tradition as dogma and sacred history, is the starting point for theological knowledge. And progress from this starting point in theology can be none other than what it is in philosophy, namely, the progress of a negative mediation, which reduces that starting point to something subordinate that is not truth on its own grounds. ...Whoever does not recognize this, whoever conducts only an affirmative mediation between the point of departure and the endpoint, whoever wants to see immediately, by a kind of intellectual intuition, the absolute truth in the gospel history as such, denies the <u>Phenomenology</u> in the realm of theology.[62]

Strauss also accepted Hegel's identification of incarnation as the essential idea of religion. Moreover, he followed Hegel in naming Christianity the absolute religion since it had rendered explicit this truth, which was only implicitly understood in other religions.[63] Strauss's appropriation of this Hegelian idea underlines not only Strauss's indebtedness to Hegel, but also the degree to which he went beyond Hegel's own written statements. For Strauss did not stop with affirming the idea of divine–human union as central to religion; he went on to assert that Jesus the Christ was not the only one to effect such a union.[64]

What led to Strauss's going beyond Hegel was his integration of Hegelian philosophical insights with a thoroughgoing historical criticism of the gospel stories about Jesus. This confluence of historical criticism and philosophical speculation is reflected in what Strauss regarded as the most important question that could be asked about the gospels: Does their historical character belong merely to the form or also to the essential content of the truth of Christian claims about the Christ? Since Strauss could not find a clear answer to this question in Hegel's writings, he turned to Hegel's disciples in theology.[65] But they too disappointed Strauss. Philip Marheineke and other theological Hegelians did not seem to understand properly Hegel's distinction between representation and concept. If they had understood it properly, then, when they applied it to the story of Jesus' life in the gospels, they would have come to the same conclusion as

Strauss: the apparently historical nature of the story was nothing more than the pictorial, and inferior, form for presenting the Christian idea. Not to pass on to the "idea," but to remain standing at the historical "facts," was to betray the principles of Hegel's philosophy of religion.[66]

Whether this allegation by Strauss against the right-wing Hegelians is correct is not easily determined. On the one hand, Hegel did affirm the crucial importance of Christianity as an historical religion and as the occasion for mediating the implicit human awareness of the truth about God.[67] He was critical of Gnostics for dehistoricizing the incarnation and evaporating the concrete actuality of the Christ into a universal thought.[68] On the other hand, Hegel was insistent that the historical elements of religions were insufficient to produce the conviction of truth. Only the inner testimony of Spirit could provide the sufficient cause of that conviction.[69] Faith, Hegel averred, is "by no means a bare assurance respecting finite things . . . as, e.g., the belief that such or such a person existed and said this or that," but rather "the subjective assurance of the Eternal, of Absolute Truth, the Truth of God."[70]

Strauss capitalized on this tension in Hegel's writings. In an effort to justify his own preference for holding to the unimportance of historical knowledge about Jesus, Strauss highlighted those texts in which Hegel either made clear distinctions between the speculative and historical realms of truth or criticized the sensuous and external as grounds of faith.[71] The result was an undialectical reading of Hegel and historical skepticism about the gospel stories. Whereas Hegel seemed to grant pictorial representation a function independent of concepts, via the elements of feeling and sensuality, Strauss viewed the former merely as the primitive precursor of the latter.[72] Once the level of concept (Begriff) had been reached, representation (Vorstellung) was no longer necessary. By identifying myth as an historical type of representation, Strauss concluded that the evangelical myth of Jesus needed to be replaced by the concept of divine-human union. Consequently, he did not relate the philosophical form of the Christian claim, i.e., the concept of divine-human union, in a dialectical way to the traditional, orthodox form of the Christian claim, i.e., the historical veracity of the gospels' presentation of Jesus as Son of God. Instead of sublating or transcending the latter, the former simply destroyed it.[73]

Strauss was aware that his conclusion would not receive the approbation of all Hegelian theologians.[74] He knew that his resolve to let the discipline of history determine whether the gospel story of Jesus' life was accurate distinguished him most clearly from the right-wing Hegelians. A philosophy of religion could do nothing more than suggest whether something like an actual incarnation of God _must_ take place; only history, Strauss argued, could decide whether Jesus was an instance of that incarnation.[75] To defend the tenability of this view, Strauss was compelled to dispel misrepresentations of it by other Hegelian theologians.

First, he had to combat the charge that his brand of historical criticism was incapable of admitting the presence of God in the events of history. Strauss responded that his position, rather than limiting the presence of God in history, granted it the fullest scope. Strauss held that "all history is considered to be divine activity." He strongly objected, therefore, to the theory "that any one part of history is distinguished as an immediate divine revelation from all the other parts as merely mediate revelations," and he rejected the idea that God attains full expression in any one finite existent.[76]

> This is indeed not the way in which Idea realizes itself—
> to lavish all its fullness on one exemplar and to be stingy
> towards all others. It rather loves to distribute its riches
> among a multiplicity of exemplars, which reciprocally
> complete each other, in the alternate appearance and dis-
> solution of a series of individuals. And that is not a true
> realization of the idea? Is not the idea of the unity of the
> divine and human nature a real one in an infinitely high-
> er sense when I grasp the whole of humanity as its real-
> ization, than when I single out a solitary human being as
> such?[77]

Second, Strauss had to refute the insinuation that he could not accept traditional christological doctrine because he mistakenly thought that it denied to the rest of humanity a share in divinity. Strauss labelled this charge an "almost deliberate misinterpretation" of his position. He replied that he did not deny that orthodox doctrine granted a share of divinity to human beings besides Jesus; what he rejected was orthodoxy's assertion that this divinization was realized perfectly in Jesus alone and only imperfectly in all other persons.[78]

Third, Strauss had to correct the claim that his mythical theory left nothing historical remaining in the gospel presentation of Jesus' life. Strauss let his Life of Jesus speak for itself on this point.[79] There the following elements were preserved as historical: Jesus' early development in Nazareth and his discipleship under John the Baptist; Jesus' initial adoption of John's preaching of repentance and the approach of God's kingdom; his gradually developing consciousness of himself as the messiah; Jesus' gathering of followers around himself; and his death on a cross.[80] Strauss's failure to weave these elements into a cohesive portrait of Jesus' life contributed to the impression that his book was more historically destructive than it actually was. If one had to err, either retaining everything in the gospels as historical or allowing it all to collapse as unhistorical, Strauss preferred the latter alternative, whereas Bruno Bauer and other critics opted for the former.[81]

Strauss, however, did not confine himself to a defensive posture. He aggressively argued for the greater philosophical adequacy of his case concerning the status of Jesus within human history. He insisted that his assessment of the significance of the historical Jesus was in accord with Hegel's statements concerning world-historical geniuses insofar as it held that some individuals—in this case, Jesus—are preeminent bearers of the divine life.[82] Preeminence, Strauss reminded his Hegelian critics, did not, however, entail exclusivity.[83] Moreover, Strauss argued that his christology was founded upon a more adequate understanding of God since it ascribed no narrow limits to the expression of the divine life in the finite world.[84] Although some areas of human life and some individuals may be more disclosive of the divine than others, no single area or individual could be viewed as the exclusive, self-sufficient embodiment of the divine life.

> Even presupposing the religious realm as, in the highest sense, that of the incarnation of God, still, the divine life imparted within a single sphere is not exhausted in one great individual but is presented in a series of them. Members in this series can be ranked in an ascending order but not so that anyone ever presents a decisive non plus ultra.[85]

The christological import of Strauss's conviction was that Jesus, in theory, could be accorded the comparatively highest rank in the hierarchy of divine embodiments up to the present point in time. It would, however, always remain uncertain whether, "even after such a long interval, someone else could still surpass him."[86] Consequently, Jesus was to be regarded in practice only as an embodiment of the divine-human unity, and that only on the basis of an historical-critical examination of his life.[87]

Did Strauss, then, write The Life of Jesus Critically Examined as a good Hegelian? In many ways, yes. Strauss adopted Hegel's Vorstellung-Begriff distinction, which, when integrated with his conception of myth, became the guiding principle of his book. Strauss also shared Hegel's dynamic conception of Spirit, whose activity is eternally self-diremptive and self-reconciling. And Strauss aspired to the Hegelian ideal of a conceptually appropriate grasp of final truth. But if we ask whether an application of these Hegelian ideas to the gospel narratives must necessarily yield the same results as Strauss's investigation, our answer is no. And this is for two reasons. First, Hegelian speculation constituted one important component in Strauss's work; the other major component, the techniques of historical criticism, Strauss had acquired elsewhere. Thus, Strauss's historical-critical investigation of the gospels went beyond the scope of Hegel's philosophy of religion.[88] Second, Strauss overemphasized the negative aspect of Hegelian Aufhebung in his interpretation of the gospel narratives, and he radically devalued the importance of real history in the life of reason. Whereas Hegel sought to maintain a firm bond between reason and history, Strauss loosened, if not dissolved, it.[89] Insofar as Strauss came to regard positive religion as dispensable, we are justified in concluding that, although Strauss shared many of Hegel's principles and although these principles did not exclude the direction Strauss took with them, his separation of Christianity's "eternal truths" from the gospel story is more the heritage of the wedge G. E. Lessing had begun to drive between event and truth in the preceding century.

Strauss's Christological Proposal

Strauss's book expressed a challenge both to the theologians of his day and to the faith of educated Christians. For the latter, Strauss formulated the challenge in terms of decision between personal, religious growth or stagnation; for the former, in terms of an argument against conceiving the essence of Christian faith as bound up with assertions about the messianic activity of the historical Jesus. For both audiences, Strauss's aim was to raise their consciousness to a recognition of their potential as embodiments of the unity of humanity and divinity. The crowning achievement of The Life of Jesus Critically Examined, then, was its offer of liberation from submission to traditional dogmatic christology and from the concomitant stagnation of one's own religious development.

Strauss intended to make this offer attractive by evaluating critically the connection between Christian truth and historical event. With the aid of the representation-concept distinction, Strauss sought to persuade his readers that the truth of Christian faith is separable from its historical origin. In fact, Strauss argued that the true core of faith (the idea of divine-human unity) was not merely separable, but indeed had to be separated from the husk of faith (the historical form in which that idea had been originally expressed) if Christianity were to perdure in the modern world. To choose "the holy history in its biblical form" meant that Christianity would languish, but to choose "the concept which is true in and for itself" meant that it would thrive. Strauss's own choice was clear: "What is essential in Christianity, for the philosophical point of view, are the idea and its eternal realization in humanity."[90]

What, then, is the significance of Jesus for Christian faith? Strauss held that the historical person Jesus provided the impulse for elevating the idea of humanity as the union of infinite and finite spirit into the general consciousness of people. He claimed that the church's myth of the historical God-man was only the sensible presentation of the philosophical truth of the union that exists between Absolute Spirit and the human species.

> This alone [i.e., the Gottmenschlichkeit of the human species] is the absolute content of christology. That the same appears bound to the person and history of an individual has only the subjective cause that this individual,

through his personality and his fate, became the occasion
of raising that content into the general consciousness and
that the intellectual level of the ancient world--and of the
people in every age--was capable of viewing the idea of
humanity only in the concrete figure of an individual.[91]

In Strauss's view, the primitive church did not consciously misrepresent
Jesus when it presented him as the unique Son of God; it singled him out
because his life made explicit for it the implicit truth of the unity of God
and all humanity. Strauss drew an analogy between the demiurge of Plato,
who formed the world "while looking upon the Ideas," and the early Christian community, which formed its picture of Jesus as the Christ while "the
idea of humanity in its relation to divinity hovered unconsciously" before
it.[92] In both cases, the _idea_ was what is important. Therefore, Western
civilization, since it had advanced far beyond the limitations of primitive
thought, no longer needed to be bound to a past historical figure. In fact,
the increase in human knowledge since the dawn of the modern period
had made the miraculous portrait of Jesus unacceptable. Insofar as the
bond of unity exists in principle between every human being and God,
Strauss believed that people no longer needed a special mediator between
them and the deity.

> Christ in himself may have been who and what he wills.
> That can be a matter of indifference to our religion be-
> cause we don't need any more a reconciler besides our-
> selves ...This, dear friend, is my way.[93]

After the publication of the first edition of his _Life of Jesus_, Strauss
retreated somewhat from its radical christology. The ecclesiastical and social ostracism that Strauss endured in response to his book, the repeated
failure to gain a professorship in theology after his dismissal from the
Tübingen seminary, and the numerous books and pamphlets written
against him caused him to waver in his views.[94] As he prepared the third
edition of his book, Strauss confessed that "the entire basis" of his thinking
was no longer the same as when he wrote the first edition.[95] In the former edition, Jesus was granted provisional importance as the fortuitous
vehicle for expressing explicitly the already intuited idea of the divinity of

the human species; in the third edition, he was given lasting significance as the decisive factor in the development of humankind's religious-spiritual life.[96]

Strauss chose the concept "genius" to describe Jesus because it allowed him to highlight Jesus' lasting significance without lapsing into orthodoxy's supernaturalistic portrayal of him.[97] Strauss, however, was not reticent in his praise of Jesus. He suggested not only that Jesus stood above the geniuses in other spheres of human activity, but also that he outstripped other religious geniuses by founding the "most perfect religion."[98] Without Jesus, who, Strauss now insisted, is "an historical individual," not "a mere symbol," religion was unthinkable.[99] Strauss even conceded Jesus' insurpassability:

> If, however, Christ endures for us and if he remains for us the highest that we can know and conceive of in reference to religion; [if he endures] as the one without whose presence in the soul no perfect piety is possible: then indeed in him there remains for us the essential matter of Christianity.[100]

When the Zurich debacle was over and Strauss had commenced work on the fourth edition of his Life of Jesus, he abandoned the concessions of the third edition and reasserted the principal claim of his 1835 christology.[101] The focus of christology is not the personality of the historical Jesus, but the idea of the "incarnation," i.e., the progressive realization of the unity of divine and human nature in all humanity. That Strauss regarded the radical christology of his 1835 Life of Jesus to be his authentic position is supported by his reaffirmation of the substance of that position in the fourth and final edition of The Life of Jesus Critically Examined, and by the directions of his will that any future editions of his work be made according to the original edition.[102] Strauss's enduring theological challenge was thereby preserved in its most pointed form, namely, the assertion that it was neither theologically necessary nor historically possible to demonstrate that Jesus of Nazareth was the Christ and that he belonged to the core of Christian faith. It was to this proposal that Strauss's Catholic contemporaries had to reply.

NOTES

[1] Contrary to the date given on the title page, the second volume was also published in 1835. See the testimony of Adolf Hausrath, _David Friedrich Strauß und die Theologie seiner Zeit_, 2 vols. (Heidelberg: F. Bassermann, 1876–78), 1:182.

[2] Ziegler, 1:178. In a letter to a close friend in 1832, Strauss indicated that he imagined that he might be expelled from the lecture hall for what he planned to say in his lectures about Jesus. Strauss to Christian Märklin, 6 February 1832, in: Jörg F. Sandberger, _David Friedrich Strauß als theologischer Hegelianer_, Studien zur Theologie und Geistesgeschichte des Neunzehnten Jahrhunderts, vol. 5 (Göttingen: Vandenhoeck & Ruprecht, 1972), p. 197. Five months later Strauss came into conflict with his Tübingen colleague J. C. F. Steudel (1799–1837) over his allegedly cavalier treatment of some supernatural events in Jesus' life. Since Strauss refused to dissimulate in class, he fully expected to be dismissed from the Protestant seminary in Tübingen. See Strauss's letter to Steudel, 3 July 1832, in: D. Traub, "Die Stiftsakten über David Friedrich Strauß, Nachtrag," _Blätter für württembergische Kirchengeschichte_, Neue Folge, 28 (1924):17.

[3] Friedrich Nippold called Eschenmayer's _Der Ischariothismus unserer Tage_ a "masterpiece of revilement, with the tone of the Old Testament prophets." _Handbuch der neuesten Kirchengeschichte seit der Restauration von 1814_, 2d revised ed. (Elberfeld: R. L. Friderichs, 1868), p. 266. See also Harris, p. 77.

[4] Richard S. Cromwell, _David Friedrich Strauss and His Place in Modern Thought_, with a Foreword by Wilhelm Pauck (Fair Lawn, N. J.: R. E. Burdick, 1974), p. 15.

[5] The numerical equivalents of the Hebrew letters forming Strauss's name added up to 666, which is the number of the beast in Rev. 13:18. Furthermore, some people pointed out that ostriches inhabit the God-forsaken wasteland described in Is. 13:21 and 34:13 and that "Strauss" is the German word for "ostrich." See Harris, p. 67.

[6] David Friedrich Strauss, _Das Leben Jesu kritisch bearbeitet_, 2 vols. (Tübingen: C. F. Osiander, 1835), 1:v. Hereafter the different editions of Strauss's _Life of Jesus_ will be identified by the date of publication given in parentheses.

[7]"The main distinction between Strauss and his predecessors consisted in the fact that they asked themselves anxiously how much of the historical life of Jesus would remain as a foundation for religion if they dared to apply the conception of myth consistently, while for him this question had no terrors." Schweitzer, p. 79.

[8]See Marilyn Chapin Massey's fascinating study Christ Unmasked: The Meaning of the Life of Jesus in German Politics (Chapel Hill: The University of North Carolina Press, 1983). Massey's thesis is that the first edition of Strauss's Life of Jesus implied a radical democratic politics similar to that espoused by Heinrich Heine and the young Karl Marx. Strauss's text had this unintentional political meaning in that it liberated its readers from submission to an exalted figure of the past and from the concomitant stagnation of their own religious development as well as raised their consciousness to a recognition of their own potential as agents of historical change. Massey's interpretation notwithstanding, it must be rememberd that Strauss was politically conservative, even aristocratic. This became especially apparent in the Robert Blum affair, which led to Strauss's resignation from Württemberg politics. Moreover, Wolf claims that Strauss's poetic affinities were with the camp opposed to Heine's. Ernst Wolf, "Die Verlegenheit der Theologie. David Friedrich Strauss und die Bibelkritik," in: Libertas Christiana: Festschrift für Friedrich Delekat, Theologische Abhandlungen, vol. 26 (Munich: Christian Kaiser, 1957), pp. 219-20.

[9]Harris, p. 70.

[10]Ferdinand Christian Baur, Kritische Untersuchungen über die kanonischen Evangelien, ihr Verhältniss zu einander, ihren Charakter und Ursprung (Tübingen: Ludw. Fues, 1847), p. 49. Strauss to F. C. Baur, 1 May 1836, Baur-Nachlass, Ms. 750, University of Tübingen Library, Tübingen, Federal Republic of Germany. This letter is cited in its entirety by Ernst Barnikol, "Der Briefwechsel zwischen Strauss und Baur," Zeitschrift für Kirchengeschichte 73, Vierte Folge 10 (1962):82-84. See also J. M. Robertson, A History of Freethought in the Nineteenth Century, 2 vols. (London: Watts & Co., 1929), 2:500.

[11]Strauss to Christian Märklin, 15 November 1831 and 6 February 1832, in Sandberger, pp. 189 and 194.

[12]The structural changes were these: the first part of the project was drastically modified; the third, constructive part became, by Strauss's own admission, a "mere appendix;" while the critical second part, swelling to 1,300 pages, became "the real body of the book." Streitschriften, 3:59.

Concerning the reasons for these changes, see Strauss to Märklin, 6 February 1832, in Sandberger, p. 197.

[13]Ibid., p. 196.

[14]Friedrich Wilhelm Graf, Kritik und Pseudo-Spekulation: David Friedrich Strauß als Dogmatiker im Kontext der positionellen Theologie seiner Zeit, Münchener Monographien zur historischen und systematischen Theologie, vol. 7 (Munich: Chr. Kaiser, 1982), especially pp. 81–105. Cf. Schweitzer, p. 70.

[15]Peter Hodgson has pointed out important support for this view in Strauss's 1832 lectures on "Logic and Metaphysics." In these lectures, Strauss confessed that for him it was "equally comforting" to conceive the unity of the divine and the human in the form of concepts as it was to imagine it in the form of an image of Jesus' ascension. See his "Vorlesungen über Logik und Metaphysik," unpublished lectures (University of Tübingen, 1832) in Schiller National-Museum, Marbach, Federal Republic of Germany, No. 6828, 15th folio, pp. 15–6; 16th folio, pp. 1–2. Cf. Hodgson, Introduction to Strauss's Life of Jesus (1972), p. xxxv.

[16]Strauss had already planned to execute a life of Jesus prior to obtaining notes from Schleiermacher's lectures on the subject. See Strauss, Streitschriften, 3:60. With Ziegler's qualification in mind and despite the fact that Strauss did not personally hear Schleiermacher's lectures on Jesus' life, Massey's claim for Schleiermacher's significant influence on Strauss's historical method can be nonetheless affirmed. See Marilyn Chapin Massey, "David Friedrich Strauss's Christological Thought: The Influence of Friedrich Schleiermacher" (Ph. D. dissertation, University of Chicago, 1973), pp. 4, 28–9, 51–4, 59, 98–9, 119, 128. Cf. Ziegler, 1:131.

[17]Concerning Schleiermacher's lectures, Strauss said: "The truth is that I found myself repelled by them at almost every point, and the careful for-mulation of my view in distinction from Schleiermacher's in many parts of the life of Jesus is, to be sure, due to this repulsion. ...In the conception of the most remarkable events in Jesus' life, such as the transfiguration, res-urrection, and things of that kind, he agreed openly or covertly with Dr. Paulus--a point of view I believed I could prove to be untenable." Strauss, Streitschriften, 3:60. Upon his departure from Berlin in 1832, Strauss said this to his friend Wilhelm Vatke, the Old Testament scholar: "Schleiermacher has powerfully stimulated me, and I owe him many thanks; but the man still has not satisfied me. He remains standing at the halfway mark; he does not say the final word. I will say that word." The

conversation is quoted by Heinrich Benecke, Wilhelm Vatke in seinem Leben und seinen Schriften (Bonn: Emil Strauss, 1883), p. 75.

[18]Strauss, Leben Jesu (1835), 1:x.

[19]Strauss, Streitschriften, 3:37.

[20]Strauss, Leben Jesu (1840), 1:81–82; Life of Jesus (1972), pp. 74–79. There is a difference between using this principle to deny the historical probability of miracles (and thus to disallow miracles as historical causes) and using it to assert the metaphysical impossibility of miracles. Strauss does the latter and, to that extent, is open to the criticism of John T. Noonan. "Hegel and Strauss: The Dialectic and the Gospel," Catholic Biblical Quarterly 12 (1950): 144–45.

[21]Strauss's scientific examination planned to cleanse Christianity's essential truth from historical claims about Jesus so that that truth, now expressed in its most appropriate form, might stand out all the more clearly and admirably. It would say what the gospels really wanted said, only better. See Müller, p. 9.

[22]Strauss, Leben Jesu (1835), 1:vii.

[23]Strauss, Leben Jesu (1840), 1:81; Life of Jesus (1972), p. 78.

[24]The first approach had become infamous with Reimarus's essays, published as the Wolfenbüttel Fragments by G. E. Lessing. But by the 1830s it had lost ground to the approach epitomized by H. E. G. Paulus (1761–1851), who maintained in his Das Leben Jesu als Grundlage einer reinen Geschichte des Urchristentums (1828), that insufficient knowledge about the laws of nature and "secondary causes" prevented eyewitnesses from perceiving the natural cause of Jesus' alleged miracles.

[25]Strauss argued that no truly historical consciousness was possible without recognition of the inviolability of the nexus of finite causes. See Leben Jesu (1837), 1:75. The supernaturalists did not possess this recognition. Moreover, Strauss rejected their conception of God's activity in the world. For Strauss, God acts upon the world as a whole in an immediate fashion, but upon the various individual parts of the world in a mediated way, i.e., through the laws of nature. Ibid., 1:86. It is important to note that Strauss introduced these clarificatory arguments as well as his statement concerning the inviolability of the causal nexus beginning only with the second edition of his Life of Jesus. Hence, as Hodgson rightly comments, the

dialectical procedure of playing the supernaturalistic and rationalistic interpretations off of each other is the true method of the first edition of Strauss's book, and not the careful application of historical criteria to the individual gospel stories. See Hodgson, Introduction, Life of Jesus (1972), p. xxv.

[26]See Strauss's statement of self-defense to the royal Board of Studies on July 12, 1835, quoted in: Carl Weizsäcker, "David Friedrich Strauß und der württembergische Kirchendienst," Jahrbücher für deutsche Theologie 20 (1875):651.

[27]Strauss acknowledged that the rationalistic exegesis of Eichhorn was an advance over the naturalistic exegesis of Reimarus because the former recognized myth production as innocent and natural in the ancient world, whereas the latter held it to be contrived and deceitful. See Leben Jesu (1835), 1:18-19. Still, both interpretations were inferior to the mythical interpretation because they stripped the biblical stories of their true, divine content. Ibid., p. 52.

[28]For a detailed exposition of Heyne's contribution and of the adoption of his ideas by Eichhorn, Gabler, and others, see Hartlich and Sachs, pp. 5, 11-32.

[29]Strauss, Leben Jesu (1835), 1:28-29.

[30]Ibid., p. 46. Historical myths were the exaggerated and distorted embellishments of a story that had an historical event at its core. Philosophical myths were stories, sometimes also in historical garb, which expressed ethical convictions or speculative explanations of nature.

[31]Ibid., pp. 49-50. The article, "Die verschiedenen Rücksichten, in welchen und für welche der Biograph Jesu arbeiten kann," which appeared in the fifth volume of Dr. Leonhard Bertholdt's Kritisches Journal der neuesten theologischen Literatur (1816):225-45, seems to have exerted considerable influence on the formation of Strauss's own opinion.

[32]Strauss, Leben Jesu (1835), 1:75. Strauss noted that his mythological approach to Scripture was quite similar to the allegorical approach, which had received long-standing approval in the church. The only essential difference between the two methods was that the latter ascribed the inspiration of the evangelists to God, whereas the former ascribed it to the spirit of the community. In both cases, however, suprahistorical truths

were believed to be buried in the historical shell of the biblical stories. Ibid., p. 52.

[33]Ibid., p. 74. Strauss admits that the actual origin of mythical narratives is "lost in darkness." But the process is understandable--in fact, antecedently probable--in view of the uneducated nature of Jesus' disciples and the sudden, tragic nature of Jesus' end. Ibid., pp. 71-72. Cf. Life of Jesus (1972), pp. 80-84.

[34]Strauss, Leben Jesu (1835), 1:37. Cf. "Die verschiedenen Rücksichten," pp. 235-36.

[35]Strauss, Life of Jesus (1972), p. 80. Although this statement comes from a later edition of his work, the idea was already operative in the first edition of The Life of Jesus Critically Examined.

[36]He explained the omission in the first edition this way: "After this justification of the following investigation's point of view, a presentation of its leading critical principles and especially of the criteria, whereby an element of the gospel history shall prove itself to be mythical, could still be expected. But since these principles and criteria could only be abstracted from the mass of individual cases of their application that has been worked through and since, irrespective of this, they do not even permit a presentation with proper clarity, it is indeed better to weave their exposition into the course of the investigation. The learned reader will discover for him/herself whether there is unity among them and consistency in their application--without a prefatory summary from the author." (Emphasis mine.) Strauss, Leben Jesu (1835), 1:75.

[37]Strauss to Märklin, 6 February 1832, in Sandberger, pp. 195-96.

[38]By showing the supernaturalistic and rationalistic interpretations to be mutually contradictory, Strauss destroyed the tenability of both. As a result, his mythical interpretation won by default. Strauss sought to rectify the methodological weakness of his work in subsequent editions. He specified his historical criteria for the first time in the second edition of his Life of Jesus. And in the third and fourth editions, he added a typology of myths and of other unhistorical material found in the gospels. See the excellent exposition of Hodgson, Introduction, Life of Jesus (1972), pp. xxv-xxix.

[39]Baur concurred substantially with Strauss's understanding of historical process. He said of Strauss's Life of Jesus: "The entire result does not

strike me as revolutionary as it will appear to you. From my point of view, everything historical can be regarded only as an impetus for the development of Spirit, as the external but necessary impulse for bringing to Spirit's consciousness the eternal truths, which lie in it. Therefore, the entire history of development always goes in the direction of tearing Spirit, by means of repeatedly new shoves, free from the external, the given, the letter, and the tradition." Baur to W. Heyd, 10 February 1836, in: Wilhelm Lang, "Ferdinand Baur und David Friedrich Strauß," Erster Teil, Preußische Jahrbücher 160:483-85; also in Adolf Rapp, "Baur und Strauß in ihrer Stellung zueinander und zum Christentum," Blätter für württembergische Kirchengeschichte 52 (1952):102-04; here p. 103.

[40]Although he did not lecture on the Bible or on the history of the church at Blaubeuren, Baur did introduce his students to psychological and mythological interpretations of the doctrines of pagan religions. See Cromwell, pp. 20-23. In his Symbolik und Mythologie, which appeared the year before Strauss's graduation from Blaubeuren, Baur presented myth as the pictorial representation of an idea.

[41]See F. C. Baur, Symbolik und Mythologie oder die Naturreligion des Altherthums, 2 parts in 3 vols. (Stuttgart: J. B. Metzler, 1824-25), 1:27-28. At the time of his graduation (1825), Strauss still believed in the literal truth of the Bible. See Strauss's Gesammelte Schriften: Nach des Verfassers letztwilligen Bestimmungen zusammengestellt, 12 vols. (Bonn: Emil Strauss, 1876-78), 1:125-26.

[42]As he was preparing the second edition of the Life of Jesus, Strauss thanked Baur for his critical comments on the first edition, and he asked Baur for suggested readings on myth, besides his Symbolics, that would benefit him. Strauss to Baur, 1 May 1836, in Lang, Erster Teil, pp. 486-87.

[43]Baur, Symbolik, 1:98-99.

[44]In his official capacity as member of the board of inspection for the Tübingen seminary, Baur defended his former pupil's academic freedom and argued against his dismissal as instructor. See Weizsäcker, pp. 644-48. Baur reiterated this view in his letter to W. Heyd of Markgröningen, 10 February 1836, in Lang, Erster Teil, p. 484. Baur noted that Strauss should not be singled out for censure; all that Strauss's Life of Jesus had done was to weave together into one fabric all the individual threads that had been previously spun by other Protestant scholars. Strauss by and large concurred in this judgment. In his self-defense before the royal board of studies, Strauss pointed out that the tendency to "idealize" the factual

character of Christianity had its origin in the eighteenth century. His blame was only that of being the first to synthesize coherently this tradition and to elucidate its natural conclusion. See Weizsäcker, pp. 648-49.

[45]Baur, "Abgenöthigte Erklärung," Tübinger Zeitschrift für Theologie (1836):179-232, reprinted in: Klaus Scholder, ed., F. C. Baur: Ausgewählte Werke in Einzelausgaben. Historisch-kritische Untersuchungen zum neuen Testament (Stuttgart: Friedrich Frommann, 1963), pp. 267-320. The exact nature of Baur's view of Strauss has been muddied by different researchers into that relationship. Wilhelm Lang has argued that Baur did not air his theological differences with Strauss in his earliest writings so as not to strengthen the attack against Strauss. Lang, Erster Teil, p. 483. Although this is true to a certain extent, one needs to heed Barnikol's caution. He warns that Lang has a decided preference for Baur, whereas Ziegler favors Strauss. Zeller, on the other hand, tends to paint a picture of harmonious unity between Baur and Strauss. Barnikol's particular criticism of Lang for often not indicating omissions in his version of the Strauss-Baur correspondence is well-founded. See Barnikol, pp. 74-76.

[46]"Internal criticism" refers to the attempt to judge the historical validity of the gospel stories according to evidence internal to those stories, e.g., the contradiction of one evangelist's report by another's portrayal of the same event, or the presence of miracles in the reported story. "External criticism" refers to the judgment concerning the gospels' historical validity on the basis of external evidence, e.g., ancient testimony concerning the authorship of the gospels, the age of the gospel texts, etc. Baur distinguished his work from Strauss's in this way: "But now I ask: Where is my criticism—even in one single place of my writing—based upon the mythical view? Where do I reject even one single historical fact, which is of importance for the critical judgment concerning these letters, simply because it is a miracle? Or where do I argue simply and solely from the inner contradiction of the content? At every point I proceed from definite historical facts that have been sifted out and seek only then upon this basis to draw together the different threads of my critical combinations into a single whole. This holding fast to the historically given is what is characteristic of my criticism. And it seemed to me timely to maintain the principle of this historical criticism not only vis-à-vis the criticism current until now ...but also vis-à-vis Strauss's (with which, in general, even that which is characteristic of the object of study permits no totally adequate comparison with mine)." Baur, "Abgenöthigte Erklärung," p. 294.

[47]Strauss to Baur, 17 November 1846, in: Wilhelm Lang, "Ferdinand Baur und David Friedrich Strauß," Zweiter Teil, Preußische Jahrbücher 161

(1915):125–26. Cf. Strauss's poem, "Negative und positive Kritik," of 1844: "(Dr. Baur spricht:) Wie Nein und Ja sind wir, wie Sturm und Regenbogen; Er sagt: est ist nicht wahr; ich sag' : es ist erlogen." "Poetisches Gedenkbuch," Gesammelte Schriften, 12:27.

[48]Strauss to Märklin, 22 July 1846, in Rapp, p. 119. The letter is also available in: Eduard Zeller, Ausgewählte Briefe von David Friedrich Strauß (Bonn: Emil Strauss, 1895), p. 183. Cf. Strauss to Baur, 17 November 1846, in which letter Strauss openly confessed that he used "history only as the means to a dogmatic, i.e., anti-dogmatic purpose." Lang, Zweiter Teil, p. 126.

[49]Baur did precisely that in his letter to Märklin, 26 November 1846: "The result of Strauss's investigation, insofar as it takes all the evangelists together and always refutes one with the other, is simply this: that all report in the same fictitious way. I, however, have sought to give the question a different turn. Now the question is no longer, what have they reported, but how have they reported, i.e., to what extent at all did they intend to report. ...In this sense I call my criticism positive in distinction from negative criticism, because it does not immediately deny historical credibility to at least one gospel, but rather grants it only relative credibility--as everything here is to be taken merely relatively. What injustice have I thereby done to Strauss?" Ibid., p. 129. Cf. Strauss to Baur, 17 November 1846, ibid., pp. 125–26.

[50]"Baur's overemphasis of 'tendency criticism' (or redaction criticism) should be viewed as a reaction to Strauss's one-sided criticism of stories apart from their literary context and traditio-historical development. The best results can be obtained from a combination of the two methods and indeed Strauss and Baur together lay the foundations of modern form criticism and redaction criticism." Hodgson, Introduction, Life of Jesus (1972), p. xxxi.

[51]Baur, Kritische Untersuchungen, p. 41.

[52]Baur's view is expressed in his 1844 study of John's gospel in the Theologische Jahrbücher. See Rapp, pp. 117–18 for an account.

[53]Strauss to Märklin, 22 July 1846, ibid., p. 119.

[54]Using a political analogy drawn from the situation in the French Parliament, Strauss distinguished three different directions in Hegelian interpretation with regard to Jesus the Christ. The right, represented by C.

F. Göschel (1784–1862), G. A. Gabler (1786–1853), and Bruno Bauer (1809–1882), held that the entire gospel history of Jesus was proven as history by the necessary truth of the idea of the unity of the divine and human natures. The center, occupied solely by Karl Rosenkranz (1805–1879), maintained that only a part of the gospel story can be validated as historical from the truth of the philosophical concept. Strauss, who represented the left, rejected both positions. His claim was that no part of the gospel story can be established as history by the truth and meaningfulness of an idea. Only historical criticism could accomplish that. The philosophical idea of the unity of divine and human natures can do nothing more than ground a searching christology. Strauss discussed in detail the three christological directions emanating from Hegel in his Polemical Writings. See Streitschriften, 3:95–120 for the right-wing Hegelians; 3:120–26 for the center; and 3:126 for Strauss's brief statement concerning his own view.

[55]See Hartlich and Sachs, pp. 122–23; Hugh R. Mackintosh, Types of Modern Theology: Schleiermacher to Barth, 8th ed. (London: Nisbet and Co., 1937; reprint ed., 1952), p. 118; Harris, pp. 52–3.

[56]Strauss, Leben Jesu (1835), 2:729.

[57]Although Strauss denied God's individual personality, he did not dismiss God's "personal," i.e., spiritual qualities. See his Die christliche Glaubenslehre in ihrer geschichtlichen Entwicklung und im Kampfe mit der modernen Wissenschaft, 2 vols. (Tübingen: Osiander, 1840), 1:523–24. Cf. Gesammelte Schriften, 10:214–16. In a letter to his friend Rapp, 27 February 1840, Strauss confessed that he had done away with traditional theism. He admitted, however, that, despite the propriety of pantheistic language in reference to God, he was cautious with its use in the Christian Faith out of fear that his book might be banned. Zeller, p. 90.

[58]See Carl Ullmann, "Das Leben Jesu," Theologische Studien und Kritiken 9, no. 3:813; Friedrich Vorländer, "Über die philosophisch-theologische Theorie des Dr. Strauß, Verfasser des Lebens Jesu," Zeitschrift für Philosophie und spekulative Theologie 111, no. 1:95.

[59]G. W. F. Hegel, The Logic of Hegel, translated from the Enzyklopädie by William Wallace, 2d ed. (Oxford: Clarendon Press, 1892), p. xxi.

[60]See Hegel's Lectures on the Philosophy of Religion, translated by E. B. Speirs and J. B. Sanderson, 3 vols. (New York: Humanities Press, 1962), 3:148, where Hegel explains: "Philosophy has been reproached with setting itself above religion; this, however, is false as an actual matter of fact,

for it possesses this particular content only and no other, though it presents it in the form of thought; it sets itself merely above the form of faith, the content is the same in both cases."

[61]By 1840 the distinction between religion and philosophy seems no longer to be merely something formal for Strauss. The relation of pictorial representation to speculative concept is replaced by the relation of illusion to reality. Hence, in Christian Faith Strauss referred to dogmas no longer as the product of creative Idea, but as the product of the "worldview of idiotic consciousness." Glaubenslehre, 2:624. The influence of Ludwig Feuerbach and burgeoning hostility to theology, as a result of his failure to obtain the teaching post in dogmatics at Zurich (1839), were factors in this shift. See Franz Courth, "Die Evangelienkritik des D. Fr. Strauß im Echo seiner Zeitgenossen," in: Georg Schwaiger, ed., Historische Kritik in der Theologie (Göttingen: Vandenhoeck & Ruprecht, 1975), pp. 38–41. Cf. also Wolf, pp. 226–27.

[62]Streitschriften, 3:65–66; In Defense, p. 11.

[63]According to Hegel, all religions share the notion of an incarnational relation between God and humankind; the comprehension of this truth, however, varies widely from religion to religion. Philosophy of Religion, 1:77. In the Christian proclamation of Jesus as the Son of God, the form and content of human religious consciousness adequately mirrors for the first time the form and content of God's consciousness of self as living Spirit. See The Philosophy of History, trans. and with a Preface by J. Sibree (New York: Dover Publications, 1956), p. 319. Cf. James Yerkes, The Christology of Hegel (Albany: State University of New York Press, 1983), p. 119.

[64]Strauss, Leben Jesu (1835), 2:734–36.

[65]Strauss, Streitschriften, 3:57 and 95.

[66]Ibid., p. 58.

[67]See Hegel's The Philosophy of History, p. 319, and Philosophy of Religion, 1:164.

[68]Hegel, Lectures on the History of Philosophy, 3:17.

[69]Hegel, Philosophy of Religion, 1:165 and 3:113.

[70]Hegel, The Philosophy of History, p. 415.

[71]Strauss, Streitschriften, 3:87, 89-90. Although Strauss cannot be faulted for this tactic, he is to be criticized for failing ultimately to formulate a synthetic explication of the tensions and textual difficulties that he uncovered in Hegel. Instead of doing this, he merely set one passage against another. Ibid., pp. 90, 93. The end result was a dismembered Hegel. In contrast to Strauss's approach, Hegel's thought has been fruitfully explicated by focusing on the distinction he posited between the ultimate source and the actual occasion of consciousness of the Christian truth. The source of such religious knowledge is internal whereas the occasion is external; both elements, however, are essential. See James Yerkes's lucid and suggestive interpretation, pp. 121-47.

[72]Christian Hermann Weisse (1801-66) emphasized this difference between Strauss and Hegel in his article, "Strauß und Bruno Bauer. Eine kritische Parallele," Zeitschrift für Philosophie und spekulative Theologie 10, no. 1:44-45. Hegel had insisted that philosophical reflection, "in comprehending the popular religious idea . . . does not keep to the forms of the popular idea, but has to comprehend it in thought, though in doing this it recognises that the form of the popular idea is also necessary." (Emphasis mine.) Hegel, Philosophy of Religion, 3:147.

[73]See Edwina Lawler, "Critical Response to Schleiermacher and Strauss, 1800-1850" (Ph. D. dissertation, Drew University, 1980), pp. 188-90. Cf. Sandberger, pp. 100-01. Whether Strauss's interpretation of Hegel on the question of history and historicity is correct depends heavily upon the intended subject of Geschehensein in the following passage: "Nämlich nicht, ob dasjenige, was die Evangelien berichten, wirklich geschehen sei oder nicht, kann vom Standpunkte der Religions-philosophie aus entschieden werden, sondern nur, ob es vermöge der Wahrheit gewißer Begriffe nothwendig geschehen sein müsse, oder nicht. Und in dieser Hinsicht ist nun meine Behauptung, daß vorerst aus der allgemeinen Stellung der Hegel'schen Philosophie die Behauptung der Nothwendigkeit, eines solchen Geschehenseins auf keine Weise folge, sondern eben jene Stellung setze diese Geschichte, von welcher, als dem Unmittelbaren, ausgegangen wird, zu etwas Gleichgültigem herunter, welches so geschehen seyn könne, aber ebensogut auch nicht, und worüber die Entscheidung ruhig der historischen Kritik anheimzugeben sei." Streitschriften, 3:68. If the subject is the various events of Jesus' life as reported by the gospels, then Strauss is correct in saying that it is ultimately a matter of indifference to Hegel whether or not they actually occurred since Hegel recognized that the historical was an area of probability and, as such, could not provide the certainty one needed concerning God's incarnational relation to the finite. See

his *Philosophy* *of* *Religion*, 1:152-53. Only inner, rational conviction could provide certainty. Ibid., p. 165. Hence Hegel could assert: "Make of Christ, exegetically, critically, historically, what you wish ...the sole question is, what is the Idea or the truth in and for itself." *Philosophy* *of* *History*, pp. 325-26. If, on the other hand, the historical attestation of the fact of God's incarnation is the intended subject, then Strauss is guilty of misreading Hegel. The fact that the consciousness of the reconciliation of the divine and the human was made explicit in the Christian doctrine of the incarnation is the presupposition of and the necessary condition for the rise of Hegel's speculative philosophy. Hegel held that the reconciliation, by which the unity between the divine and human natures is made explicitly manifest, "must become an object for the world—it must appear, and that in the sensuous form appropriate to Spirit, which is human. Christ had appeared—a man who is God—God who is man. And thereby peace and reconciliation have accrued to the world." Ibid., p. 324. Even if Jesus were not the real embodiment of that reconciliation, the actual formulation of such a conviction concerning him in Christian *Vorstellungen* and dogmas made Christianity the absolute religion and set the stage for the conceptually adequate comprehension of the universal truth of the unity of human and divine natures. If Jesus were not the historical realization of this unity and if the events reported of him in the gospels were not factually true, then Hegel had to account for the rise of such Christian ideas. Strauss accounted for their existence by defining them as the result of the non-conscious myth-production of the earliest Christians. It is doubtful that Hegel would have followed Strauss on this point. After speaking of narratives which are not to be taken seriously, although written in an historical style, Hegel averred: "But then besides this there is something historical which is a divine history, and of such a nature that it is regarded as in the strict sense a history, the history of Jesus Christ. This is not taken merely as a myth in a figurative way, but as something perfectly historical." *Philosophy* *of* *Religion*, 1:146.

[74]"I was not surprised that when my book appeared, the many opponents of the Hegelian philosophy used its conclusions to demonstrate the destructive consequences of the Hegelian method of philosophizing. I also anticipated the move of the Hegelian school to reject the point of view of my book and protect itself from being identified with it. In a certain sense, both parties are in the right. Above all, the Hegelians are right when they protest: 'It is not our opinion.' In fact, it is not. ...And when they appeal to Hegel himself and protest that he would not have recognized my book as an expression of his own feelings, I agree. Hegel was personally no friend of historical critique." Strauss, *In* *Defense*, pp. 7-8; *Streitschriften*, 3:61.

[75]Whereas Strauss's interest in Jesus' story was both philosophical and historical, Hegel's was philosophical: "The truest content of Christian faith is to be justified by philosophy, not by history [Geschichte]. What Spirit does is no history [Historie]; it has to do only with that which exists in and for itself—not something past, but something simply present." Hegel, Sämtliche Werke, ed. Hermann Glockner, 20 vols. (Stuttgart-Bad Canstatt: Friedrich Frommann, 1965), 16:328. Yerkes has argued that Hegel seems content to let historical inquiry sift the data, confident that such sifting will not substantially erode the basic outline of the Christ. "Hegel's position seeks to be neither a gnostic nor an historicist form of reductionistic interpretation of the Christ event. Religious meaning and historical data are distinguished, but not disintegrated in his position." P. 147; see also pp. 141-42.

[76]See Strauss's rebuttal of Göschel's and Gabler's charge in Streitschriften, 3:97; In Defense, pp. 39-40. Cf. his similar rebuttal of the right-wing Bruno Bauer, ibid., p. 119, and of the centrist Karl Rosenkranz, p. 125, whom Strauss otherwise praises for his clarity and liberality, pp. 120-21.

[77]Strauss, Leben Jesu (1835), 2:734.

[78]Strauss, Streitschriften, 3:119.

[79]Ibid., 3:60.

[80]Strauss, Leben Jesu (1835), 1:355-63, 469-81; 2:480-89, 511-53.

[81]Strauss, Streitschriften, 3:65, 120.

[82]Ibid., 3:70-71.

[83]Strauss believed that an idea was made no less real simply because it was represented in a multiplicity of embodiments, not all of which existed at the same time. In fact, multiplicity of embodiments is the way we first come to formulate a particular idea as real, namely, through collecting its reality from a number of phenomena. Ibid., 3:99-100; In Defense, p. 15.

[84]Strauss, Streitschriften, 3:124-26.

[85]Strauss, In Defense, p. 17; Streitschriften, 3:72.

[86]Ibid., 3:73.

[87]Ibid., p. 126.

[88]Hartlich and Sachs are, therefore, right to assert: "Entgegen einer nahe-liegenden und immer wieder geäußerten Ansicht, daß Strauß' Kritik in en-ger Abhängigkeit von Hegel zu sehen sei, ergibt unsere Untersuchung, daß Strauß gerade in Abwehr der unklaren Hegelschen Speculation über das Verhältnis von Idee und Geschichte im Christentum und ihrer exegetischen Konsequenz auf die Linie der 'mythischen Schule' zurücklenkt." P. 5. It is, however, too much to say that Strauss's mythical interpretation of the gospels was "not at all dependent upon the premises of Hegelian specula-tion." (Emphasis mine.) P. 122. Strauss had been freed from the need of holding fast to the historical veracity of the gospels by Hegel's philosophy of religion.

[89]Gotthold Müller formulates this conviction in the sharpest possible terms: "Damit is auf einen wichtigen Divergenz-Punkt zwischen Hegel und Strauß hingewiesen: auf ihre verschiedenartige Bewertung der 'Geschichts-tatsachen,' denen bei Hegel im Rahmen des dialektischen Geistprozesses (noch) eine gewiße Bedeutung zukommt, während Strauß sie für völlig entbehrlich hält, so daß er die Hegelsche 'Dialektik' monistich auflöst." P. 28. Müller acknowledges Strauss's Hegelianism only in a restricted sense: "...nämlich so, daß er [i.e., Strauss] bei einem 'Hegel' angekommen war, den er von seinen eigenen anti-dualistischen Prämissen aus in einer höchst ein-seitigen Weise auffasste und ausdeutete." P. 228.

[90]Strauss, Streitschriften, 3:65, 160.

[91]Strauss, Leben Jesu (1835), 2:735-36. It is important to note that this passage appears only in the first and second editions of The Life of Jesus. In the third edition, it was replaced by a paragraph in which strauss ad-mitted that Jesus continued to have a lasting significance for contemporary Christianity in that he originally constituted and unsurpassably exempli-fied true Christian consciousness. Strauss removed this christological con-cession from the fourth edition of his work, without restoring, however, the long paragraph from the 1835 edition. This omission is puzzling since the paragraph presents, more clearly and forcefully than the fourth (1840) edition, what appears to have been Strauss's true view of the matter. Thus, the first edition: "...Science of the present age, however, can no longer suppress the consciousness that the relationship to an individual belongs only to the form of this doctrine, as it has been conditioned by time and the needs of the people."

[92]Ibid., p. 736.

[93]Strauss to Märklin, 3 November 1839, in Ziegler, 2:334-35.

[94]This is reflected in the reversal of his earlier appraisal of the authentic-ity of John's gospel and his admission that there might be more historical material in all the gospels than he had at first acknowledged. Strauss to Rapp, 17 March 1838, in Zeller, p. 58. In the third edition of his book, Strauss also fell occasionally into the kind of strained rationalistic inter-pretation that he had earlier scorned. See Harris, pp. 117-21; Cromwell, pp. 82-88; Hodgson, Introduction, Life of Jesus (1972), pp. xlii-xliii.

[95]Strauss to Rapp, 17 March 1838, in Zeller, p. 58.

[96]Hodgson, in his Introduction to Strauss's Life of Jesus (1972), p. xxxvi, observes that the concessions in the third edition were initially unrelated to any specific chance of employment as a professor of theology. Strauss had begun his revisions in the summer of 1837, "at a time when he was not being actively considered for an appointment at Zurich and had very little hope of being called." Strauss had completed the third edition by the spring of 1838 (the Preface is dated 8 April), whereas the final possibility of an appointment at the University of Zurich did not materialize until the summer of the same year. When it did appear that he was under consid-eration for the job, Strauss used the changes in the third edition to his ad-vantage. See his letter to Professor Hitzig of Zurich, 14 June 1838, in Hausrath, Pt. I, Appendix, p. 18. Strauss further sought to strengthen his case by publishing at the same time the essay "Transitory and Permanent Elements in Christianity (1838)," in which he described Jesus in terms not unlike Schleiermacher's. When public opinion sought to coerce the Zurich government to rescind its decision to hire him, Strauss prepared an ex-panded re-issue of this 1838 essay, in which he offered his mediating view of Jesus. Strauss completed the Preface to the volume that contained the essay, Zwei Friedliche Blätter, on March 15, 1839. But three days later the Large Council of Zurich decided to retire Strauss before the assumption of his academic duties. See Hans J. Hillerbrand, A Fellowship of Discontent (New York: Harper and Row, 1967), pp. 142-45.

[97]That Strauss did not want to begrudge Jesus some permanent signifi-cance, while still repudiating supernaturalistic christology, is revealed in the section entitled "Attempts at Mediation," which Strauss wrote for the third edition of his Life of Jesus as a replacement for his earlier demolition of dogmatic christologies. See Hillerbrand, p. 142. Cf. Zwei Friedliche Blätter (Altona: J. F. Hammerich, 1839), pp. 100-01.

[98]Ibid., p. 108. Strauss claimed that Jesus' superiority over other founders of religions consisted in the harmonious equilibrium of his inner life, wherein he possessed the closest relationship to God. Strauss later repudiated this evident approximation to Schleiermacher's christology. See pp. 116-17.

[99]Ibid. As this passage indicates, Strauss still found unconscionable the category of absolute miracle and the literal idea of resurrection and ascension. What made Jesus a significant religious figure was his speeches and his ethical life.

[100]Ibid., p. 132. Cf. Ziegler, p. 279. Courth, Leben Jesu, p. 122, alleges that the shift in Strauss's evaluation of Jesus is incipiently present in the first edition; he further maintains that myth begins to yield to history. If Courth means to suggest that the historical Jesus now has greater importance in Strauss's christological position, he misleads. Although Strauss now presents a more positive historical picture of Jesus and is motivated to find some connection between Jesus and the content of Christian faith, he does not argue that this connection is necessary; if not simply fortuitous, it is at best tenuous.

[101]The fourth (1840) edition followed primarily the second edition in substance and the third edition in format (i.e., preserving the third's formal and stylistic improvements). Christologically, the fourth edition closely approximated the first edition. See Life of Jesus (1972), pp. xlvi-xlvii.

[102]See Das Leben Jesu für das deutsche Volk bearbeitet (1864), l:ix, cited by Hodgson, Introduction, Life of Jesus (1972), p. xlvii, note 103. Even though the 1835 book offered the most critical historical portrait of Jesus and the most drastically pared view of Jesus' relation to contemporary Christian faith, it proved not to be Strauss's most radical statement on Christian faith. In his final work, Der alte und der neue Glaube (1872), Strauss abandoned Christianity altogether and adopted a Darwinian, nontheistic worldview.

CHAPTER 2

JOHANNES KUHN: A "SCIENTIFIC" RESPONSE TO STRAUSS

Johannes Kuhn (1806-1887) was one of the first Catholic theologians of the
nineteenth century to pay serious attention to Strauss's Life of Jesus.
While still a professor of New Testament exegesis at the University of
Giessen (1832-37), Kuhn referred to Strauss in his lectures; and shortly
after the appearance of the latter's book, he issued two major articles that
grappled with the methodological and hermeneutical issues Strauss had
raised.[1] The mature fruit of his debate with Strauss came two years later
with The Life of Jesus Scientifically Examined (1838).[2] Although only the
first of the projected three volumes was ever published, this one volume
won recognition as the best of the Catholic critiques of Strauss.[3] The book
was indeed remarkable for its avoidance of personal invective, its objective approach to the subject matter, and its perspicacious analysis.

Kuhn undertook the debate with Strauss because he realized that the
issues Strauss raised were more than exegetical. Among the most important were the determination of the relation of faith to knowledge, religion
to philosophy, and history to idea. These issues were important because
they went to the heart of every conception of Christian faith. Kuhn
thought that Strauss's handling of them constituted a critical version of
Hegelianism. He understood his own task to be the scientific scrutiny of
the adequacy of this critical, Hegelian approach for Christian faith.[4]

Kuhn's Exegetical Essays

The primary concern of Kuhn's early essays was the literary character of
the New Testament, specifically, the historical character of the gospels. In
his first exegetical essay (1834), Kuhn announced that he wanted to
"establish a new view concerning the character of the historical writing in
the New Testament," a perspective that would set limits to the credibility
of these texts.[5] Such a new perspective was demanded by honest biblical
criticism, which recognized that the biblical authors creatively manipulated

traditions about Jesus for a specific confessional end. Kuhn suggested that there is a higher and a lower interest in history. The New Testament authors possessed the former interest, because they did not intend to present an exact, detailed chronicle of events, but only their essential heart. Consequently, their writings could claim only a limited "historical fidelity."[6] The "pragmatism" of the biblical authors, the desire to heighten the effect of a story in order to reveal its "higher reality," sometimes led the authors to use "a rearrangement, modification, and--from an empirical point of view--a real falsification of details."[7] Kuhn insisted, however, that this pragmatism was not falsifying because it retained the essential historical core of the reported event.[8]

Although Kuhn had formulated this basic view of the historical material of the New Testament prior to his debate with Strauss, the latter's Life of Jesus challenged him to define his own position more carefully. Kuhn began to spell out his position vis-à-vis Strauss in his two major essays of 1836. In light of Strauss's work, Kuhn thought that the decisive question for any interpreter of the gospels was whether the evangelists intended to write "history" and, if so, in what sense.

Kuhn laid out his answer to this question in his essay "Concerning the Literary Character of the Gospels in Relation to Apostolic Preaching and the Apostolic Letters." He argued that the gospels were historical, but neither in the pure nor in the conventional sense. With Strauss he acknowledged the confessional character of the gospels; against Strauss he asserted that they possessed considerable historical content. Kuhn's starting point in his response to Strauss was the conviction that the gospels were the organic development, in form and content, of the orally transmitted apostolic kerygma. This conviction permitted Kuhn to argue that the gospels, like the kerygma, had both an historical and a didactic purpose.[9] The didactic purpose, although primary, was dependent upon the historical. According to this perspective, the gospels are historical presentations with the specific purpose of demonstrating the reasonableness of faith. Consequently, the "selection and arrangement of what is purely historical" in the gospels "has proceeded according to the principle of its suitability or appropriateness for the production of the proof of faith."[10]

Kuhn's point was that the evangelists wanted to write a history of Jesus the Christ, not a history of Jesus of Nazareth. Consequently, the evangelists' historical narrative differed from biography both quantitatively and qualitatively. It reported only those facts from the life of Jesus that were "fit for demonstrating his messiahship." Hence, the evangelists were virtually silent about Jesus' life prior to his baptism.[11] And unlike common history, which presents the facts as the result of finite causes relative to specific contexts, the evangelists' "sacred history" presented the facts in the context of divine providence.[12] In short, the gospels were as much theological documents as they were historical documents. Strauss's Life of Jesus challenged Kuhn to defend his view that the confessional aim of the evangelists had only caused a constriction of the scope of events reported from Jesus' life and a qualitative enhancement of those features that exhibited Jesus' messianic character, but had not vitiated the substantial accuracy of what the evangelists reported.

Kuhn responded to Strauss's challenge by attempting to undermine Strauss's explanation of myth-formation, which Kuhn regarded as the Achilles' heel of Strauss's book. Kuhn criticized Strauss's description of how oral tradition could produce myths unconsciously. He specifically objected to Strauss's assertion that the final product of the process of oral transmission was different in essence from the original form of the story about Jesus. His point was this: If, as Strauss admitted, the basic story of Jesus' life was not altered essentially at any point in the process of oral transmission, then the final form of the transmission could not be myth, as Strauss alleged, since the transformation of a basically historical story into a myth is a change in essence.[13]

Kuhn's second line of attack against Strauss's view of myth-formation was to contest his claim that the Old Testament provided the richest material for the mythicization of Jesus' life. In particular, he rejected Strauss's claim that many of the events of Jesus' life depicted in the gospels were fictively modeled after Old Testament stories about Moses. Although he admitted that there was at least one isolated parallel between the adult lives of Moses and of Jesus, Kuhn insisted that, in general, the gospels eschewed presenting Jesus as the natural successor of Moses.[14] Instead, they presented him as a revolutionary counterpoint to Moses.[15] Kuhn argued that the Sermon on the Mount, that occasion on which the conjunction of Moses and Jesus was the closest and the most natural, supported his view. It did not present Jesus simply as the second Moses, but rather as the messiah who was so far exalted above Moses that his "fulfillment" of the Mosaic Law constituted its simultaneous abolition.[16] If there were indeed any systematic distortion in the gospels, Kuhn suggested that it was the distortion of Old Testament texts to fit the actual course of Jesus' life and not the distortion of the facts of Jesus life to fit the prophecy of the Old Testament.[17]

Kuhn's own view of the influence of Hebrew scriptures on the shape of the gospels was that they functioned in a confirmatory, rather than in a creative fashion. According to this view, the evangelists drew parallels between Jesus and Old Testament prophets only where an objectively real basis for such parallels existed. This hypothesis rested upon two warrants: 1) the presumption that the apostles and evangelists would not have been able to demonstrate convincingly that Jesus was the messiah if they had fabricated Jesus' history, and 2) the observation that some aspects of Jesus' life ran counter to prevailing conceptions of the messiah.

The probative force of the warrants for Kuhn's hypothesis was not as strong as he imagined. The former warrant erroneously presumed that ancient culture shared the same historical consciousness and concomitant skepticism characteristic of contemporary Western culture, and it assumed that the predominantly Gentile audience was still capable of verifying the historical truth of the evangelists' reports. Its persuasive inefficacy notwithstanding, this warrant reveals that Kuhn thought that Christian faith was dependent upon personal certainty about the historical truth of the story of Jesus' life.

The second warrant, however, was not quite as vulnerable. It acknowledged what modern biblical scholarship has confirmed, namely, that early Christians had difficulty reconciling certain scandalous aspects of Jesus' life with prevailing messianic conceptions and that, as a result, they sometimes had to scour Scripture assiduously to find support for their confessional claims about Jesus. Kuhn identified the concept of a suffering messiah, the betrayal by an intimate friend, and the crucifixion as elements difficult to reconcile with then current messianic expectations. The conclusion Kuhn drew from this insight was that "the fact conditioned the interpretation of prophecy, and not the reverse—-that the latter called forth the former."[18] Nonetheless, Kuhn's first essay against Strauss did not vanquish his opponent, although it did point out the need for Strauss's argument to be moderated.[19]

Kuhn concluded his essay with a reassertion of his basic understanding of the gospels. Insofar as the gospels were dogmatic and didactic, they were not history in the narrower sense of the word; insofar as their confessional interpretations were built upon historical reminiscences of Jesus' life, they were not simply myths.[20]

> The gospel presentation cannot, therefore, be characterized as history in the narrower and stricter sense of the word for the reason given. And, in fact, [it is not history] to the extent that use was made of the prophetic aspect. According to the gospel descriptions that are at hand, however, history does not at all evaporate in the prophetic aspect, as little as the latter evaporates in the former. And Justin's view is one that has been advanced far beyond the truth, ...from which—-if it were true—-a concept for the gospel history would follow that is completely different from the one that corresponds to the truth. According to Justin, the literary character of the gospels would be dogmatic-historical, but it is, in fact, historical-dogmatic.[21]

Kuhn's second major essay of 1836, "Hermeneutics and Criticism in their Application to the Gospel Story," dealt even more directly with the claims of Strauss's Life of Jesus. It demonstrates that Kuhn, unlike his conservative Catholic contemporaries, did not reject the tools of historical criticism, but that he, unlike Strauss, also did not apply them radically. Kuhn welcomed the rise of biblical criticism as necessary and integral to the theological enterprise. He observed that theology could no longer be satisfied simply with discovering the apparent meaning of biblical passages; it had to raise hard questions about the truth of biblical stories. On the other hand, Kuhn insisted that the critical task was not the only task for the biblical theologian. The critical question (Is the story true?) was secondary and subsequent to the hermeneutical question (What does the story mean?).

What Strauss observes in this regard is perfectly correct:
that in every act of faith in itself ...doubt is co-posited,
even if it is not developed. But this must be defined
more closely in the sense that every interpretation that
does not have criticism in itself and does not allow it to
function as an internal fire of purification is like the dead
letter and cannot be called a knowledgeable interpretation. Similarly, on the other hand, this restriction must
be valid: that every criticism that does not proceed from
the hermeneutical function, but forces itself in an external manner upon it as an already formed point of view, is
to be regarded as an alien element, which makes the interpretation unscientific.[22]

Kuhn charged Strauss with the failure to observe the proper roles of
hermeneutics and criticism in his book. In this regard, Strauss's mythical
interpretation followed in the mistaken path of its predecessors, the allegorical and naturalistic interpretations of Scripture. Like them, Strauss's
mythical interpretation failed to distinguish between the supernatural
form and the supernatural content of a story; correlatively, it failed to appreciate the true intent of the biblical authors.[23] Kuhn did not mean to
suggest that these different modes of interpretation had no place in scriptural exegesis. On the contrary, he admitted that naturalistic exegesis operated from some correct principles and--like mythological exegesis--was
applicable to Scripture in some cases.

But does it follow that each and every interpretation,
which declares something mythical that has been presented as purely historical, is in itself subjectively arbitrary and unscientific in a contradictory way? Not at all.
We distinguish the mythical interpretation as a standpoint from the interpretation of a myth as an individual
result. The latter appears via the process of immanent
explanation and is thereupon inescapable; the former,
however, rests upon a position external to the material to
be interpreted, ... whose objective reality, with reference to that material, is simply presupposed.[24]

Kuhn's point was that any interpretation that rested upon an a priori presupposition about the text failed to be scientific hermeneutics. Kuhn averred:

> We have already seen above how every so-called interpretative standpoint rests upon a bias [Vorurtheil], upon an unscientific presupposition; how a thoroughly unprejudiced explanation ceases to be one precisely then when it makes its appearance at the outset as a standpoint [Standpunkt]. Scientific exegesis protests, therefore, just as much against the exclusively supernaturalistic and rationalistic interpretation as it does against the exclusively mythical. And it protests against them precisely on account of their exclusivity, i.e., their characteristic as standpoints.[25]

Kuhn objected to Strauss's reading of the gospels for the very reason Strauss held his reading to be superior to the alternatives, namely, its consistency and comprehensiveness. Kuhn held that it was impermissible to infer the mythological character of most of the gospel story from the mythological character of one part of that story. Even if the beginning and the end of the gospel stories were myth, Kuhn refused to surrender the narrative of Jesus' public ministry to a mythological reading. His reason for this refusal was that the story of Jesus' public life "rests upon the eyewitness testimony of the apostles," whereas the story of Jesus' birth and childhood does not. Kuhn's conclusion: "the latter can be mythical while the former is not by a long shot."[26] Kuhn found Strauss's case for a consistently mythical reading of the gospels unpersuasive. Strauss's appeal to "the necessary progress of interpretation" from the supernatural to the rational to the mythical reading did not constitute proof of the tenability of Strauss's case.[27]

Kuhn's cautious median position between the supernaturalistic interpretation of orthodoxy and Strauss's mythological interpretation reflects his understanding of faith. Just as faith does not require a comprehensive picture, but rather a basic historical outline of Jesus' life, so too exegesis does not require a consistently literal or supernaturalistic approach to the gospels, yet does demand that their historical core be left intact.[28] Kuhn's understanding of faith implicitly informed the attitude with which he approached the gospels. That attitude, in turn, shaped his reading of the gospels and explains his divergence from Strauss.

Kuhn approached the gospels with a fundamental willingness to accept their content as historically true. To reject the presumption of the gospels' historicity before conclusive proof to the contrary had been adduced was, in Kuhn's mind, a failure to keep the critical function of exegesis in its properly secondary and dependent relation to the hermeneutical function. According to this view, one was entitled to begin with the traditional, historical reading of the gospel narrative, which was then to be subjected to the objections of modern historical criticism. The basis of the historical reading of the gospel narrative had traditionally been the apostolic authorship of the gospels. Consequently, Kuhn agreed with Strauss that the mythical reading of the gospels and the origin of the gospels from eyewitnesses were "mutually exclusive" points of view, and he identified apostolic authorship as the issue from which the question of the historical character of the gospels could find "its only scientifically certain and completely decisive resolution."[29] As warrant for his own approach to the gospels, Kuhn stated his conviction that most of the gospel stories derived ultimately from eyewitnesses to Jesus' life.

Strauss, on the other hand, came to the gospel texts with a fundamental suspicion about their historical veracity. This suspicion prompted him to consider whether the category of myth might properly be extended to the account of Jesus' public life, as it had been applied by his predecessors to the stories of Jesus' birth and ascension. The warrant for his suspicion about the historical truth of the gospels was his conviction that the gospel texts did not derive from eyewitnesses.[30]

The backings that supported Strauss's and Kuhn's different assessments of gospel authorship were, of course, divergent. Whereas Strauss made evidence internal to the gospel stories his primary criterion for determining whether the reports stemmed from eyewitnesses, Kuhn made primary appeal to the external evidence. This divergence mirrors again the differences that obtained in Strauss's and Kuhn's respective conceptions of the hermeneutical task: Strauss was concerned first with the question of the historical truth or believability of what was reported, whereas Kuhn was concerned first with the question of the reporter's identity and intent. Thus, Kuhn held Strauss's denial of the apostolic origin of the gospels of Matthew and John to be illegitimate since Strauss had come to that conclusion on the basis of (from Kuhn's point of view) questionable internal evidence. Kuhn argued that it was Strauss's obligation as a scientific exegete to determine the quantity and quality of external evidence in support of apostolic authorship and then to modify the conclusion which that evidence suggested by means of an appraisal of the internal evidence. Kuhn believed that if Strauss had followed this procedure, he would have concurred that apostolic authorship of two of the gospels was probable.[31]

Although biblical scholarship has since demonstrated the correctness of Strauss's view, Kuhn had a valid reason for rejecting Strauss's case against apostolic authorship in his Life of Jesus. Strauss had insisted that the external evidence render total certainty of apostolic authorship. Kuhn reminded him, however, that historical judgments could never yield more than probability; consequently, insistence upon irrefutable testimony from people who had known the apostles to be the authors of the gospels was simply unreasonable.[32] Kuhn apparently had an inkling that Strauss's theological agenda was behind his unreasonable demands.[33]

Kuhn hoped to blunt further the destructiveness of Strauss's view of the gospels by challenging his understanding of myth. It is at this point, however, that Kuhn's naiveness as a critic is revealed. Kuhn argued that Strauss's understanding of the Jesus myth as the unconscious and unintentional creation of the primitive Christian community was untenable in the light of the Prologue to Luke's gospel, in which the author promised to provide Theophilus with an ordered account of the events of Jesus' life as they had been handed down to him from eyewitnesses (Luke 1:1-4). Kuhn took this prologue as evidence that someone involved in handing on the traditions about Jesus really knew what was true and false and wanted to convey this information. Following the Protestant rationalist H. E. G. Paulus, Kuhn claimed that Luke would not have written this prologue if he were going to include mythical fabrication in it.[34] Strauss had pointed out, however, that the truth of this claim depended upon Luke's knowing that what he was about to report was mythical. Strauss's point, of course, was that Luke did not recognize that mythical elements were already present in the oral traditions he received.[35]

The root of Kuhn's flawed historical judgment was his insistence that the core of Christian faith depended upon the historical truth of the gospel and his concomitant conviction that the earliest Christian community agreed with him.

> The historical character of Christianity rests namely upon the historical truth of the gospel story, and Christianity itself is nothing without it. The apostle Paul says in I Cor. 15:14, if Christ is not raised, then our preaching and your believing is illusory, and he conceives Jesus' resurrection only as the highest expression of the historical in his life. Consequently, if the historical content of the gospel story is essentially curtailed, then the specific character of Christianity, its essence, its truth, its effect and fruit— which altogether rest upon this historical component-- falls completely away. It is a thoroughly vain attempt to dissolve historical Christianity into an ideal Christianity and to want to cover the loss of the former by the mag - nificent appearance of the latter. The former is no more as soon as it ceases to be historical. And what is substi- tuted is something completely different, which bears the name of Christianity with gross injustice.[36]

This firm theological judgment impelled all of Kuhn's various critical and hermeneutical strategies of attack against Strauss. It constituted the core of his own theological position and, although it did not completely preclude his ability to formulate defensible interpretations of the gospel texts any more than Strauss's theological starting-point prevented him, it did deeply influence his reading of the gospels. Because of his theological starting-point, Kuhn deferred to the more benign conception of the historical ve- racity of the gospel narrative, whereas Strauss took an opposing position because of his different starting-point. That their respective theological convictions shaped their hermeneutical projects is reflected not only in their divergent historical judgments on a variety of individual points,[37] but is also patently manifest in their overall willingness or unwillingness to let tradition decide those cases where certainty in historical judgment is im- possible. Kuhn enunciated this difference programmatically in his analysis of Strauss's view of the authenticity of Luke's gospel:

When we, however, read the arguments which Strauss brings against the genuineness of the third gospel, it becomes completely doubtful which is greater: the embarrassment created for the mythical point of view by the composition of the gospel story by apostles and students of the the apostles or the boldness of criticism, whereby the most decisive historical facts are contradicted and a more than sufficiently established historical content is exchanged for a mere, vain possibility. The impression that this type of argumentation and subjection of historical objects to suspicion infallibly makes upon everyone who has a concept of the certainty of historical transmission achieves here its maximum: all history and every historical transmission is subjected to a boundless skepticism ...[38]

Whereas Kuhn could accuse Strauss of facilely converting "mere suspicion" about a text's historical truth into a certain judgment that the text was mythical, Strauss could alternatively fault Kuhn for being too willing to accept the text's content as historically true. Although Kuhn was not an uncritical interpreter of the gospels, he was nonetheless less skeptical than Strauss about the corrupting influence of Christian tradition upon the ancient deposit of historical reminiscences of Jesus. Kuhn, of course, did not see this lack of skepticism on his part as a defect. Rather, he understood it to be the result of keeping in balance the two functions of interpretation, and appreciating the Church's role as preservation of the tradition. Strauss, by contrast, had upset the balance of scientific interpretation, for he let its hermeneutical function be consumed by its critical function. Kuhn incorporated these insights into the writing of his own Life of Jesus.

The Life of Jesus Scientifically Examined

Kuhn, unlike some of his Catholic colleagues, recognized that Strauss's work not only challenged exegetes to defend their own manner of biblical interpretation, but also challenged theologians to define the proper relationship between theology and philosophy. More specifically, he perceived that

Strauss's book raised the question of the place of historical knowledge about Jesus in Christian faith.[39] As a person who was primarily interested in speculative theology, but was teaching New Testament exegesis at the time, Kuhn was ideally equipped to detect the wider theological significance of Strauss's work. His concern to give younger theologians some orientation in this matter prompted him, while still in Giessen, to lecture on the life of Jesus in the summer semester of 1836, and, after his arrival in Tübingen, to publish his presentation.[40] Kuhn's Life Of Jesus Scientifically Examined (1838) was, therefore, designed to counterbalance Strauss's onesidedly critical Life of Jesus. It aimed to do this, not by refuting Strauss's presentation in detail, but by offering a life of Jesus that was more appropriate in structure and content.

Kuhn's Life of Jesus was a truncated work. Only the first of the three planned volumes in response to Strauss was published. This first full book consisted of a lengthy introduction and five chapters. In the introduction, Kuhn handled the question of the gospels' authorship and historical character; in the chapters he dealt with the messianic inauguration of Jesus' ministry. Kuhn had omitted the genealogies of Matthew and Luke from consideration since they did not derive from the original apostolic kerygma, and, as such, they had no claim to being a necessary historical component of the gospel narrative. Kuhn began instead with an analysis of John the Baptist's public ministry, which was followed by a careful study of John's relation to Jesus and an exposition of the stories of Jesus' baptism and temptation. At that point Kuhn's presentation broke off, leaving many significant topics, e.g., a full analysis of the New Testament foundations for a christology, the exposition of Jesus' miracles, and an investigation of the death and resurrection of Jesus, untouched. Kuhn fitted his critique of the deficiencies of Strauss's work into this incomplete framework.[41]

As the title of his book suggests, Kuhn saw the chief deficiency of Strauss's presentation to be its failure as "scientific" scholarship. According to Kuhn, a scientific life of Jesus required attention to both the historical and the theological dimensions.[42] Strauss's work, however, was nothing more than a "mere critique of the gospel history." The christological survey at the end of Strauss's Life of Jesus, although it appeared at first glance to give the theological moment its due, was related to the rest of the work only externally and accidentally.[43] By neglecting the theological, construc-

tive task, Strauss's book became, in Kuhn's estimation, onesidedly negative.[44]

> Therefore, those presentations of Jesus' life which, with
> regard to the main question, behave merely negatively
> towards the content of the same and do not rise above
> the meaning of a critique of the gospel story, lack above
> all a strictly scientific and theological character. To that
> group belongs the most recent work of Strauss, which can
> in no way be taken for an examination of Jesus' life—for
> which it passes itself off . . . The critique of the gospel
> history as such, however, is likewise not theological, but
> only becomes theological when it steps out of its negative
> sphere, refers unremittingly that which has been criti-
> cally confirmed back to the middle point of the theologi-
> cal circle of ideas, and establishes its [i.e., what has been
> critically confirmed] meaning according to it.[45]

Kuhn identified three underlying causes of Strauss's excessive negativity. First, Strauss had transformed the legitimate principle of criticism
into a mania for finding "contradictions" among the various gospel accounts, thereby replacing balanced criticism with radical skepticism as a
principle of historical scholarship.[46] Second, Strauss had inverted the
proper order and relationship between internal and external criticism in
his study of the gospels, thereby begging the question of gospel authorship.[47] Third, Strauss failed to grasp the literary character of the gospels.
He failed to perceive correctly the gospels' intermingling of historical
reminiscence with didactic or theological presentation.[48]

Kuhn found Strauss's deficiencies at these three points to be the result
of presuppositions no less dogmatic than the orthodox ones Strauss castigated.[49] Specifically, Kuhn rejected Strauss's philosophical determination
of the relationship of spirit and history, which magnified the former at the
expense of the latter. Kuhn did not think that ideality and factuality could
be neatly separated when asking fundamental questions about reality; for
him, a factual or experiential basis was indeed relevant to assertions of religious truth.

> Now if we posit a philosophy, which has taken as its prin-
> ciple absolute opposition towards everything factual, as
> existents in themselves having primordial significance,
> then such a philosophy will hold it at least for equivalent

> whether myths or true histories testify to the truth of
> certain ideas ... For in the former as well as in the lat-
> ter, Spirit only wants to reveal itself; and they, equally
> worthless, fall away like the skin of a snake in order to
> make room for other forms, which immediately share the
> same fate. Spirit alone is alive for it ... But if the divine
> Spirit, which reveals itself in history, speaks to us
> through facts, which are dissolved in ideas for our mind,
> then it is just as difficult--on account of this primordial
> relation of Spirit to history--to separate the idea from the
> truth of the fact as it is to separate the fact from the
> truth of the idea.[50]

Kuhn suggested that the Hegelian philosophy of history that Strauss had adopted so emphasized Absolute Spirit or Idea that the traditional Christian understanding of history, as the _free_ work of the self-revealing God and of responsible human agents, was seriously threatened.[51] In a similar way, the pantheistic bent of Hegelianism threatened to erase the hard distinctions between divine and human and to destroy the category of miracle.[52] In such a system, it was a matter of indifference whether a myth or an historical fact was the bearer of the truth of Idea; for only the Idea mattered in the self-enclosed system of objective spirit's activity.[53]

Kuhn's position, by contrast, was built upon the rival presupposition that God was revealed only in the events of history and that God's revelation was a free decision. This outlook was, according to Kuhn, theologically more adequate than Strauss's not only because it upheld God's freedom and integrity, but also because it had surer safeguards against subjectivism and ideology. Insofar as his view coincided with the traditional Christian view of God active in history, Kuhn saw it not as an unwarranted dogmatic presupposition, but as an appropriate and established thesis. Kuhn, therefore, discounted Strauss's challenge to traditional orthodoxy and simply articulated his position without seeing the necessity to bolster it with detailed argumentation. Applied to the case of Jesus, Kuhn's presupposition made historical knowledge about Jesus a constitutive part of faith.[54]

Although he did not explicitly acknowledge his own philosophical premises, Kuhn was keenly aware that Strauss's book was not without presuppositions, as Strauss had proudly claimed. In fact, Kuhn thought that he could demonstrate that Strauss's philosophical perspective prevented him from correctly comprehending the relation between the kerygma and the historical events of Jesus' life. Kuhn explicitly rejected Strauss's claim that philosophical study, which clearly had freed him from orthodoxy, made him better able than other theologians to comprehend the true meaning of the gospels. On the contrary, Strauss's philosophical premises encouraged him to conceive of Christian truths allegorically and to force upon the historical study of Christian origins an interpretation that dissolved facts into ideas, which were the alleged higher, yet unconscious, referents of the narrative about Jesus.[55]

Kuhn acknowledged the legitimacy of philosophical reflection in a scientific examination of Jesus' life, but he insisted that its proper domain was small and its role in the exposition of faith minor.[56] He approvingly cited Schleiermacher in support of his view that philosophy ought never to play a substantial material role in the explication of faith.[57] This delimitation of philosophical presuppositions did not mean, however, that Kuhn felt entitled to approach the gospel texts with all the biblical presuppositions of traditional orthodoxy. On the contrary, he agreed with Strauss that the gospels were not to be treated with hermeneutical principles different from those used when dealing with other historical documents. Historical criticism, evenly and universally applied, meant that the absolute truth of Scripture could not be accepted as the precondition of Christian exegesis.[58] This theoretical agreement notwithstanding, Kuhn refused to approve of Strauss's practical execution of the critical task. Unlike him, Kuhn presupposed the truth of the traditional view of the gospels until it was decisively disproven, and he gave the miraculous a limited role as a category of historical explanation.[59]

Kuhn's understanding and use of miracle effectively discloses the distinctive characteristics of his concept of historical criticism. He agreed with Strauss that a miracle, by definition, transcended the natural causal nexus, whereas human explanation was restricted to the cause-and-effect connection of natural things.[60] But he disagreed with Strauss in affirming the possibility of miracle and conceding its conditional use in historical explanation. Kuhn conceived the essence of the miraculous to consist in the interior, invisible operation of God within human beings. His view therefore fell between Strauss's, which denied the possibility of miracles, and the strict supernaturalists', which emphasized the objective facticity of miracles and seemed to see direct divine intervention everywhere. Kuhn thought it just as irreconcilable with a proper idea of the divine activity to "multiply miracles unnecessarily" as it was irreconcilable with educated thought to "think that something is miraculous when it is comprehensible as something natural."[61]

Kuhn's treatment of the events surrounding Jesus' baptism illustrates his approach. Rejecting the supernaturalistic interpretation of the voice from the clouds as thunder, Kuhn insisted that neither the open heavens, the dove, nor the voice were objective phenomena; rather, they were the subjective form in which the Baptist's disposition was expressed. This interior state of mind, however, was not self-produced. Kuhn explained:

> In unusually heightened states of mind, that which a person has experienced interiorly with a force that overpowers quiet recollection appears to the person in an external fashion. John was put into such a state at the baptism of Jesus. And precisely this--that what occurred at this moment in his inner self transcended these bounds--provides the proof that it was not an idea which was presented to him in a natural fashion, not a mere self-produced reflection, but rather a divine idea that simultaneously was pressed upon him and that, therefore, overpowered and enchanted his spirit.[62]

Kuhn felt justified in finding the "miraculous" in Jesus' baptism. How else, he queried, could John the Baptist, who as yet had no knowledge of Jesus' messianic character, have recognized Jesus as the messiah except through an extraordinary revelation? Kuhn similarly maintained that the event was extraordinary for Jesus as well, in that it gave him the impetus to step forward openly as the messiah.[63] Kuhn's psychological interpretation of miracles distanced his view from the usual supernaturalistic and naturalistic interpretations; it did not, however, bring him any closer to Strauss's mythological interpretation. Whereas Strauss sought to demonstrate that the stories of the miracles were, on the whole, not historically true, Kuhn accepted the facticity of the stories containing miracles and sought to discover their meaning.

In light of the serious deficiencies he detected in Strauss's work, Kuhn held it necessary to begin his own Life of Jesus with the question Strauss had handled most poorly, namely, the nature of the gospels. Here Kuhn built upon the results of his earlier study of the literary character of the gospels. He reiterated his conclusion that the gospels were the written expression and supplementation, in both form and content, of the original oral kerygma, which, in turn, derived from personal witnesses to Jesus' ministry.

To warrant this conclusion, Kuhn offered the principle proposed by Schleiermacher: the degree of congruence between the external and internal evidence determines the question of gospel authorship.[64] In Kuhn's estimation, Strauss violated this principle by giving insufficient consideration to the external evidence and by inappropriately considering the question of the credibility of the gospels' content before determining the authenticity of their authorship.[65] For his part, Kuhn stated that the congruence of external and internal critiques indicated that there was a high degree of probability that the bulk of the stories reported in the gospel narrative derived from eyewitnesses, but he cautioned that this judgment had to remain tentative since new data concerning the gospel texts might be discovered later, which would require a revision in the previous historical judgment.[66]

Kuhn offered several reasons for concluding that the external evidence supported the apostolic authenticity of the gospels. First, heretics recognized the Christian gospels as genuine writings. That they, as opponents of orthodoxy, did not contest the gospels' authenticity gave greater weight to their testimony than that of orthodox Christians. Second, the outspoken pagan enemies of Christianity, who--unlike the heretics--had no regard for the Christian church, also did not contest the authenticity of the gospels. Third, the entire church since the middle of the second century recognized all four gospels (not just one or the other in this or that part of the Christian world) as authentic. This datum acquired special weight since the second-century church was more attuned than the first-century church to the differences between genuine and inauthentic gospels and since the second-century church did not accept into its canon all the writings which bore the names of the apostles.[67] Individually, these various testimonies yielded a high degree of probability; collectively, they provided historical certainty for the ancient authenticity of the canonical gospels. Kuhn's point was that no other writing of antiquity possessed as many old and credible vouchers for its authenticity as did the gospels.[68]

In answering the question of whether the evangelists intended to report history, Kuhn repeated his view that the gospels were not history in the strict sense. Following his Scripture teacher A. B. Feilmoser (1777-1831), Kuhn asserted that the purpose of the gospels was to provide a justification of Christian faith in Jesus.[69] This didactic, theological purpose guided at every point the evangelists' reporting of historical reminiscences of Jesus; and it required the evangelists to report only those reminiscences that disclosed Jesus as the messiah. Consequently, the evangelists restricted their attention to Jesus' public ministry and, within that ministry, to Jesus' miracles and his fulfillment of Old Testament prophecies.[70]

Kuhn anticipated the objection that his theory of gospel composition as a conscious, theological enterprise might lead to the same conclusion as Strauss's theory of their unconscious, mythological formation. Drawing upon his previous exegetical essays, he conceded that the authors might have embellished their historical reminiscences, but he staunchly denied that they thereby distorted the historical substance of their portrait of Jesus.[71] To Strauss's objection that the disparity among the various gospel accounts destroyed the historical credibility of all, Kuhn retorted that the disparity did not imply objective contradiction of fact, but was the reflection of the selectivity and normal divergence of individual authors in the pursuit of the same literary goal, namely, the presentation of Jesus as the proper object of faith.[72] The task of the critical exegete was, therefore, not to dismiss the historical truth of the gospel core on account of this occasional disparity, but rather to discover the particular "purposive conception" that guided each evangelist in his writing.[73] Kuhn insisted that, although the individual creativity of the author shaped the historical narrative, it did not fabricate the historical facts.

Kuhn thought that the gospels of Matthew and John demonstrated his point. The "dogmatic character" of the first gospel so dominated over its historical aspect that Kuhn was ready "to concede still greater infringements of the concrete, external truth of history" in this gospel "than one has been able until now to expose with more or less probability." Nonetheless, Kuhn insisted that this infringement affected only the particular details in Matthew; it did not include the essential core of the story.[74] Kuhn's argument was basically the same for the gospel of John. Although it was influenced by Gnosticism and although it differed significantly from the synoptic gospels, John still possessed an historical substratum that was reliable.[75]

The assumptions behind this endeavor to preserve the historical substance of the gospel narrative were philosophical and theological. Kuhn assumed that the evangelical story was effective in achieving its theological purpose only if it were substantially true historically. Kuhn held that the strength of the Glaubensbeweis depends "entirely upon the certainty of what has happened," and that historical certainty, "in turn, depends upon the degree of testimony to the same."[76] The testimony of the apostles had to confirm historically that Jesus possessed the most elevated natural condition if a person were reasonably to claim that Jesus was the Christ or Son of God. For this reason, establishing the substantial historical veracity of the gospel narrative about Jesus was a matter of utmost theological concern to Kuhn.[77]

Kuhn believed that an adequate theology of history could simultaneously dislodge Strauss's mythological theory and meet the demands of both reason and faith. In a chapter entitled "The Deduction of the Christ Idea," Kuhn sketched part of a theology of history that, he thought, would demonstrate that the theological significance attributed by the evangelists to the historical narrative of Jesus' life was credible to objective human reason. His central presupposition was that historical process and human development had purposive direction, which was neither linear nor circular. Kuhn argued that history could not have such order unless there existed a higher, guiding reason that provided general cohesion to the diverse, subjective intentions of human agents. In short, subjective and objective reason had to cooperate in giving order and purpose to history.

In view of the order and non-linear development of history, Kuhn postulated that it was reasonable to expect a middle point in the process by which the whole was borne. Kuhn offered the idea of the Christ as this bearer of the highest development of human history.78 Just as the moral world order was advanced by paradigmatic human individuals, so too the highest development of which humans were capable was to be exemplified by an individual. In the Judeo-Christian world, such an individual was called "Christ." Kuhn concluded his sketch of a theory of history with the thesis that the highest world-historical function implied the highest natural endowment and, correlatively, that the attainment of the highest human capability presupposed propinquity to divinity.[79]

Kuhn's desire to verify the gospel story historically did not mean that he simply read the text in the traditional dogmatic way. He approached the question of Jesus' messianic consciousness, for example, psychologically.[80] Kuhn's reasoning was that whatever entered into the finite world and produced a definite effect in it had to traverse a temporal, finite development. His exposition focused, therefore, on Jesus' natural human capacity as the zenith of human possibility. He placed Jesus' humanity into the foreground of his presentation without denying Jesus' divinity. Nonetheless, his christology "from below" drew criticism from the conservative journal The Catholic, which accused Kuhn of christological heterodoxy and claimed that his view bordered on Nestorianism.[81]

The specific complaint of Kuhn's anonymous Catholic critic was that the idea of a gradual development of Jesus' consciousness was incompatible with orthodox Catholic teaching. The critic argued that consciousness was thoroughly determined by one's personality. In Jesus' case, that meant that Jesus' consciousness was shaped and determined by the Logos, which--as divine--did not permit the gradual awakening of messianic self-consciousness in response to the influence of external causes, as Kuhn had suggested.

Kuhn's rebuttal was twofold. First, he averred that his position would be objectionable if he had asserted Jesus' humanity exclusively. He, however, had not done that. He had only highlighted Jesus' humanity, as was appropriate for an historical presentation of Jesus' life. Second, Kuhn argued that the denial of a gradually developing human consciousness in Jesus bordered on Eutychianism. If Jesus possessed a complete human intelligence (as orthodox doctrine affirmed), and if self-consciousness were essential to intelligence, then, concluded Kuhn, Jesus had to have a human self-consciousness. And a human self-consciousness entailed development in time via environment, education, and language. Jesus' childhood, therefore, was not merely physically, but also spiritually and psychologically different from his adulthood.[82]

Kuhn's conflict with conservative Catholicism discloses his median position between traditional supernaturalism and Straussian radicalism in
the investigation of the gospels. That Kuhn agreed in principle more with
Strauss than with the conservative Catholics is suggested by his rejection
of the anonymous Catholic critic's assertion that the entire course of higher
biblical criticism opposed the Catholic spirit. Kuhn defended the propriety
of the application of historical-critical principles to the New Testament for
the sake of writing a scientific life of Jesus; he labelled its prohibition a
sign of conservative dogmatism.[83] Kuhn refused to accept the authority of
scholastic theologians, since their exposition of Jesus' divinity was exaggerated; and he refused to regard traditional supernaturalism as normative.[84]
By contrast, Kuhn advocated an understanding of Jesus in which neither
his divinity nor his humanity was unduly emphasized. If Strauss had
gone too far in eliminating the distinctions between Jesus and the rest of
humankind, the scholastic and conservative Catholics were in danger of
going too far in asserting those distinctions.

Kuhn, then, concurred with Strauss in the use of historical criticism.
They disagreed, however, on the precise specification of what constituted
the necessary principles and conclusions of such criticism of the gospels.
That divergence had its root in different conceptions of faith and christology.

An Assessment of Kuhn's Disagreement with Strauss

Kuhn's debate with Strauss was ultimately about the core of Christian faith.
In the words of Franz Courth, it addressed the fundamental question of
Christian dogmatics: "whether the truth of Christianity ... is an idea that
can be separated from history, or whether the Christian truth remains,
necessarily and for all time, bound to the concrete history of Jesus of
Nazareth."[85] Kuhn thought that Strauss had released the essential truth of
Christianity from its anchoring in history and had eviscerated the historical
content of faith, namely, its assertion that Jesus was the Christ. For that
reason, Kuhn could not regard Strauss's construal of faith Christian in the
strict sense.[86] Although it referred to the story of Jesus and used the cate-
gories of Christian theology, Strauss's construal of faith was a philosophical

construct of ideas. Kuhn believed that it made the connection to Jesus tenuous at best and irrelevant at worst, and for this reason Kuhn judged Strauss's conception of faith to be discontinuous with the past tradition of the Church and inappropriate to the present needs for a Christian dogmatics. According to Kuhn, not only the proper use of the name "Christian," but also the ability reasonably to affirm the truth of Christianity required every modern formulation of faith to ground itself in the actual facts of Jesus' life and of the movement it spawned.[87] Whereas Strauss' faith in the truth of Christianity was established primarily by his particular appropriation of Hegelian philosophy, Kuhn's faith in it was established primarily by the testimony of the apostles (originally) and the witness of the Church (contemporaneously).[88]

The constitutive reference to history had been the most essential characteristic of Kuhn's conception of faith since his earliest days as a theologian.[89] In his first publication, Kuhn asserted that history is "the fundamental characteristic and simultaneously the primordial element of Christianity."[90] In fact, it was its focus upon history that distinguished theology from philosophy in Kuhn's mind. Although both disciplines studied God, as Hegel had claimed, the latter proceeded in an abstract fashion, while the former examined God's concrete activity in the historical process. To deny or to diminish the importance of history thus constituted a violation of the very nature of theology.[91]

In support of his view of the importance of history in general and of Jesus' history in particular, Kuhn appealed to the Judeo-Christian heritage and to apostolic tradition. The former held that the deity revealed itself only in history; the latter claimed that the deity expressed itself most clearly and most fully in and through the historical person Jesus. It was this identification of history as the primary locus of God's activity that distinguished Jewish and Christian faith from other forms of belief in God. And Christian faith was distinguished from Jewish faith by its "idiosyncratic, historically given essence," the affirmation of Jesus of Nazareth as the Christ. Kuhn conceived of faith neither as a general faith in God nor as an abstract belief that existence is worthwhile. On the contrary, its peculiar character consisted in "the immediate connection of faith to Jesus Christ and in this [connection]--that is, mediately--to God."[92]

Kuhn therefore objected to Strauss's construal of faith because it made Jesus at best the historical occasion for raising the idea of the unity of humanity and divinity into general human consciousness, but it did not make him part of the content of faith. Kuhn, on the other hand, held that faith made the claim that Jesus mediated the presence of God. For Kuhn, this christological claim had an historical as well as an existential character. Its historical aspect comprised the conviction that "the messianic age is inaugurated through the messiah Jesus" and that through him "everything formerly promised by God has been fulfilled." Even the existential aspect, the experience of being regenerated and the adoption of a new understanding of life, was tied to Jesus.[93] Historical knowledge about Jesus was therefore both relevant and necessary.

In his response to Strauss, Kuhn generally presumed, rather than cogently argued for, the greater adequacy of his understanding of faith. His presumption, however, was made explicit in other contexts. In reviewing a Protestant book on the Christian teaching concerning faith in 1835, Kuhn claimed greater adequacy for his position since it corresponded better with the New Testament understanding of faith and with the apostolic tradition.

> New Testament faith, where it appears in a characteristic way, is essentially a faith in Jesus the messiah, the reconciler and also the only necessary mediator of the salvation of humanity. Not a single apostle has preached, none of the New Testament authors has taught that general faith as confidence in God, i.e., in eternal truth and the highest good. Their preaching and teaching is, in general and in its deepest roots, not abstract but historical: a simple reference to the gracious action and mighty deeds of God in the course of time ...[94]

The implicit basis of Kuhn's presumption was the conviction that Christian faith lost religious force and form if it were construed as presenting only an ideal or possible mode of living in the world rather than a way of living that had been realized in the past (by Jesus) and that now stood before people as a challenging demand. Such a conviction seems to have been operative when Kuhn claimed, on the one hand, that "the truth, effect, and fruit" of Christianity deteriorated if the historical content of the gospel story were curtailed;[95] on the other, when he asserted that the mere image of Jesus, the story about him, and his teaching by themselves were all devoid of redemptive force.

> Of course, an exalted personality can have a mighty effect upon his contemporaries; his example can powerfully stimulate through the magic of reality. But the magic no longer helps the succeeding generations; they have only a picture of him, which exercises no greater effect than the ideal of a perfect human being, such as the philosophers are concerned to set up in their writings. Then for what reason is Christ for us? Will his image redeem us?--But his teaching, they say, can do that. Then that, which is determined now in one way, now in another, is supposed to produce a very definite, one and the same effect! In this case it is just like with reason, to which all appeal and each understands by it his own opinion.[96]

By appealing to what was "objectively given" in the story about Jesus, Kuhn gave the impression that for him faith was, to a great extent, a matter of historical knowledge. But he conceived of faith and knowledge as related, yet distinct.

Both faith and knowledge were built upon an intuitive knowing.[97] Faith differed from knowledge, however, insofar as its truth and certainty were not established solely by the human mind. Kuhn held the distinction between knowledge and faith to be roughly analogous to Thomas Aquinas' distinction between a science in the strict sense and a subalternate science.[98] Since the nature of faith was both similar and dissimilar to the nature of knowledge, theology's task was accordingly analogous to philosophy's. Just as philosophy moved from perception (_Anschauung_) to concept (_Begriff_), so theology moved from positive faith (_positiver Glaube_) to known faith (_gewusster Glaube_).[99]

Strauss had also spoken of philosophy's need to move beyond sense knowledge to true knowledge, and he had applied this idea analogously to theology's task.

> Rather, just as sense certainty, the 'this' and the 'supposing that,' showed itself, in the course of things, to be the poorest and emptiest mode of cognition, so too believing certainty, holding fast to the indicated 'this,' to this miracle, to this person, in general to this portion from the rest of history and reality, must be recognized as a relatively needy form of the religious life.[100]

Hence:

> Contemporary christology wants to be led to the idea in the fact, to the race in the individual. A dogmatics which, in its doctrine of Christ, remains standing alongside him as an individual is not dogmatics, but a homily.[101]

Strauss and Kuhn clearly meant different things by the movement of faith from a simple to a mature stage. The disputed issue between them was whether the reformulation of faith entailed a change in faith's content. Strauss insisted in the Preface to his Life of Jesus that the reformulation involved merely a change in the form in which Christian truth was presented. In actuality, it entailed a material change in the traditional understanding of faith, consisting in the replacement of Jesus the Christ with the idea of the divine humanity (Gottmenschlichkeit) of the human race as the content of faith.[102] In this process, faith became knowledge; believing in Jesus as the Christ became knowing the divinity of the human species.[103] With reference to the "divine humanity" of the human species, Strauss claimed:

> This alone is the absolute content of christology. That the same appears bound to the person and history of an individual has only the subjective cause that this individual, through his personality and his fate, became the occasion of raising that content into the general consciousness and that the intellectual level of the ancient world--and of the people in every age--was capable of viewing the idea of humanity only in the concrete figure of an individual.[104]

Kuhn argued that this formulation of christology expressed a radical transformation of the nature and content of faith. Faith was not a matter of philosophical knowledge, even though knowledge was not totally alien to it. And although theology was not satisfied with simple, intuitive faith, it could not allow the movement from simple to mediated faith to entail a change in the content of Christian faith.[105] Mature or mediated faith recognized that the gospel narrative was not entirely true historically, and it articulated the nature of the Christ's relationship to God in a much more sophisticated and philosophical way than that of simple or unmediated faith. Nonetheless, both forms of faith asserted that God was active in a special way in the person of Jesus of Nazareth. For Kuhn, this specific focus upon Jesus and the assertion about the special status of Jesus was an integral part of the content of faith.

The adequacy of Kuhn's understanding of the relationship of history and faith depends in large part upon the way faith is construed. Kuhn held that the belief that Jesus was the Christ was integral to full Christian faith. Because faith therefore seems to make assumptions about an historical person, Kuhn inferred that historical knowledge about Jesus has a bearing on faith. The weakness of his view, however, was that he failed to appreciate that faith was also a matter of existential orientation, which did not require historical analysis as a condition of its possibility. Kuhn did not consider seriously enough that faith and Christian living might be possible on the basis of an existential appropriation of Jesus' example, without a verification of the historical accuracy of the gospel's portrayal of Jesus. Having assumed that his view had the full support of the tradition, Kuhn neglected to offer decisive arguments for the inadmissibility of Strauss's understanding of faith. He did offer, however, a few considerations in support of the adequacy of his own interpretation of Christian faith.

The most important consideration Kuhn put forth was the necessary role of the present church's proclamation and witness as a source of faith. Kuhn observed that when faith is shaped and nourished by the larger Christian community it is more reliable since it is less vulnerable to the subjective distortions of individuals. He claimed that the individual "is what it is only as a living member of the community," and he drew the conclusion that the faith of the individual "is not independent of the faith of all and is not true and valid for itself beyond the common consciousness."[106] According to this line of the thought, Protestants who relied on Scripture as the exclusive source of faith were mistaken, and individual interpretations of Scripture which were not generated by or nourished in the Christian community were unfounded. In short, Kuhn asserted that the faith of the individual Christian was dependent upon the Church, and the church of the present, in turn, was dependent upon the church of the past. Whereas the source of Christian truth is found primarily in Scripture (and secondarily in complementary traditions), the source of faith is located in Tradition, the proclamation and witness of the contemporary church.[107]

Kuhn alleged that Strauss had distorted the Church's faith by claiming that his particular appropriation of an Hegelian philosophy of religion was identical with it. Against this temptation to make out of faith what one wanted, Kuhn appealed to the givenness of Tradition and the importance of "ecclesial consciousness." And in response to the thoroughgoing critical character of Strauss's book, Kuhn asserted that if one's starting point was not the present consciousness of the Church, but rather one's own radical doubt about the truth of that consciousness, then "such a person not only never comes to faith itself and to the truth and certainty characteristic of it," but also transforms faith into "a merely natural product of science and of human reason."[108] For Kuhn, acceptance of the historical claims of Christian faith depended in part upon one's trust in the fidelity of the Tradition to the actual story of Jesus' life and teaching. In his Life of Jesus, Kuhn attempted to demonstrate that the Tradition, although not necessarily true in the literal sense, was nonetheless fundamentally trustworthy. In his later reflections on faith and knowledge, he advanced the thesis that acceptance of the existential and religious claims of Christian faith depended upon the medium through which those claims were communicated. For Kuhn, the principal medium was the church community.[109]

Just as Strauss used exegesis to support his theological case about Christian faith, so too Kuhn turned to exegesis to refute Strauss and to establish his own interpretation. And the weakness of Kuhn's case becomes apparent at this point. His conviction about the importance of the historical content of faith and Jesus' role therein led Kuhn to overestimate the significance of historical knowledge about Jesus. Correlatively, he failed to appreciate that living in a Christian manner today was possible and meaningful even if history could not verify that Jesus had lived that way. Moreover, his theological presuppositions prevented him from living up to the critical rigor demanded of him as a biblical critic.

Kuhn's theological premises made him willing as an exegete to accept the Tradition's account of Jesus' story in cases where high historical proba- bility simply did not exist. Kuhn narrowly construed the New Testament meaning of "eyewitness," and he accepted Luke's self-proclaimed intention to report the testimony of eyewitnesses uncritically. Although he recog- nized that a theological aim guided, and sometimes dominated, the gospel narrative, Kuhn failed to perceive that the evangelists not only could dis- tort the details of Jesus' life, but also could generate entire stories about him or accept unknowingly a story generated in the oral tradition. Other weaknesses of Kuhn's work were its tendency to presume that its case was proven once the deficiencies in his opponent's position had been re- vealed,[110] and its tendency to overstate its case.[111]

On the other hand, there are a number of positive and praiseworthy features about Kuhn's response to Strauss. In the first place, he was fre- quently convincing in his critique of Strauss. Kuhn rightly criticized Strauss for failing to admit his own presuppositions about Christianity and Scripture as well as for letting his philosophical speculation subvert the exegetical task. Kuhn was also correct to oppose the mythical view (as well as the supernaturalistic view) as the _exclusive_ standpoint from which to interpret the gospel texts. Similarly, he was justified in taking Strauss to task for not undertaking a serious literary-critical analysis of the gospels and not exercising caution when talking about possibilities and probabili- ties. In this regard, Kuhn, more than Strauss, shared the same concern as modern form criticism with the history of the form and content of the syn- optic tradition.[112]

For his part, Kuhn was a sympathetic interpreter of the gospels' pur- pose. He recognized that the evangelical proclamation about Jesus had both an historical starting point and a theological intent, and he averred that the loss of either element entailed a serious alteration in the original nature of Christian faith. Although Kuhn was insufficiently critical by modern standards, he did recognize the creative element in the process of tradition.

Moreover, Kuhn clearly acknowledged the need for and the propriety of historical criticism of the Bible. He refused to acquiesce to the demands of those more conservative Catholics, who declared that "higher criticism" had no place in Catholicism.[113] It was to Kuhn's credit that he attempted to define a median position between Strauss and the conservative Catholics. He neither relinquished what he perceived to be the essence of the Catholic understanding of Christian faith nor allowed his theology to harden into a narrow Catholic dogmatism, at once anti-modern and anti-critical. Rather, Kuhn's theology was in open dialogue with modern scholarship and with Protestant theology, and it accepted as much from each as he deemed appropriate.[114]

In the final analysis, Kuhn's response to Strauss, despite its limitations, is worthy of consideration and of praise. Insofar as Kuhn understood the gospels not as biographies, but as documents written by people of faith, who consciously selected their materials for the promulgation of faith, Norman Perrin's appraisal of Kuhn's Life of Jesus is accurate: in many ways Kuhn's book is a hundred years ahead of its time.[115]

NOTES

[1]Johannes Kuhn, "Von dem schriftstellerischen Charakter der Evangelien im Verhältniss zu der apostolischen Predigt und den apostolischen Briefen," Jahrbücher für Theologie und christliche Philosophie 6 (1836):33-91; "Hermeneutik und Kritik in ihrer Anwendung auf die evangelische Geschichte," ibid. 7 (1836):1-50. Although M. J. Mack also referred to Strauss's Life of Jesus in his 1836 article on the messianic views of Jesus' contemporaries, Kuhn's first essay appeared earlier in the year. See Franz Courth, Leben Jesu, p. 272, note 3. Cf. Josef Rupert Geiselmann, "Der Glaube an Jesus Christus--Mythos oder Geschichte? Zur Auseinandersetzung Joh. Ev. Kuhns mit David Friedrich Strauß," Theologische Quartalschrift (1949):261.

[2]One can only speculate about the reasons for Kuhn's failure to finish his reply to Strauss. A major factor was probably his assumption of the chair for dogmatics at the University of Tübingen in 1839. Kuhn took over this post from his mentor, the founder of the Catholic Tübingen School, Johann Sebastian Drey; he continued in this position until the end of his life (1887). The time consumed by his professorial duties, his work with the small Catholic community in Tübingen, and his involvement in church-political affairs of the 1840s apparently precluded Kuhn's further involvement with Strauss's work. For a detailed sketch of Kuhn's life, see August Hagen, Gestalten aus dem schwäbischen Katholizismus, Zweiter Teil (Stuttgart: Schwabenverlag, 1950), pp. 59-95. For a good sketch of his theological work, see Franz Wolfinger, "Johannes Evangelist von Kuhn (1806-1887)," in: Heinrich Fries and Georg Schwaiger, eds., Katholische Theologen Deutschlands im 19. Jahrhundert, 3 vols. (Munich: Kösel Verlag, 1975), 2:129-62.

[3]"Among the Catholic Leben Jesu, of which the authors found their incentive in the desire to oppose Strauss, the first place belongs to that of Kuhn of Tübingen ...Here there is a serious and scholarly attempt to grapple with the problems raised by Strauss." Schweitzer, p. 107, note 5. See also Karl Adam, "Die katholische Tübinger Schule" in his Gesammelte Aufsätze zur Dogmengeschichte und Theologie der Gegenwart (Augsburg: P. Haas & Co., 1936), p. 402. Stephan Lösch judged Kuhn's Life of Jesus to be not only the most technically refined contemporary criticism of Strauss, but also one of Kuhn's best works ever. "Die katholisch-theologischen Fakultäten zu Tübingen und Giessen (1830-50)," Theologische Quartalschrift 108 (1927):177.

[4]Kuhn, "Ueber Glauben und Wissen, mit Rücksicht auf extreme Ansichten und Richtungen der Gegenwart," Theologische Quartalschrift 21 (1839):421.

[5]Kuhn, "Über Apostelgeschichte 5, 36.37," Jahrbücher für Theologie und christliche Philosophie 1 (1834):4.

[6]Ibid., p. 28. See also "Über Matth. 23, 35," Jahrbücher für Theologie und christliche Philosophie 1 (1834):339-40.

[7]Ibid., p. 340.

[8]Ibid., pp. 340 and 370. Cf. "Über Apostelgeschichte," p. 28.

[9]Kuhn, "Von dem schriftstellerischen Charakter," pp. 34-37. Despite their basic coherence, Kuhn admitted that the gospels and the apostolic kerygma differed in certain respects. He thought that the latter was more tapered to the needs of individual communities, whereas the former were more general and abstract demonstrations of the reasonableness of Christian faith. See pp. 89-90.

[10]Ibid., p. 43. Kuhn meant "proof" [Beweis] in the sense of a justification of the possibility of faith rather than a scientific demonstration of its necessity. See Franz Wolfinger, Der Glaube nach Johann Evangelist von Kuhn. Wesen, Formen, Herkunft, Entwicklung (Göttingen: Vandenhoeck & Ruprecht, 1972), pp. 86-90. Kuhn, moreover, did not fail to emphasize the supernatural quality and gift-character of Christian faith. See his "Über Glauben und Wissen," pp. 405-06, 418-20.

[11]Kuhn, "Von dem schriftstellerischen Charakter," pp. 47-48. Cf. Kuhn's Das Leben Jesu wissenschaftlich bearbeitet (Mainz: 1838; reprint ed., Frankfurt: Minerva, 1968), pp. 127-28.

[12]Kuhn, "Von dem schriftstellerischen Charakter," pp. 56 and 59.

[13]Ibid., p. 65.

[14]That parallel was Matt. 4:2 and Deut. 9:9, 18. The specification of Jesus' adult life is significant since Kuhn restricted the history of Jesus' life to the period that commenced with his baptism by John. Thus, any possible parallels between the birth narratives of Moses and of Jesus were ruled out of consideration. Ibid., pp. 44 and 46. Cf. Strauss, Leben Jesu (1835), 1:72-73.

[15]Kuhn, "Von dem schriftstellerischen Charakter," p. 67. Kuhn's refutation of Strauss's claim is built primarily upon evidence from John's gospel, whose historical reliability is today held suspect. Kuhn considered John to be the only gospel that could claim a direct apostolic origin in the strict sense since he did not think the Greek version of Matthew (in its present form) originated with the apostle Matthew. See ibid., p. 46.

[16]Ibid., pp. 67-68. Similarly, Kuhn opposed Strauss's claim that Deut. 18:15 provided the motive force for the evangelists' desire to portray Jesus as a prophet like Moses. See Strauss, Leben Jesu (1835), 1:72-73, especially note 31 on p. 72. Kuhn argued that this text naturally referred to the entire series of prophets who would succeed Moses, but that it had acquired a messianic interpretation by the time of Jesus. Since the actual characteristics and activity of Jesus' life suggested that he too was a prophet, it was natural enough to apply this passage also to Jesus.

[17]Kuhn, "Von dem schriftstellerischen Charakter," p. 70.

[18]Ibid., p. 75. Kuhn's argument has merit, but it does not thoroughly refute Strauss's case. One can accept Kuhn's basic point without following him to the conclusion that no specific conception or expectation of the messiah influenced the gospel picture of Jesus in a significant way. Insofar as both Kuhn and Strauss overstated their cases, each provided an important counterbalance to the other's claims.

[19]Kuhn's refutation of Strauss's explanation of myth-formation was, at best, only partially successful. His first foray, although it uncovered a weakness in Strauss's logic, could do nothing more than require Strauss to modify his strong claim; it did not require a rejection of Strauss's basic insight about the distorting capacity of tradition. In fact, Kuhn's line of argument left him open to Strauss's criticism for presupposing the historical veracity of the first link in the chain of oral transmission of the story of Jesus' life. Kuhn thereby begged the question Strauss had raised. Similarly, Kuhn's second foray against Strauss's explanation of myth-formation required, at most, the moderation of Strauss's view, not its rejection altogether. Moses and the Hebrew prophets may not have been the models according to which each event in the gospel portrayal of Jesus' life was creatively fashioned, but to deny altogether that they exercised considerable influence on the portrayal of those events was naive from the perspective of rigorous historical criticism.

[20]To allege that the formula "it happened so that Scripture might be ful-filled" was the result of myth-production constituted one of the most seri-ous hermeneutical errors Kuhn could imagine. See ibid., pp. 82-84. For support of his view, Kuhn appealed to Ammon, whom Strauss had criti-cized for inconsistency and lack of clarity in his treatment of myth. P. 84, notes 1 and 2.

[21]Ibid., p. 86.

[22]Kuhn, "Hermeneutik," p. 2.

[23]Ibid., pp. 10-15.

[24]Ibid., p. 19. Concerning the naturalistic interpretation, see ibid. pp. 9 and 15.

[25]Ibid., p. 25.

[26]Ibid., pp. 25-26.

[27]Ibid., p. 22.

[28]Ibid., pp. 19 and 25.

[29]Ibid., p. 37.

[30]Strauss, Leben Jesu (1835), 1:59-66.

[31]Kuhn, "Hermeneutik," p. 39. Cf. Kuhn's Leben Jesu, pp. 6-8. Although Kuhn's appeal to the consensus understanding concerning the authenticity of John's gospel has been vitiated by contemporary scholarship, his argu-ment against Strauss could reckon with considerable scholarly approval in the nineteenth century (e.g., from Schleiermacher). The Protestant Ull-mann, for example, agreed with Kuhn that Strauss's handling of the exter-nal evidence for apostolic authorship was inappropriate. See Ullmann's re-view of Strauss's Life of Jesus in the third Heft of Studien und Kritiken (1836):789.

[32]Strauss said: "Man wird die Forderung überspannt nennen, für die Au-thentie eines Buchs ein Zeugniss von einem Bekannten des Verfassers, also gleichsam von einem Augenzeugen des Aktes der Abfassung und einem Ohrenzeugen der Versicherung des Autors, es geschrieben zu haben, zu verlangen. Sie wäre es, wenn es sich nur um Wahrscheinlichkeit, wenn

auch noch so hohe, der Authentie einer Schrift handelte: hier aber wird
Nothwendigkeit, oder ein Zeugniss verlangt, welches uns auch gegen das
etwaige Ergebniss der inneren Kritik doch bei der Annahme eines apostolischen Ursprungs der genannten Evangelien zwingend festhielte. Ein
zwingendes Zeugniss müßte die angeführte Beschaffenheit haben, und da
ein solches fehlt: so bleibt uns die Möglichkeit offen, je nach der inneren
Beschaffenheit jener Evangelien sie als Werke von Aposteln oder Nichta-
posteln zu behandeln." Leben Jesu (1835), 1:64.

[33]Kuhn, "Hermeneutik," pp. 37-38.

[34]Kuhn defended Paulus' interpretation by citing those New Testament
passages that seemed to voice strong opposition to the inclusion of myths
in Christian teaching (e.g., I Tim. 1:4, 4:7; Titus 1:14); by using II Peter
1:16-18 to make a case that, already in the apostolic age, the difference
between authentic and fabricated stories was recognized; and by highlighting the preference of the primitive Christian community for the dis-
courses of Peter or James over those of Paul, since the latter had not been
an eyewitness of Jesus' life. Ibid., pp. 28-32.

[35]Strauss, Leben Jesu (1835), 1:57.

[36]Kuhn, "Hermeneutik," p. 33.

[37]For example, Kuhn held that the possibility of myth-formation should not
be judged according to the time that elapsed between the death of Jesus
and the writing of the gospels, but according to the relation of the persons
reporting to the history reported. Ibid., note 1. Moreover, Kuhn argued
that even Paul, as a preacher of the good news, had to have been interested in the historical details of Jesus' life and would not have allowed the
historical knowledge he gained from others to be tainted with mythical
additions. Ibid., p. 48. In both cases, Kuhn presumed that ancient Christians were interested in history and thought historically in a manner
closely akin to the historical thinking of his nineteenth-century contemporaries.

[38]Ibid., p. 43.

[39]See Kuhn, "Ueber Glauben und Wissen," p. 421.

[40]See Kuhn's "[Selbstanzeige über] das Leben Jesu, wissenschaftlich bearbeitet von Dr. Johannes Kuhn," Theologische Quartalschrift (1838):567, 564.

[41]Consequently, it was impossible to find an independent, comprehensive appraisal of the concept of myth in Kuhn's Life of Jesus. Kuhn was concerned to criticize the foundations upon which Strauss's mythical theory was built, rather than the concept itself: "Dieser [i.e., Mythosbegriff] ist, wie gesagt, bei weitem nicht das wichtigste und bedarf streng genommen gar keiner Widerlegung; er ist nur ein wiewohl glänzender Lückenbüsser für die tiefe Leere, welche die herrschende Philosophie unter dem unfreiwilligen Beistande der veralteten Theologie erzeugt hat. Alles kommt vielmehr darauf an, zu untersuchen, ob sich das große Loch in der Urgeschichte unserer Religion wirklich findet, oder ob man es ihr nur angedichtet hat." Ibid., p. 570. Insofar as myth's function was, according to Strauss, to express in religion what the concept expressed in philosophy, Kuhn was correct in detecting the secondary importance of myth in Strauss's Life of Jesus. Myth had a subordinate function in Strauss's system vis-à-vis the idea of the unity of humanity and divinity. Cf. Courth, Leben Jesu, p. 130.

[42]"Wie schon das Evangelium, auf dessen Grund sie allein gebaut werden kann, wesentlich zwei Seiten hat, eine historische und eine didaktische, so muß die wissenschaftliche Darstellung von der Kritik des Geschichtlichen zu dem theologischen Momente, der speculativen Erörterung des Glaubensbeweises, fortschreiten." Kuhn, Leben Jesu, p. iv.

[43]Ibid., pp. 117–18.

[44]In censuring the one-sidedness and negativity of Strauss's work, Kuhn was advancing a criticism similar to F. C. Baur's. See Baur's letter to Märklin, 26 November 1846, in Lang, Zweiter Teil, p. 129. Cf. Baur's "Abgenöthigte Erklärung," in Scholder, p. 294.

[45]Kuhn, Leben Jesu, pp. 117–18.

[46]"Die Sucht, Widersprüche in den Evangelien aufzufinden, muß auf den höchsten Gipfel gestiegen sein, wenn sie sich wie hier auf durchaus klare Dinge wirft, welche überall keinen Verdacht erwecken, außer wo die Skepsis zum Princip gemacht worden." Ibid., p. 347.

[47]Here Kuhn reiterated his critique from his earlier essay on hermeneutics. See "Hermeneutik," pp. 37–39. Strauss began with the internal evidence and gave it the predominant role in forming his judgment about the gospels' derivation from apostles or from their associates: "Die dabei zum Grunde liegende Ansicht über den Ursprung unsrer Evangelien wird theils

auf innere Gründe, theils auf äußere Zeugnisse gestüzt. In ersterer
Beziehung sind alle diejenigen Stücke in den Evangelien, welche sich
weigern, anders als mythisch sich auslegen zu lassen, eben so viele innere
Gründe gegen die Voraussetzung einer Abfassung derselben durch Apostel
oder solche, welche unmittelbar von Aposteln ihre Erkundigungen eingezo-
gen hätten; auf innere Gründe also kann die Authentie der Evangelien
nicht gebaut werden, ehe sämmtliche Erzählungen derselben darauf ange-
sehen sind, ob sie eine historische oder eine mythische Auffassung verlangen." Strauss, Leben Jesu (1835), 1: 62-63. This strong statement and the
lengthy section that followed appears only in the first edition of Strauss's
Life of Jesus, though some of that subsequent material appeared in a re-
worked form in the second edition. Kuhn responded to Strauss: "But what
authorizes him [i.e., Strauss], already here at the beginning of the investigation, to presuppose the result of his internal critique and to make it the
criterion for the external critique? That rests essentially upon the presupposition of the inauthenticity of our gospels (Strauss, p. 62). How is it possible to determine according to it the principle for investigating authenticity? This is a striking case of petitio principii." Kuhn, Leben Jesu, pp. 9-10.

[48]Misunderstanding in such a fundamental area doomed to failure any scientific critique of the gospels: "Ueber den schriftstellerischen Charakter
der Evangelien sind die Urtheile noch eben so schwankend als falsch, und
nur diess Eine entgeht Niemand, daß sie die Seele der Kritik der evangelischen Geschichte berühren, deren Erfolg zuletzt ganz allein von ihnen ab-
hängt." Ibid., p. viii. In particular, Kuhn faulted Strauss for demanding
total harmony among the various accounts of Jesus' life as the requisite for
the gospels' historical credibility. In this regard, Kuhn perceived a basic
similarity in principle between Strauss and gospel harmonists. Whereas
the latter thought such harmony was an actual characteristic of the
gospels, the former insisted that it was not an actual characteristic, but a
necessary (and lacking) requirement for the gospels' credibility. See ibid.,
p. 187. See also p. 343, where Kuhn says in exasperation: "So zeigt sich
auch hier wieder als eine über alles Maass reiche Quelle von Irrthümern
und Anklagen gegen das Evangelium, die unberechtigte Voraussetzung, daß
jeder Evangelist eine vollständige und genaue Geschichte des Lebens Jesu
habe geben wollen und müssen!"

[49]For Strauss, "scientific" connoted total freedom from dogmatic presuppositions and the acceptance of the uniformity of all events as the principal
tool of historical criticism. See his Leben Jesu (1835), 1 : x. Cf. Kuhn,
Leben Jesu, p. 340, note 3: "How little of a genuinely critical content the
more recent, namely Strauss's critique is entitled to claim is most apparent
from the unlimited accumulation of dogmatic decisions. Criticism and

dogmatism are known opposites and we want only to remind one not to confuse the latter with the former."

[50]Ibid., pp. vi–vii.

[51]See Courth, Leben Jesu, pp. 163–65. Courth sketches both Kuhn's distancing of himself from Hegel and his critical appropriation of the same, including Hegel's role in freeing Kuhn from the Romantic conception of history. Cf. Wolfinger, Der Glaube, p. 93.

[52] See Kuhn's "Selbstanzeige," pp. 565–66, where he admitted that the pitiful exposition of miracles by theologians was also partly responsible for Strauss's rejection of them. For Kuhn's understanding of pantheism, see "Ueber Glauben und Wissen,' p. 396. See also pp. 432–35, where Kuhn alleged that the Hegelian philosophy of religion did not correspond to the Church's consciousness of the truth about God, humans, and their relationship. Correlatively, Kuhn suggested that the difference between philosophy and theology was perhaps more than a mere matter of form. In an earlier essay, "Über den Begriff und das Wesen der speculativen Theologie und (oder) christlichen Philosophie" (1832), Kuhn admitted that theology and philosophy had common truths and were subject to the same laws of knowledge. Their difference was the way they viewed their object: philosophy proceeded in a more abstract fashion, investigating the existence of God in nature; theology, on the other hand, proceeded more concretely, investigating God's existence in the dynamics of historical process. See Wolfinger, Der Glaube, p. 301.

[53]See Kuhn, Leben Jesu, pp. vi–vii.

[54]Strauss, by contrast, had suggested that the ascertainment of historical knowledge about Jesus was ultimately irrelevant for Christian faith. See Franz Courth, Leben Jesu, p. 75: "Für das Straußsche Geschichtsverständnis ist kennzeichnend, daß er nur dann bereit ist, Geschichte als annähernden Ausdruck der Idee gelten zu lassen, wenn man sie als universalgeschichtlichen Prozeß versteht. Nicht das Individuelle, Einmalige und Unwiderrufliche kann die Wirklichkeit der Idee widerspiegeln, sondern nur das Allgemeine und Unpersönliche." Thus: "Aufgrund dieser Einstufung von Idee und Geschichte ist für Strauß eine notwendige Verbindung der überzeitlichen Wahrheiten des Christentums mit konkreten Ereignissen der Geschichte undenkbar. Nie kann Geschichte für das Sein der Idee konstitutiv sein." Ibid. p. 77.

[55]Kuhn, Leben Jesu, p. vii.

[56]"Das Philosophische, welches in einer wissenschaftlichen Bearbeitung des Lebens Jesu in Betracht kommt, betrifft lediglich das Verhältnis der Idee zu der Thatsache, des Geistes zu der Geschichte, aber dieses in einem solchen Umfange und in einer Tiefe, wie nirgends sonst." Ibid., p. vi. Kuhn demonstrated his own use of philosophical reflection in establishing the relationship of idea and history in section 39 of his Life of Jesus, entitled "Deduction of the Christ Idea," pp. 129-40. Moreover, he noted that his particular use of philosophy would be revealed in his treatment of the Glaubensbeweis from the stories of Jesus' baptism, temptation, death, and resurrection as well as in his analysis of miracles and fulfilled prophecies. See pp. vii-viii. Unfortunately, we possess only Kuhn's discussion of the baptism and temptation stories; the rest, including his intended exposition of miracles, was never published. Kuhn, however, discussed in detail the role of philosophy in theology in his lengthy article, "Ueber Glauben und Wissen" (1839).

[57]Kuhn, "Ueber Glauben und Wissen," pp. 452-54.

[58]Kuhn, "Hermeneutik," p. 2.

[59]Although his full treatment of the question of miracle had been postponed to the (never published) third volume, Kuhn gave some indications of his view on this matter in the first volume of his response to Strauss. See his Leben Jesu, p. 312.

[60]"Zwar liegt es schon im Begriffe, daß das Wunder uns über den natürlichen Causalnexus hinausführt, während all' unser Erklären und Begreifen auf den ursächlichen Zusammenhang der natürlichen Dinge eingeschränkt ist, woraus folgt, daß eine Wundererklärung entweder gar nicht oder nur bedingter Weise möglich ist." Ibid., p. 310.

[61]Ibid., p. 321. See also p. 311.

[62]Ibid., pp. 319-20.

[63]Ibid., pp. 326-27, 332-34.

[64]Kuhn referred approvingly, ibid., p. 6, note 2, to Schleiermacher's Kurze Darstellung des theologischen Studiums, par. 113. See Friedrich Schleiermacher, Brief Outline on the Study of Theology, trans., with introductions and notes by Terrence N. Tice (Atlanta: John Knox Press, 1977), p. 52.

65"Dann aber ist es entschieden ein verfehlter, unwissenschaftlicher und unkritischer Standpunct, welchen die neueste Kritik der evangelischen Geschichte eingenommen hat, indem sie von vorne herein die Evangelien darauf ansieht, ob sie eine historische oder eine mythische Auffassung verlangen. Von vorne herein sage ich; denn ihre Prüfung der äußern Beweismittel steht in gar keinem Verhältnis zu der Freiheit, die sie sich nimmt, die evangelische Geschichte darauf anzusehen, ob sie nicht mythisch sei. Es ist diess also reine Willkür und der eingenommene Standpunct ein willkührlicher." Kuhn, Leben Jesu, pp. 84-85. See also pp. 6-8.

66"Hat man dann mit Berücksichtigung aller Umstände die Grenze der möglichen und den Grad der wirklichen Beglaubigung eines Buches ausfindig gemacht, so tritt die innere Kritik auf, welche aber, ihrer Natur nach, niemals das Resultat der äußeren Kritik gänzlich aufheben, sondern lediglich verstärken oder abschwächen kann. So wird erst durch beide die Stufe bestimmt, welche ein Schriftwerk auf der Stufenleiter der verschiedenen Modalitäten historischer Beglaubigung für uns einnimmt, bis neue Entdeckungen vorher nicht bekannter Zeugnisse gemacht werden, oder der Inhalt einer Schrift mit Rücksicht auf ihren Ursprung richtiger als bisher erkannt und beurtheilt wird." Ibid., p. 11. See also "Hermeneutik," pp. 37-39. Kuhn opined that the gospels had been composed, beginning about thirty years after the ascension, in the following order from the earliest to the latest: Matthew, Luke, Mark, and John. Leben Jesu, pp. 37-39. For Kuhn's analysis of Matthew, see ibid., pp. 13-17; Mark, pp. 31-33, 40-41; Luke, pp. 50-51, 61-63; John, pp. 65-69. Kuhn noted, p. 50, that the external evidence for Luke's gospel was weaker and not as old as the evidence for both Matthew's and Mark's gospels.

67Ibid., pp. 75-76, 78-83.

68Ibid., p. 84. See also pp. 5, 8, 20, and 286.

69See Wolfinger, Der Glaube, p. 86, note 49 and "Johannes Evangelist von Kuhn," p. 131.

70Again it should be noted that Glaubensbeweis did not connote for Kuhn the proving of one's faith. Faith was fundamentally a supernatural gift of God. Kuhn, therefore, insisted that a scientific presentation of Christian faith could never establish it, but could only help to remove hindrances to it. See his "Ueber Glauben und Wissen," p. 404, note 11 and pp. 420, 455-56.

[71]Kuhn, Leben Jesu, pp. 219, 286. Kuhn suggested, in a phrase reminiscent of Strauss's description of the function of myth, that the evangelists sometimes used material objects in their gospel narrative to symbolize abstract ideas. See pp. 313-14, where Kuhn says the following about the story of Jesus' baptism: "der offene Himmel und die Stimme gehören also nicht einmal zu der unmittelbaren Erscheinung, dem subjektiv Aeußerlichen, sondern sind Produkte der spätern Reflexion des Täufers oder der Evangelisten, und entweder als bloß ergänzende Züge der Erscheinung oder als sinnbildliche Darstellung abstrakter Ideen zu betrachten; oder es findet vielmehr beides statt. Denn wie schon die Erscheinung der Taube nur der entsprechende sinnliche Ausdruck des geistigen Eindrucks auf den Täufer ist, so sind die Ergänzungen jener Erscheinung zugleich Erweiterungen der einfachen Bedeutung derselben." (Emphasis mine.) Cf. Geiselmann, "Der Glaube an Jesus Christus," p. 427.

[72]Kuhn, Leben Jesu, pp. 86-87. See also pp. 185, 187, 343.

[73]Ibid., pp. 357-58.

[74]Ibid., p. 90. See also pp. 89, 92-93, 99-100.

[75]Ibid., pp. 107-08, 113. Concerning differences between John and the synoptic gospels, see pp. 230, 264-68, 285.

[76]Ibid., p. 156.

[77]Ibid., pp. 122-23.

[78]Ibid., pp. 133, 135-36. Kuhn's ideas here bear some resemblance to the transcendental, searching christology and to the concept of an absolute savior in the theology of Karl Rahner. See Rahner's Foundations of Christian Faith: An Introduction to the Idea of Christianity, trans. William V. Dych (New York: Seabury Press, 1978), pp. 178-203, especially pp. 179, 190-95.

[79]"Dieses Gesetz läßt sich durch den Satz ausdrücken: die erhabenste welthistorische Stellung des Menschen involvirt die höchste Naturbegabung. Auf den Messias angewandt ergibt sich der Satz: seine eminente, absolute Bestimmung setzt eine absolute, göttliche Natur voraus. Während aber jene historisch vorliegt und augenscheinlich durch die Apostel bezeugt ist, beruht die Annahme von dieser auf einem Schluß, dessen historische Fassung als Ueberlieferung (Matt. 1:2; Luke 1,2) dargeboten wird." Kuhn, Leben Jesu, p. 138.

[80]This section, pp. 419-44, which was not significantly altered in Kuhn's book, had originally been Kuhn's inaugural lecture at the University of Tübingen in the summer of 1837. See ibid., p. 419, note 1.

[81]This charge was made by an anonymous reviewer of Kuhn's Life of Jesus in Der Katholik 71 (1839):66-80, 209-19. See especially pp. 72-78 and 210-11. Although the terms "christology from above" and "christology from below" are anachronistic, they accurately correspond to Kuhn's meaning. Kuhn noted that a Life-of-Jesus approach to christology differed from a dogmatic approach in that it presents Jesus' life primarily as the ideal human life, whereas the latter presents his life as a divine life. Moreover, the truly adequate dogmatic approach ultimately unites the human and divine aspects, whereas the other approach, by its very nature, allows the divine aspect to retreat somewhat--without completely elimi-nating it. See Kuhn's "Ueber Glauben und Wissen," p. 491.

[82]Ibid., pp. 492-96.

[83]"Er [i.e., Kuhn's Catholic critic] hat die--für mich wenigstens--unerhörte Behauptung gegen mich geltend gemacht, daß 'die ganze sg. höhere Kritik ganz gegen den katholischen Geist' sei, und von diesem Gesichtspuncte aus gegen das Kritische in meinem Leben Jesu mehrere Einwendungen er-hoben, die ich bei solchen Prämissen ganz natürlich finde, die aber auch nicht mehr Bedeutung und Gewicht haben, als dieser sein bloßer Macht-spruch. Das sieht Jeder wohl ein, daß es um die wissenschaftliche Schrift-auslegung geschehen wäre, wenn die Behauptung des Ungenannten Grund hätte, und daß wir Katholiken wenigstens auf sie für immer verzichten müßten, wenn die Kritik gegen den Geist und das Princip unseres Glaubens verstiesse. Aber zum Glück ist es nicht ... Gegen unsern frühern Plan müssen wir uns übrigens für jetzt ... einer Auseinandersetzung dieses Gegenstandes enthalten und mit dem Versprechen schliessen, demnächst das Verhältniss der Kritik zur Auslegung auf dem katholischen Stand-puncte zu beleuchten, wo alsdann auch die Einwendungen ihre Erledigung finden werden, welche der Ungenannte in dieser Beziehung gegen die Kri-tik in meinem Leben Jesu aus dogmatischen Gründen gemacht hat." Ibid., pp. 502-03. Cf. Der Katholik (1839):74. Johann Sebastian Drey (1777-1853), the founder of the Catholic Tübingen School, had also welcomed the rise of the historical and exegetical disciplines. He advocated the study of the Bible as ancient literature; and he rejected the use of Scripture as a catalogue of proof-texts. "Noting the poor state of biblical criticism, he complains: how long has it been since Richard Simon, and there is still no reliable theory of biblical criticism?" James Tunstead Burtchaell, "Drey,

Möhler and the Tübingen School," in: Ninian Smart, John Clayton, Steven T. Katz, and Patrick Sherry, eds., Nineteenth Century Religious Thought in the West, 3 vols. (Cambridge: Cambridge University Press, 1985), 2:116. Cf. Friedrich Heyer, The Catholic Church From 1648 to 1870, trans. by D. W. D. Shaw (London: Adam & Charles Black, 1969), pp. 126-27, especially note 2 on p. 126.

[84]In the dispute about Kuhn's presentation of Jesus' self-consciousness as developing gradually, the critic in Der Katholik had appealed to scholastic theologians in support of his view that the reference in Luke 2:52 to Jesus' growth in wisdom only meant that Jesus' acquired knowledge was not the result of the appropriation of something outside himself, but the result of self-productive knowledge from inside. To that appeal, Kuhn responded: "If some scholastics have taught this concerning human knowledge, does it follow that one may not teach anything different? And have even all the scholastics and all the teachers of the church taught this way? Not at all!" "Ueber Glauben und Wissen," p. 501. Kuhn later became embroiled in a dispute with neoscholasticism and with Der Katholik concerning the relation of knowledge to faith and of philosophy to theology. See Wolfinger, Der Glaube, pp. 220-35, especially pp. 233-35. Cf. also Hagen, p. 84. Some Hermesian theologians also sent a notice to Rome against Kuhn's Life of Jesus. See Theologische Quartalschrift 22 (1840):282-311; 24 (1842):489-515. Cf. Wolfinger, "Johannes Evangelist von Kuhn," pp. 132-33, 137-38. Kuhn's opposition to the establishment of a free, Catholic university in Germany also brought him into conflict with the "Mainz School" and neoscholasticism. Kuhn's works, however, were not placed on the Index apparently because even some of his opponents recognized his great love of the Church and his contributions to the theological discipline. See Hans-Jürgen Brandt, Eine Katholische Universität in Deutschland? (Cologne: Böhlau Verlag, 1981), pp. 320-29, especially pp. 321-22.

[85]Courth, Das Leben Jesu, p. 16. Courth notes, moreover, that the question of faith's historical character and its rootedness in Jesus took precedence for Kuhn over the question about the range and activity of oral tradition (contra Geiselmann) and the questions of theism and pantheism (contra Wolfinger). Ibid., pp. 248-49. Cf. Geiselmann, "Der Glaube an Jesus Christus," p. 258; Wolfinger, Der Glaube, pp. 91-92, especially note 74 on p. 92, and p. 299.

[86]See Kuhn, "Hermeneutik," p. 33.

[87]Kuhn, Leben Jesu, p. vi; "Von dem schriftstellerischen Charakter," pp. 42-44.

[88]The distinction between the ground and the means of grounding faith is made quite nicely in German: Jesus is the former (Grund), while the apostles/church are the latter (Begründer).

[89]Wolfinger has remarked: "Die Frage nach Wesen und Gestalten des christlichen Glaubens ist das Grundanliegen Kuhns noch vor dem von Geiselmann genannten der Überlieferung." Der Glaube, p. 299. Cf. Fries's assertion: "Die Gottesfrage und die Frage des Glaubens erhalten in seinem theologischen Werk die größte Entfaltung und die intensivste Reflexion." Heinrich Fries, Johannes von Kuhn, Wegbereiter heutiger Theologie (Graz: Styria Verlag, 1973), p. 57.

[90]Kuhn, "Über den Begriff und das Wesen der speculativen Theologie," p. 299.

[91]See Wolfinger, Der Glaube, p. 301.

[92]See Kuhn, "[Rezension von] David Schulz, Die christliche Lehre vom Glauben (1834)," Jahrbücher für Theologie und christliche Philosophie (1835):121.

[93]Ibid., p. 119.

[94]Ibid.

[95]Kuhn, "Hermeneutik," p. 33.

[96]Kuhn, "Rezension von Schulz," pp. 122-23.

[97]Kuhn also asserted the corollary that all knowledge, including philosophical knowledge, has its beginning in an act of faith. Kuhn developed this idea under the term Vernunftglauben. See "Ueber Glauben und Wissen," pp. 393, 397, and 403, note 10. Wolfinger, "Johannes Evangelist von Kuhn," p. 136, delineates the influence of Jacobi's philosophy at this point.

[98]Kuhn, "Ueber Glauben und Wissen," p. 407.

[99]Ibid., pp. 395, 397, 418-19. The Church played a crucial role in this movement. On the one hand, the testimony of the earliest church provided the basis for the truth of the historical claims of Christian faith about Jesus. On the other hand, the individual experience of the Spirit and the communal lived witness of the Church provided the present basis for the existen-

tial and religious truth of Christian faith. Faith in the broad sense refers to that knowledge whose truth and certainty "rests immediately upon the testimony of another," what Kuhn called "historical knowing" or _fides_ _ex_ _auditu_. Faith in the narrower sense, however, refers to that supernatural knowledge which is founded upon "the rebirth of the entire person through the Spirit of God," namely, the kind of knowledge that a self-reliant individual "never has nor can produce out of him/herself." Ibid., pp. 407-08.

[100]Strauss, _Streitschriften,_ 3:68.

[101]Strauss, _Leben Jesu_ (1835), 2:738.

[102]Strauss admitted the material change in the conclusion to his work: "Die sinnliche Geschichte des Individuums, sagt HEGEL, ist nur der Ausgangspunkt für den Geist. Indem der Glaube von der sinnlichen Weise anfängt, hat er eine zeitliche Geschichte vor sich; was er für wahr hält, ist äußere, gewöhnliche Begebenheit, und die Beglaubigung ist die historische, juristische Weise, ein Faktum durch sinnliche Gewissheit und moralische Zuverlässigkeit der Zeugen zu beglaubigen. Indem nun aber der Geist von diesem Äusseren Veranlassung nimmt, die Idee der mit Gott einigen Menschheit sich zum Bewußtsein zu bringen, und nun in jener Geschichte die Bewegung dieser Idee anschaut: hat sich der Gegenstand vollkommen verwandelt, ist aus einem sinnlich empirischen zu einem geistigen und göttlichen geworden, der nicht mehr in der Geschichte, sondern in der Philosophie seine Beglaubigung hat. Durch dieses Hinausgehen über die sinnliche Geschichte zur absoluten, wird jene als das Wesentliche aufgehoben, zum Untergeordneten herabgesetzt, über welchem die geistige Wahrheit auf eigenem Boden steht, zum fernen Traumbild, das nur noch in der Vergangenheit, und nicht wie die Idee in dem sich schlechthin gegenwärtigen Geiste vorhanden ist." (Emphasis mine.) Ibid., 2:737.

[103]"Wie jede Idee wird auch die Idee des Christentums nicht geglaubt, sondern gewußt. Gerade dadurch, daß sie begrifflich, in ihrer reinen Denkbarkeit gefaßt wird, habe er, so meint Strauß, Philosophie und Theologie zu einem echten Ausgleich gebracht; dieser besteht darin, daß der Glaube durch das Wissen ersetzt wird. Glauben, die Grundentscheidung des Christen für den sich offenbarenden Gott, ist für Strauß eine Kümmerform des Wissens." Courth, _Das Leben Jesu,_ p. 130. See also pp. 64-65.

[104]Strauss, _Leben Jesu_ (1835), 2:735-36.

[105]Kuhn, "Ueber Glauben und Wissen," pp. 418-20.

[106]Ibid., p. 412.

[107]Burtchaell summarizes Kuhn's thinking on this point: "The Christian must ask two questions: Where can he find the Word of God; How can he discover its meaning? The former question seeks a source of truth (Quelle der Wahrheit), which is found primarily in Scripture and secondarily in complementary traditions. The latter seeks a source of faith (Quelle des Glaubens), which is located in Tradition, the proclamation of the contemporary Church. Protestantism's mistake had been to force Scripture to serve as a total source, both of truth and of the faith, a purely divine source free of all possible human infection. The Catholic solution was that the Bible could never be a judex controversiarum: history made it clear that every deviation in doctrine had made its case upon an interpretation of Scripture." James Tunstead Burtchaell, Catholic Theories of Biblical Inspiration Since 1810: A Review and Critique (Cambridge: Cambridge University Press, 1969), p. 31. Cf. Kuhn's "Die formalen Principien des Katholicismus und Protestantismus," Theologische Quartalschrift 40 (1858):1-62.

[108]Kuhn, "Ueber Glauben und Wissen," p. 405. See also pp. 413-14, 434.

[109]Kuhn and Strauss had similarly divergent views of the creative role of the primitive Christian community. Whereas Strauss conceived of that creativity as consisting in the replacement of the historical Jesus with the Christ of faith, Kuhn conceived of it as consisting in the demonstration of the former as the latter. See Fries, p. 33. Cf. Geiselmann, "Der Glaube an Jesus Christus," pp. 275-76.

[110]This limitation is exemplified in Kuhn's critique of Strauss's handling of the question of gospel authorship. Although Kuhn was right to excoriate the latter for demanding impossible conditions for the proof of apostolic authorship and for reversing the proper relation of external to internal critique, this did not imply that Kuhn's own conclusions were any less susceptible to criticism.

[111]One example of this is Kuhn's inversion of Strauss's theory concerning the influence of the Old Testament on the New Testament picture of Jesus. Rather than simply replacing Strauss's assertion, that Old Testament prophecies shaped or created the New Testament image of Jesus, with his own view, that the apostles' actual historical experience of Jesus caused them to select, alter, and re-interpret those Old Testament expectations,

Kuhn would have done better to affirm a reciprocal relationship of both-and.

[112]Due to the level of knowledge and tools then available, Kuhn's steps in this direction were halting and few. See Geiselmann, "Der Glaube an Jesus Christus," pp. 418-19. Cf. Courth, Das Leben Jesu, p. 212. In an inchoate way, Kuhn also anticipated some of the insights of redaction criticism. His recognition of the conscious shaping of the tradition by individual evangelists (particularly Mark and Luke, whom Kuhn did not regard as eyewitnesses) complemented Strauss's heavy emphasis upon the unconscious creativity of the community.

[113]Kuhn, "Ueber Glauben und Wissen," pp. 502-03. The conservatives claimed that a source of Kuhn's alleged heterodoxy was his appropriation of too much Protestant theology. See the anonymous review of Kuhn's Life of Jesus in Der Katholik 71 (1839):72-74, especially p. 72. Cf. Lösch, p. 177.

[114]In this regard, Heinrich Fries is right to point out that Catholic biblical scholarship of the late nineteenth and early twentieth century could have been spared many detours and blind alleys if the path Kuhn showed had not been ignored or discounted as dangerous. Fries, pp. 21-22.

[115]Norman Perrin, Rediscovering the Teaching of Jesus (New York: Harper and Row, 1967), pp. 212-13.

CHAPTER 3

THE RESPONSES OF MACK AND HAGEL

Martin Joseph Mack (1805-1885) and Maurus Hagel (1780-1842) were the
next Catholics after Kuhn who recognized the serious challenge Strauss's
book posed for orthodoxy and wrote lengthy responses to it. Mack's report
on Strauss's book appeared in 1837 in the Theological Quarterly, the journal established by the Catholic theology faculty at Tübingen. Hagel's critical review, Dr. Strauss's Life of Jesus Examined from the Catholic Point of
View, appeared two years later.[1] Although both works rejected Strauss's
thesis, the perspective of each was slightly different. Whereas Mack responded explicitly as an exegete, and only incidentally as a theologian,
Hagel responded explicitly as a dogmatic theologian, who used exegetical
objections to undermine the basis of Strauss's theological claims.

Martin Joseph Mack was a professor of exegesis at the University of
Tübingen and was co-editor of the Theological Quarterly for several years.
As such, Mack was a member of "the most educated and excellent" Catholic
faculty among German institutions in the 1830s.[2] With Kuhn and others,
he represented a new phase in the history of the Catholic Tübingen faculty,
namely, the move away from the Enlightenment theology of Feilmoser and
Hirscher towards the new ideas of Johann Adam Möhler.[3] Although not as
well known as Hagel, Mack distinguished himself during his professional
career by the objective tone and moderate position of his scholarly publications. As an exegete, Mack earned praise for his careful analysis of the
Pastoral Letters.[4] As a theologian, he advocated a forward-looking spirit
that avoided excesses. To his fellow Catholics Mack declared that both lib-
ertinism and ultramontanism were aberrations; and he insisted that, although communion with the bishop of Rome was essential to Catholicism,
blind obedience was alien to a good Catholic.[5] In his dialogue with Protestants, Mack displayed a deep concern for mutual respect and fairness. He
condemned bitter polemics, yet showed himself to be an able defender of
Catholic theology when it was under attack.[6]

The spirit of objectivity and moderation is reflected in Mack's response to Strauss. His critique not only avoided personal invective and polemical confessionalism, but also maintained an objective tone throughout. Mack acknowledged Strauss's exceptional erudition, and he remarked that Strauss had the right to expect from his critics evaluations that were "academically serious," yet "calm and respectful."[7] Since the atmosphere in 1835-1836 was too emotionally charged for Strauss to get a fair hearing, Mack delayed publication of his own analysis of Strauss's work until 1837. Being fair-minded, however, did not imply that Mack was reticent to criticize Strauss. His response to Strauss, together with Kuhn's Life of Jesus, has been hailed as "the most solid work that we have in this time period from a Catholic pen concerning the life of Jesus question."[8]

Maurus Hagel, in contrast to Mack, responded to Strauss's Life of Jesus as a veteran dogmatic theologian, who had already engaged in polemical apologetics in the defense of Catholicism against the corrosive effects of rationalism and other destructive forms of modern philosophy.[9] He spent the mature years of his career (1824-42) teaching dogmatic theology at the lyceum in Dillingen, which was the former institution of two of his mentors, Patriz Benedikt Zimmer and Johann Michael Sailer.[10] Like them, Hagel was aware of the deficiencies of sterile rationalism. But in reacting against it, Hagel failed to recognize the positive contributions other forms of philosophical thinking could make to the theological enterprise.[11] Hagel consequently resisted the strict application of historical criticism to the Bible. Just as his defense of the Mosaic authorship of the Pentateuch in his Handbook of Catholic Teaching Concerning the Faith (1838) was founded upon specious reasoning and uncritical judgments, so too his defense of the supernaturalistic interpretation of the gospels against Strauss's mythical reading was based upon similarly uncritical judgments which, in the words of Kuhn, "took notice neither of more recent philosophy nor of more recent criticism."[12]

Although neither Mack nor Hagel explicitly identified his theological motivation for writing a critical evaluation of Strauss's Life of Jesus, a careful reading of their responses makes clear that one reason for their rejection of Strauss's work was its removal of the historical person Jesus from the core of Christian faith. Mack's and Hagel's firm commitment to the traditional conception of faith, unbeknownst to them, exerted a falsifying effect upon their analysis of the gospels.

Mack's Report on Strauss's Life of Jesus

Mack was convinced that a serious examination of Strauss's Life of Jesus would uncover it as a work devoid of a "scientific basis," yet full of arbitrary judgments and accommodations to "certain favorite ideas of the age."[13] Mack generally faulted Strauss's book for omitting a careful examination of the gospel sources, for being one-sided in its exaggeration of the differences among the gospel accounts, and for failing to reach some positive result. In this latter regard, Mack saw Strauss's work as representative of a trend in Protestant biblical scholarship.[14] Since the explicit intent of his analysis of Strauss's Life of Jesus was to disclose its unsuitability as a balanced and scientific life of Jesus, Mack concentrated his critical focus upon the foundations of Strauss's mythological theory.

Mack thought that Strauss's system was built upon two assumptions that made it impossible for him to regard the gospels as basically historical. The first was Strauss's assumption that there is no such thing as direct supernatural causes. In Mack's estimation, this disallowance was the decisive reason for Strauss's dismissal of most of the gospel's story as history.[15] The second was Strauss's assumption that myths are present in every religion and, therefore, must also be found in Christianity.[16] Mack attributed this assumption to Strauss's particular construal of Hegel's philosophy of religion, which, in Mack's view, did not necessarily entail a mythical interpretation of the gospels.[17] The predisposition to find myths in religions made itself evident in Strauss's formulation of criteria for detecting mythical elements in the gospels. Mack suggested that the criteria were ordained to produce negative historical results, thus confirming Strauss's view that ancient religion is, by definition, permeated by myth. Mack summarized his analysis of the underpinnings of Strauss's book in this way:

> Thus we have as the philosophical basis of the mythological standpoint of Mr. Strauss two equally unwarranted presuppositions: 1) There can be no miracles; therefore, the gospels may not be conceived historically. 2) Every religion, every consciousness of the Absolute in the form

of representation, has myths; therefore, also the Christian; therefore, the gospel reports must be viewed mythologically.[18]

Mack saw Strauss's presupposition about miracles as the sturdier pillar of his mythological theory, and he directed his energies primarily against it. First, Mack noted that Strauss had not proven his assumption, but had merely asserted it. In response to Strauss's claim that divine causality is manifest "only in the production of the entire complex of finite causes and in their mutual effect," Mack posited the counter claim that divine causality is manifested most clearly when the usual intermediate causes are absent.[19] Mack maintained that both alternatives were possible as reasonable views, but he insisted that the burden of proof rested with Strauss, who had admitted, in the Preface to The Life of Jesus Critically Examined, that it was the responsibility of any new interpretation to rebut the older theories by means of a comprehensive debate with them.[20] By Strauss's own admission, the idea that miracles are impossible was a relatively new theory. Therefore, it could establish itself as the normative point of view only by refuting the basis that had already been adduced for the possibility of miracles. Strauss failed to do that. Rather, he merely asserted that his view was more plausible in light of the modern understanding of the world.

Mack also suggested that Strauss's theological end, which was most evident in the concluding christological survey of his book, determined Strauss's exegesis. By allowing his already formulated, philosophical construal of faith to determine his reading of the gospels, Strauss had violated the explicit intention of his Life of Jesus, which was to examine objectively the extent to which the gospels rest upon historical material.[21] Mack highlighted two indications of the fact that Strauss, instead of investigating the gospels objectively as to their historicity, sought to discredit their historical character.[22]

On the one hand, Strauss formulated no criteria for determining what was most probably historical in the gospels. Although he does offer a "positive" criterion of the unhistorical, it can achieve only negative results. This is so because Strauss's criterion, unlike the negative criterion of dissimilarity used in contemporary form criticism, did not intend to isolate authentically historical materials. Rather, it only pointed out materials that appeared unhistorical.[23] Strauss did not introduce truly historical-critical criteria into his study until the second edition of The Life of Jesus Critically Examined. And Mack used this fact to suggest that Strauss's exegesis was clearly not objectively "scientific," but rather designed to serve Strauss's theological ends.[24]

On the other hand, Strauss failed to conduct an extensive and careful evaluation of the external evidence in support of the apostolic authorship of the gospels. This convinced Mack that it really did not matter to Strauss whether the gospels derived from apostolic times or not. In either case, Strauss was convinced that the gospels were permeated with myths and legends.[25] Mack attributed this proclivity for finding myth rather than history to Strauss's unproven theological and philosophical assumptions.[26]

Mack found further evidence of Strauss's faulty method in the inconsistency with which Strauss applied his so-called positive criterion of the unhistorical. Mack complained that it was not at all clear why Strauss regarded certain parts of the gospel narrative as historical, when there was no greater warrant for so doing than was available for other elements that Strauss dismissed as mythological. If Strauss's criterion were applied more consistently, one would even have to question whether the person Jesus ever lived.

> At this point, one must immediately ask with what right does Strauss assume that a man by the name of Jesus ever existed, and that the same distinguished himself by the greatness of his spirit and his character. Indeed it pleases him not to extend his critical operations to the fact that a man named Jesus existed, and he allows this same Jesus to have the simple skeleton of a life story, which we have already highlighted above. But it simply pleases him to do this. For another, operating according to his point of view and presuppositions and in accord with his procedure, will demonstrate that the person Jesus himself, and also that which Strauss still permits to count as his history, is nothing more than the history-like clothing of mental images formed in unintentional or innocently creative saga.[27]

Mack also found Strauss's historical inferences from the form of gospel stories to be arbitrary. Strauss had maintained that the legendary character of a story was revealed if its form was "poetical" or if the agents in the story conversed in a "more elevated strain than might be expected from their training and the situations."[28] Mack replied that the judgment of what was poetical or inappropriate for a person's station in life was largely an uncertain and subjective matter. Although Mack admitted that legends could appear both in poetic form and in straightforward narratives, he refused to concede that the expression of an emotionally charged experience in poetical language automatically disqualified the experience as historical.[29]

Similarly, Mack objected to Strauss's principle of coherence, which stated that even a narrative which contained no distinct trace of myth could be held to be mythical if it were connected with other narratives, or proceeded from the author of other narratives, that exhibited unquestionable marks of a legendary character. Mack thought that this principle was influenced by Strauss's prior assumption that every religion contains myth, and he objected to this and all of Strauss's other criteria because they were designed to produce negative results.[30] Considering Strauss's criteria cumulatively, Mack remarked that

> one will easily discover that, with the application of a touchstone thus procured, no single component of our gospels can extort for itself the recognition of its historical character, but rather each [component] must submit to the discretion of the examiner whether and what in it he wants to let count for historical because, in the very best case, only the possibility that it is historical remains.[31]

Not only Strauss's method, but also his substantive thesis about the nature of the gospels aroused Mack's criticism. Mack found Strauss's view of the influence of messianic expectations upon the New Testament picture of Jesus to be both unhistorical and uncritical. It was unhistorical because Strauss made the conception of the expected messiah so broad that everything Jesus did could fit into it. It was uncritical because it presented as messianic expectations elements that could appear so only in a later age or only from a Christian perspective.[32] Specifically, Mack labelled as far-fetched a number of Strauss's alleged parallels; for example, the parallel between the flight of Jesus' family to Egypt and their return to Palestine and Moses' flight from Egypt and his return there from Midian. At best, this and other parallels adduced by Strauss were "pure possibilities," not actual probabilities.[33] Moreover, even if there existed a drive among the early Christians to portray Jesus' life as paralleling the lives of important Hebrew prophets, Strauss's theory still could not explain why Jesus sometimes appeared inferior to Moses and the prophets or why the evangelists sometimes failed to use an Old Testament parallel, when one was readily available.[34] In Mack's estimation, Strauss's view faltered most seriously in its treatment of Jesus' suffering and death. Although Strauss admitted that it was neither demonstrable nor probable that the ideal of a suffering messiah was current among the Jews of Jesus' day, the passion narrative paradoxically makes more references and allusions to the Old Testament than other parts of the gospel. The conclusion Mack drew from this fact was that "there, where it could not create from the Old Testament, the evangelical legend nevertheless had created the most from it."[35]

The point that Mack pressed home was the same one Kuhn and Hug made: the messianic expectations embedded in the Old Testament did not control the picture the evangelists made of Jesus; rather, Jesus' actual history sparked the evangelists' search for Old Testament passages that might serve as hidden "proofs" of Jesus' messiahship. Consequently, Mack rejected Strauss's claim that most of the evangelical myths were already in existence as Old Testament messianic prophecies, which only needed to be applied to Jesus. Mack had to reject this claim of Strauss since, if correct, it would blunt the rebuttal raised by many of Strauss's critics, including Mack, that there was too little time between Jesus' death and the composition of the gospels for extensive mythicization of Jesus' life to occur.[36]

Mack hurled other weapons against Strauss's mythological theory, none of which was able individually to rout Strauss's view, but which, taken cumulatively, Mack believed capable of defeating it. He observed that Strauss's mythological interpretation could not always account adequately for the shape of a specific gospel story. To Strauss's explication of Mary's visit to Elizabeth as Luke's attempt to symbolize the Baptist's subordination to Jesus, for example, Mack replied that, if subordination were intended, Elizabeth should have come to Mary, rather than the reverse. Mack had similar criticisms of Strauss's handling of the story of Jesus' presentation in the Temple and of his resurrection.[37]   Mack also found Strauss's interpretation to be frequently inconsistent. Strauss had asserted, for example, both that the performance of miracles was a requirement of the messianic myth and yet that Jesus, from the point of view of historical criticism, actually performed none . Mack wanted to know how Jesus could have claimed to be the messiah, which Strauss accepted as historical fact, if he had not performed any real miracles.[38] Similarly, Mack thought it inconsistent of Strauss to hold that the majority of Jesus' speeches in the synoptic gospels were historically authentic, when so many things in them were comparable to what could be found in the rabbinic or other literature of the period. Mack believed that this material could be regarded as "fabricated" just as much as Strauss regarded the stories of Jesus' miracles to be fabricated.[39]

Mack's final criticism was directed against Strauss's view that Christian myth was formed unconsciously. Mack held that it was more likely, at least in some cases, that stories were consciously structured in a particular way by their authors than that they were unintentionally so formed by the community. He used Strauss's explication of the relationship between Jesus and John the Baptist to make his point. Strauss maintained as historical fact that Jesus was attracted to the Baptist's message, was baptized by him, and (perhaps) became his disciple for awhile. The "Christian legend," however, wanted to present John the Baptist as acknowledging his inferiority to Jesus. This conflict between historical fact and mythical requirement resulted in the evangelical depiction of John as possessing a partial, wavering recognition of Jesus as the messiah. The gospel narrative achieved its theological end, i.e., the Baptist's admission of his inferiority vis-à-vis Jesus, by depicting the Baptist as sending a delegation from prison to ask Jesus whether he was the messiah (Matt. 11:2-15, par.). Mack wanted to know how Strauss could assert that myth formation was "unintentional" or "guileless" when manipulation of the facts seemed so apparent. Even if the facts were unintentionally fabricated, the story still failed to achieve the end Strauss predicated of it. John's sending of a delegation of disciples to Jesus did not demonstrate forcefully enough Jesus' superiority over the Baptist.[40]

Mack's own view of the gospels and of the method appropriate to their examination becomes apparent indirectly from his critique of Strauss. Unlike Strauss and modern form critics, Mack presupposed the historical truth of the gospel accounts until their falsehood could be decisively demonstrated. He refused to acknowledge suspicion about the historical veracity of a text as sufficient grounds for presuming its unhistorical character. For Mack, the burden of proof rested with the critics, not with the supporters of the tradition. Hence, although he conceded that Strauss's mythological interpretation might seem defensible on occasion, Mack declared that Strauss nowhere proved the superiority of his reading over the alternative interpretations.[41] Similarly, Mack's criteria for determining the unhistorical differed from Strauss's. Mack suggested that a report be considered unhistorical if it contradicted a report that had already been historically authenticated or if it contradicted "the laws of existence and history, which have been firmly established by pertinent experience and unprejudiced science."[42] Despite superficial similarity with Strauss's positive criterion of the unhistorical, Mack's criterion differed in that it did not denote the impermissibility of the miraculous.[43] On the contrary, Mack, like Hug, thought that the historicity of an event was established primarily by weighing the number and reliability of the witnesses.[44]

Insofar as he confined his "Report" to an exegetical assessment of Strauss' Life of Jesus, it is difficult to determine in detail and with precision Mack's understanding of Christian faith. There are, however, emphases in his analysis which serve as indications of Mack's theological views. On the one hand, Mack clearly wanted to preserve the orthodox doctrine of Jesus' divinity. He defended Jesus' early messianic consciousness and the compatibility of the omniscience of Jesus' divine consciousness with his human consciousness. That this conviction partly motivated his critique of Strauss is suggested by his remark that one of Strauss's chief difficulties in accepting the historical truth of the gospel narrative was that it attributed to Jesus a "superhuman power and wisdom."[45] Mack, by contrast, accepted the superhuman portrayal of Jesus; correlatively, he did not hesitate to accept a supernaturalistic reading of the gospels, which supported such a view of Jesus. Mack indicates that a reason for his defense of the traditional christology and of the concomitant supernaturalistic reading of the gospels was that it validated the superiority of the Christian religion, which Mack believed was concretized in its moral code. Mack perceived Strauss's mythical reading of the gospels to be more damaging than that of his predecessors precisely because it removed a unique, higher morality from Jesus' message and effect.[46] On the other hand, Mack resisted Strauss's proposal to eliminate or minimize the historical foundation of faith. Not all modern, speculative reformulations of Christian faith were to be rejected, but only those that threatened faith's traditional anchor in history. This was so because, in Mack's view, Christian faith entailed reference to the activity of God in Jesus. To remove christological assertions about Jesus from the act of faith was to eviscerate faith's core.[47]

How, then, is Mack's "Report" on Strauss ultimately to be evaluated? Exegetically, Mack was successful in identifying places where Strauss's view was overstated or inapplicable, and he was somewhat effective in disclosing the distortional effect of Strauss's philosophical and theological views upon his exegesis. But Mack's various strategies for deflecting the force of Strauss's thesis succeeded only in demonstrating that the thesis needed to be modified at a number of points.[48] They did not rout the central point of Strauss's book, namely, that there is more myth than history in the gospels' presentation of the life of Jesus.

Although his own criticism of the texts appears not to be critical at all when compared with Strauss's, Mack's exegesis was not unaffected by the higher criticism of the Bible. Higher criticism, as embodied in Strauss's Life of Jesus, forced Mack to recognize that the evangelists did not always report everything as it happened. Mack came to admit that the authors of the gospels were sometimes inexact or inaccurate in their presentations, and often one evangelist added to or subtracted from the narrative of the others. Nevertheless, Mack could not bring himself to admit that the substance of Jesus' history was falsified in the process.[49] Mack used the basic agreement of the evangelists concerning the chief points of Jesus' public ministry and their reporting of events that did not put Jesus in the best possible light as warrants for his judgment.[50] In the end, Strauss and Mack were worlds apart, and Strauss was shown to be more adept at biblical criticism: whereas Mack presupposed the credibility and accuracy of the evangelical presentation of Jesus' life, Strauss was suspicious of it; whereas Mack placed the burden of proof upon those who denied the historical truth of the gospel story, Strauss place it upon those who upheld the tradition of the story's accuracy.

Theologically, Mack suggested that the person of Jesus belonged to the core of Christian faith. Since the Christian tradition had generally made christological claims about the historical person Jesus, Mack thought it appropriate that any reformulation of Christian faith retain a focus or ground in Jesus. He unfortunately did not specify the precise nature of the grounding of faith. It is clear, however, that he was dissatisfied with Strauss's vision of Jesus because it made him simply the historical occasion for the idea of divine-human union to rise into general human consciousness. In this way, Strauss made the person Jesus largely irrelevant to the content of contemporary faith. To combat this move, Mack thought it was necessary to uphold the historical veracity of the gospels because they seemed to make Jesus of Nazareth the ground and principal content of faith. His stubborn insistence upon the historical accuracy of the gospel presentation of Jesus' life, however, implied that the truth of Christian faith was completely dependent upon the historical truth of the story of Jesus' life. Mack's staunch resistance to Strauss's idealization of Christian faith led him to use history to prove faith.

The Mack-Strauss confrontation consisted in two different readings of the gospel and two different conceptions of faith. Although contemporary biblical scholarship has validated Strauss's hermeneutics of suspicion, the question remains whether the conception of faith that Strauss proposed is satisfactory. Mack felt that it was not. But the exegetical path he chose for undermining it was unsuccessful; and he refrained from mounting an explicitly theological assault. Thus, the Mack-Strauss debate ended not with the cooperative venture of constructing a christology that was biblically sound and theologically appropriate, but rather with the hardening of lines and the listing of weaknesses in the proposal of the opponent.

Hagel and the "Catholic" Defense of Faith

Maurus Hagel divided his response to Strauss, The Life of Jesus Considered From the Point of View of Catholicism (1839), into two parts. The first part addressed the question of whether the supernaturalistic view really was outdated; the second, whether Strauss's mythical interpretation of the gospels could withstand criticism. Although the division of the work ostensibly places it in the same category as Mack's, Hagel's critique of Strauss is much more explicitly theological. Hagel wanted to refute Strauss's reading of the gospels because he realized that it shook "the religious life in its innermost foundation."[51] Hagel perceived that Strauss had a theological axe to grind, that his exegesis was intended to serve a particular theological end.[52] He opposed Strauss's view in exegetical matters because that exegesis supported theological convictions opposed to his own.

The opposition between Strauss and Hagel was rooted primarily in their different answers to the question whether claims about the historical person of Jesus were integral to Christian faith. Hagel thought they were integral, and he expressed his disapproval of Strauss's position by likening it to the christologies of Kant and Fichte. Strauss's Christ, like theirs, was an "ideal Christ" and, in Hagel's opinion, no less unreal than theirs, despite Strauss's protestation to the contrary.[53] Hagel rejected all these ideal conceptions of the Christ because they substituted an idea for the real individual and were, therefore, inadequate.

The inadequacy pertained to several areas. Practically or psychologically, idealized christology was inadequate because it failed to fulfill one of the functions of religion, the enabling of people to live nobler and better lives. If humanity were to be helped in living out an appropriate religious and moral life, it needed "an individual, not an idea" for "in speculation there is no salvation."[54]

> People need, in their internal turmoil and spiritual need,
> a redeemer. And this [redeemer] can only be an individ-
> ual who, himself sinless and perfect, has the power to
> free people from sin and to make them perfect, or, as
> Schleiermacher says, to strengthen God-consciousness in
> them. They are not helped with abstractions.[55]

Theologically, idealized christology was inadequate because it failed appropriately to express the Christian conviction that God had acted redemptively in and through the historical person Jesus.

Hagel, therefore, rejected Strauss's suggestion that the transformative power of Christian faith was adequately expressed in the idea of divine-human union. Following Schleiermacher, Hagel referred the powerful

Christian experience of being redeemed back to the person capable of producing such an effect. Hagel's claim was that only a real person could produce a real effect.

> It is, however, fact that those who believe in the personal God-man become entirely different people. They feel their God-consciousness strengthened and it is for them an easy thing to break the superior strength of sinfulness. This change in the interior of the Christian is something real; therefore, Christ, who effects this change, must also be a real principle and, concomitantly, an individual.[56]

Hagel further insisted that this redeemer had to be divine (or as he put it more modestly, "more than a mere human being") if he were to be able to communicate to contemporary Christians the strength of his God-consciousness. Hagel then attempted to use this theological premise to support the credibility of his supernaturalistic reading of Jesus' life in the gospels.[57] His procedure was, therefore, circular. On the one hand, the reality of the internal transformation of Christians suggested for Hagel the truth of the scriptural portrayal of Jesus as redeemer. The supernaturalistic reading of the gospels, on the other hand, authorized the claim that divine power produced the redemptive transformation.

Hagel, no less than Strauss, sought to bolster his theological views with a particular reading of Scripture. The force of the scriptural warrant for a high christology depended, of course, upon the historical accuracy of the gospels. In this regard, Hagel agreed, albeit only partly, with Strauss, who had opposed the attempt of right-wing Hegelians to establish by means of philosophy, instead of history, that Jesus was the Son of God.[58] In order to demonstrate historically that Jesus was the Son of God, Hagel had to establish the historical authenticity and credibility of the gospels' presentation of Jesus.[59] Hagel attempted to do this in the same way that other Catholic respondents to Strauss had, i.e., by examining the external and internal evidence pertinent to establishing the apostolic origin of the gospels.

Hagel, however, distinguished himself from Kuhn and Hug in that his treatment of the evidence was exceedingly brief and quite perfunctory. It was more a statement of conclusions than a critical examination. In fact,

Hagel seemed to possess few, if any, truly critical principles for reading ancient documents. Unlike Mack, he offered no criteria for separating the
unhistorical from the historical. His exegesis was dominated by uncritical
presuppositions, and he believed that there was better testimony in support of the authenticity and trustworthiness of the gospels than for other
ancient documents.[60] Hagel thought that the evangelists had first-hand
information about Jesus' life and reported it.[61]

Strauss's pivotal objection to the traditional, supernaturalistic reading
of the gospels was that the inclusion of miracles destroyed the claim of any
text to recognition as history. Hagel's defense of supernaturalism, therefore, entailed defense of Jesus' performance of miracles, both as metaphysically possible and historically real. As Hagel saw it, the miracles
were so inextricably woven into the fabric of the gospel narrative that "one
could not remove them without tearing it apart."[62] Hagel sought to justify
his acceptance of miracles as historical reality by proposing a counter claim
to Strauss's principle of the uniformity of events and by arguing that the
burden of proof rested upon those who contested traditional supernaturalism.

On the first point, Hagel said that the proper principle of historical
criticism is the inverse of what Strauss proposed: What _can_ happen is to
be determined not by what happens today, but by what has already happened. Hagel, of course, thought that Jesus' miracles had happened.[63]
Strauss rejected the idea of external divine intervention because it violated
his understanding of the world as a closed system and his understanding
of God as radically immanent. Hagel, by contrast, emphasized God's transcendence, which made both miracles and an incarnation possible; and he
labelled Strauss's position pantheistic.[64]   Whereas Hagel claimed that
the quality of the testimony to an event determined its historicity, Strauss
insisted that no testimony was sufficiently reliable and credible to establish the historical actuality of alleged miracles. Their opposition was complete. Whereas Strauss denied the possibility of miracles, metaphysically
and historically, Hagel affirmed it on both counts.

Hagel further sought to defend supernaturalism by declaring that the
burden of proof fell upon those who contested the supernaturalistic view.
In order for his rejection of the miraculous to be valid, Hagel claimed that
Strauss had to demonstrate the impossibility of the miraculous. Hagel in-

sisted upon the actuality of the miracles recorded in the gospels because he thought that the gospels derived from reliable, first-hand witnesses to those events. And, like Mack, he believed that actual experience, not philosophical theory, determined what is possible.[65] Hagel justified his position with a naive presumption, which he expressed in response to Strauss's call to abandon all dogmatic presuppositions before examining the gospels:

> The dogmatic presuppositions, however, are themselves never groundless and they must be tested first before one disregards them. We presuppose that the authors of the gospels were people who could know the truth and who also wanted to say it. This presupposition, however, is justified since people have a natural drive to search after the truth and to communicate to others the truth that is found. If we may or must, therefore, give the evangelists credit only for some knowledge and honesty, then the attempt to banish their reports to the realm of legends must appear to be a great and dangerous enterprise.[66]

In addition, Hagel thought it was necessary to acknowledge the limits of human knowledge. Except for logic and mathematics, there was no science in the strict sense. The so-called empirical "sciences" were, according to Hagel, nothing more than the perception of appearances and the formulation of conclusions based upon them. In this realm, but even more so in metaphysics, reason must move from knowledge to faith. Consequently, it was highly presumptuous for Strauss categorically to deny the possibility of miracles.

Hagel's defense of the historical reality of Jesus' miracles was theologically motivated; the performance of miracles validated Jesus' uniqueness and divinity. Hagel was so convinced of the proof character of the miracles that he thought that Jesus shared his view of their purpose. Like Hug, Hagel maintained that "beneficence was generally only a subordinate purpose of Jesus' miracles." Their primary purpose was to legitimate Jesus as the messiah.[67] In defense of this view, Hagel resorted to an uncritical use of John's gospel, and he appealed to the alleged self-evidence of the view that, if Jesus had not performed miracles, belief in his divinity would have been inconceivable.

> Divinity does not strike the senses. Therefore, if he [i.e., Jesus] wanted to be regarded as something more than a normal human being, he had to reveal, and simultaneously make graphic, his divine dignity through divine works. I know well that it is said that Jesus' disciples have attributed to him a superhuman essence and have fabricated miracles. But that truly means putting the cart before the horse. For it was precisely Jesus' deeds that created in the disciples faith that he is a superhuman being. If one removes the miracles or merely lets them be fabricated, then one truly no longer knows whence faith in Jesus' divinity originally came.[68]

The fulfillment of Old Testament prophecies had the same aim, i.e., to establish Jesus' divine authority.[69] Hagel explained the initial success of Christianity among Jews only a few days after Jesus' death as a result of the impression made on them by the exact fulfillment of everything Jesus had prophesied of his suffering and death. This seemed to be the only explanation since there was too little time to develop persuasive myths about Jesus that would be useful in evangelizing. Moreover, if no prophecy concerning Jesus' suffering and death had occurred in advance, then, so argued Hagel, the manner of his death would have caused the opposite effect: People would have regarded Jesus as a criminal and would have troubled themselves no more about him.[70]

Proof of Jesus' divinity was necessary not merely for the preservation of orthodox christology, but also for the maintenance of Hagel's understanding of Christian faith, of which christology was only a part. His conception of faith required claims about both Jesus and his teaching. Although he did not develop this argument explicitly in his response to Strauss, there is sufficient evidence to suggest that Hagel understood Christian faith to be a religio-moral vision of life, whose superiority over other visions was established by the unsurpassable uniqueness of its founder. Hagel viewed Jesus' speeches as "nothing but moral prescriptions or challenges for a holy transformation." Correlatively, he--like many of the liberals of the nineteenth century--conceived the kingdom of which Jesus spoke as moral in nature and present within human beings. Moral regeneration, therefore, was a significant component in the experience of redemption. Its importance in Hagel's view of faith is evident in his appeal to the history of Christianity against Strauss's idealization of faith.

> It is fact that Christianity, everywhere it went, suppressed idolatry and the dominant profligacy. And if Christianity had effected nothing else, its merit for humanity still would have been great enough, for what can denigrate the human person more than superstition and immorality? It is fact that, wherever it went, Christianity destroyed despotism, civilized nations, moderated the laws, and improved the lot of common people.[71]

The second half of Hagel's response was concerned not with the active defense of supernaturalism, but with a critical refutation of Strauss's mythological theory. Here Hagel marshalled many of the arguments that appear in the responses of fellow Catholics to Strauss. Hagel, however, often gave them a less nuanced formulation. Like Mack, Hagel rejected Strauss's contention that myths are necessarily present in religion. He pointed out that although the oldest "histories" began from myth, this did not mean that every history had to begin thus. He also held that the composition of the gospels soon after the death of Jesus prevented the intrusion of unhistorical material. More importantly, Hagel thought that the gospels were free from myth because they were written by eyewitnesses (Matthew and John) or disciples of eyewitnesses (Mark and Luke) and because they accorded with the original apostolic kerygma.[72] In short, the church's tradition vouched for the veracity of what the gospels proclaimed. Hagel's point was that the church's tradition existed before the composition of the gospels and gave rise to them; the faith of the community served as a bulwark against the possible aberrations of an individual's conception of the faith.[73]

Hagel, moreover, thought that there was internal evidence to support the view that the gospels were generally free from mythical coloration. Like Mack, he argued, on the one hand, that if the evangelists had been

disposed to work legend and myth into their narratives, then the legendary stories would have been more extraordinary than what is present
in the gospels. Especially with regard to Jesus' youth, the evangelists
would have shown little restraint in creating stories.[74] On the other hand,
Hagel argued that if the evangelists had been inclined to weave myth into
their gospels, they would have suppressed everything that presented Jesus
as less than divine or heroic.[75] They would have excluded, therefore, the
stories of Jesus' temptation in the desert and of his agony in Gethsemane,
since both stories "cast a shadow upon Jesus' superhuman nature."[76]

Hagel made two further observations, which he hoped would weaken
the cogency of Strauss's position. He first suggested that the gospel narrative would not be as cohesive as it is if it had been comprised primarily of
diverse legends that had been generated in different locations and had cir-
culated for years as oral tradition. Hagel then stated that if the fulfillment
of messianic expectations had not occurred in Jesus' actual life, it was inconceivable how people came to accept Jesus as the Christ.

> Jesus acquired for himself the reputation of the messiah.
> But this is itself only the consequence of the fact that the
> statements of the prophets had been so conspicuously
> fulfilled in him. If the Christians looked around for such
> statements in the holy scriptures of the Old Testament
> only after the fact and transferred them to Jesus, as Dr.
> Strauss says, then Jesus attained the fame of the messiah
> without it being known how.[77]

Hagel's point was the same as that of the other Catholic critics of
Strauss: the actual history of Jesus' life controlled the gospels' references
to the Old Testament messianic prophecies; the latter did not cause the
mythical generation of the former.[78] But in Hagel's case, the connection
between an "historical," supernaturalistic reading of the gospels and the
orthodox construal of faith is especially clear. As the quote above indicates, Hagel thought that Jesus' actual fulfillment of Old Testament expectations was a necessary condition for people coming to have faith in him as
lord and savior. He failed to realize that people could be attracted to
Christian faith by the actual lived example of the Christian community.

Rather, he thought that historical knowledge about Jesus, which was vouchsafed by a supernaturalistic reading of the gospels, was necessary to enable or validate the Christian vision of life. He failed to see that although such knowledge was necessary to validate specific christological claims about the historical person of Jesus, it was not necessary for validating the truth of Christian faith, if faith were conceived as a philosophy of life. Only insofar as Christian faith necessarily entails christological claims about Jesus of Nazareth is it theologically appropriate to want historical knowledge about Jesus. Hagel, however, did not make an explicit case for the necessity of this entailment.

Hagel's understanding of Christian faith shaped his reading of the gospels. Modern critical scholarship, represented by Strauss, forced him to modify, but not to abandon the supernaturalistic reading of the texts. Hagel thus admitted that the gospels were intended neither to produce a diary of Jesus' life nor to present a complete compendium of the Christian religion, but rather to present some of the major events from Jesus' ministry. On the whole, the gospels stuck to the major subject matter without worrying about secondary circumstances.[79] Hagel, like other Catholic respondents to Strauss, said that the evangelists intentionally highlighted different aspects of Jesus' life so that their accounts would supplement each other's. The purpose of Matthew's gospel, for example, was to demonstrate on the basis of prophecy fulfillment that Jesus was the promised messiah; John's was to disclose Jesus' divinity. The different purposes directed Matthew's attention more to Jesus' deeds and John's more to Jesus' speeches.[80] This difference in focus, in Hagel's estimation, satisfactorily explained the occasional silence of one evangelist about what was reported by another; it also revealed the alleged contradictions between accounts to be only apparent.[81] To Strauss Hagel therefore retorted that it was "a completely arbitrary presupposition that each evangelist must report the same thing and that only that on which all agreed is to be accepted as true."[82] Hagel, like Hug, was convinced that the various omissions and divergences of the gospels could be harmonized.

Considered as a piece of critical scholarship, Hagel's The Life of Jesus Considered From the Point of View of Catholicism was a failure. Although he identified a number of places where Strauss's skepticism was overdrawn or his interpretation was dubious, Hagel failed to overthrow

Strauss's mythological interpretation. Hagel's failure is more noticeable than that of his Catholic colleagues because he did not match their methodological care and nuanced argumentation. Unlike Mack, he did not attempt to determine what appropriate criteria could differentiate the probably unhistorical from the probably historical material in the gospels. Unlike Kuhn, he did not recognize or admit that the evangelists shaped, even altered, the presentation of Jesus' life to fit their confessional aims; nor did Hagel offer the same balanced judgment in the determination of critical issues, like the external and internal evidence pertinent to assessing the apostolic origin and historical credibility of the gospels. As a result, Hagel's book contains not only some of the same faulty, historical judgments that can be found in the work of his Catholic colleagues (e.g., the view of John's gospel as a reliable historical source, the uncritical acceptance of Luke's prologue as an accurate statement of intent); it is also replete with other arguments and judgments that are simply fallacious or specious.[83]

Theologically, Hagel's work was clear and forthright in its affirmation that Jesus is part of the content of faith. Hagel specified the connection between the person of Jesus and the message of Christianity as the relation between necessary warrant (Jesus) and affirmed truth (the Christian worldview). As we have seen, Hagel was concerned to uphold that the gospels yielded accurate historical knowledge about Jesus because the historical knowledge Hagel claimed to find in the gospels authorized the truth (and superiority) of the Christian way of life.[84]

Hagel's case, however, was unpersuasive since it did not directly refute Strauss's conception of faith as independent of the historical facts of Jesus' life. Hagel did not consider seriously that an unhistorical story about Jesus could still have religious power.[85] Instead, he averred that the historical facts could establish the content of Christian faith and that only the actual lived experience of Christianity offered "proof" of Christianity's truth.[86] Thus, his response to Strauss stands simultaneously as one more Catholic objection to Strauss's attempted idealization of the content of faith and as one more example of how theological convictions can undermine biblical criticism.

NOTES

[1]M. J. Mack, "Bericht über die kritische Bearbeitung des Lebens Jesu von Dr. Strauß," Theologische Quartalschrift 19 (1837):35-91, 259-325, 426-505, 633-686. Maurus Hagel, Dr. Strauß's Leben Jesu, aus dem Standpunkt des Katholizismus betrachtet (Kempten: Jos. Kösel'sche Buchhandlung, 1839).

[2]See Reinhardt's "Die katholisch-theologische Fakultät Tübingen im ersten Jahrhundert ihres Bestehens," in: Rudolf Reinhardt, ed., Tübinger Theologen und ihre Theologie (Tübingen: J. C. B. Mohr (Siebeck), 1977), pp. 12-13.

[3]Ibid., pp. 24-25. In fact, the Württemberg government seems to have thought that it was Möhler's influence that was evident in Mack's book Über die Einsegnung der gemischten Ehen. Ein theologisches Votum (Tübingen: n. p., 1840). This book about mixed marriages, which was censored by the government, caused Mack to be removed from his post as theologian and rector of the University in 1840. Ibid., p. 27. For a detailed account of the events that ended Mack's professional theological career, see the anonymous Memorandum über die Entfernung des Professors Dr. Mack von seinem katholisch-theologischen Lehramte an der k. württembergischen Universität Tübingen von der rechtlichen Seite betrachtet (Schaffhausen: Hurter, 1840). Concerning the difference between Mack's and Feilmoser's syle of exegesis, see Stephan Lösch, Die Anfänge der Tübinger Theologischen Quartalschrift (1819-1831) (Rottenburg: Bader'sche Verlagsbuchhandlung, 1938), pp. 35-36.

[4]See Karl Werner, Geschichte der katholischen Theologie: Seit dem Trienter Concil bis zur Gegenwart (Munich: J. G. Cotta'sche Buchhandlung, 1866), p. 539.

[5]See Mack's "Katholische Zustände," Theologische Quartalschrift (1839):3-49. Mack endorsed progress while eschewing extremes (pp. 3-5). He recognized the importance of communion with the pope (pp. 11-12), but emphasized that the Catholic has rights, and not merely duties, vis-à-vis the pope (pp. 15-16).

[6]See, for example, Mack's review of Marheineke's Zur Vertheidigung der Kirche gegen die päbstliche (Berlin: Duncker & Humblot, 1839) in the Theologische Quartalschrift (1839):504-29. Marheineke's book represented precisely what Mack wanted to avoid in his own work, i.e., groundless

invective against and caricature of one's opponent. See Mack's review, pp. 510, 516-17, 520, 528-29. Cf. Marheineke, Vertheidigung, pp. 48, 126-27.

[7]Mack, "Bericht," p. 38.

[8]Adam, p. 402.

[9]"Als Lehrer wie als Schriftsteller ging sein Hauptbestreben dahin, dem Rationalismus gegenüber die Berechtigung der Offenbarungsreligion und im Katholizismus den echten Träger der Offenbarungsreligion nachzuweisen." Thomas Specht, Geschichte des Kgl. Lyceums Dillingen (1804-1904). Festschrift zur Feier seines 100jährigen Bestehens (Regensburg: G. J. Manz, 1904), p. 167. Cf. Laurentius Stempfle, Erinnerung an Dr. Maurus Hagel (Dillingen: Joseph Friedrich, 1843), p. 10. The following works exemplify Hagel's theological concerns: Theorie des Supranaturalismus mit besonderer Rücksicht auf das Christenthum (Sulzbach: Seidel'sche Buchhandlung, 1826); Der Rationalismus im Gegensatze zu dem Christenthume (Sulzbach: Seidel'sche Buchhandlung, 1835).

[10]For a thorough sketch of Hagel's life and work, see Stempfle. Sailer and Zimmer were Catholics who, at the beginning of the nineteenth century, moved away from the Enlightenment towards the "mystical philosophy" of Schelling. See Philipp Funk, Von der Aufklärung zur Romantik (Munich: J. Kösel & F. Pustet, 1925), p. 5. O'Meara has traced the influence of Schelling in these scholars, noting that Zimmer in particular was "the clearest example of Schelling's influence upon this first generation of Catholic theologians and philosophers open to modern philosophy." Thomas O'Meara, Romantic Idealism and Roman Catholicism: Schelling and the Theologians (Notre Dame: University of Notre Dame Press, 1982), pp. 38-51, especially p. 47. Hagel imbibed some of his aversion to Enlightenment rationalism from these teachers.

[11]Kuhn saw Hagel's blindness, and he criticized Hagel for failing to see that philosophical and critical tools were not to be rejected per se simply because of their misuse by one or other theologian. The difference between Kuhn's and Hagel's perception of the philosophical and theological situation is highlighted in the former's review of Hagel's Handbuch der katholischen Glaubenslehre für denkende Christen (Augsburg: Karl Kollmann, 1838). See Theologische Quartalschrift (1838):741-51, especially pp. 743-45. Whereas Kuhn sought to use "true criticism" to refute the "false criticism" of Strauss, Hagel seemed to want to reject altogether the role of historical criticism in Christian theology. Ibid., pp. 745, 749.

[12]Ibid., p. 746. See also p. 748.

[13]Mack, "Bericht," pp. 90-91.

[14]Ibid., pp. 458 and 489.

[15]"Übrigens ist das Radicalhinderniss einer vom historischen Standpunct zu unternehmenden Erforschung und Beurtheilung der evangelischen Bericht über die an Dämonischen vollzogene Heilungen das philosophische Wider-streben des H. D. Strauß gegen die Existenz von Teufel und Dämonen ..." Ibid., pp. 496-97. See also p. 59. Cf. Strauss, Leben Jesu (1837), 1:103.

[16]Mack, "Bericht," p. 54. Cf. Strauss, Leben Jesu (1837), 1:87-89.

[17]Mack, "Bericht," pp. 56-57. See also pp. 674-75.

[18]Ibid., p. 57. See also p. 61.

[19]Ibid., pp. 52, 59-60. Cf. Strauss, Leben Jesu (1837), 1:103.

[20]The prior attempt to adjudicate the issue by means of logic had failed since the affirmative proposition requiring proof was identified differently by Strauss and Mack. Strauss's argument was: "The claim that special laws should apply for biblical history is an affirmation; the non-recognition of this claim is a negation. But according to the well-known rule, the af-firmative premise, not the negative one, must be proven ..." Leben Jesu (1837), 1:87, note 3. Mack retorted: "As if the negative assertion, viz., for biblical history the same laws are not always valid, did not already oppose at the outset the affirmative assertion of Strauss, viz., the laws which have been named are valid in all spheres of being and happening--and, there-fore, that he had to prove his affirmative premise!" "Bericht," pp. 53-54.

[21]Ibid., p. 683.

[22]"Hier ist ein schweres Mißverhältniss der von dem Verfasser deutlich genug ausgesprochenen Tendenz seines Werkes mit der Ueberschirft des-selben sogleich zu erkennen. Der Titel verspricht eine kritische Bear-beitung, und auch die Vorrede bezeichnet als Aufgabe die Untersuchung, 'ob und wie weit wir überhaupt in den Evangelien auf historischem Grund und Boden stehen.' Aber in der That liefert unser Werk weder eine Kritik der Evangelien, noch ist es seine Absicht zu ermitteln, ob wir in ihnen Geschichte haben; sondern eine Bearbeitung der Evangelien enthält es, wie

sie im Interesse der mythologischen Auffassung der Religionsgeschichte liegt, und das ist sein Begehren, zu zeigen, daß unsere Evangelien über und über mit Sagen und Erdichtungen behaftet sind." Ibid., p. 44. See also pp. 53, 657.

[23]See the good analysis of this issue in Hodgson's Introduction to The Life of Jesus Critically Examined (1972), pp. xxvi-xxviii.

[24]Mack, "Bericht," p. 88.

[25]Ibid., p. 471.

[26]Ibid., p. 64.

[27]Ibid., p. 66. See also Mack's evaluation of Strauss's exposition of the birth of John the Baptist, p. 261, and his critique of Strauss's handling of Jesus' cry of desperation from the cross, pp. 672-73. Mack railed against the arbitrariness of Strauss's historical judgments. In reaction to Strauss's natural explanation of Jesus' naming, Mack observed: "Die Willkühr aber, mit welcher der Verfasser hier der mythologischen Kritik Halt gebietet, ist beachtenswerth. Es war zu erwarten, daß er die von Lucas hier in's Gedächtnis gerufene Bestimmung des Namens Jesu schon vor seiner Geburt auch nur zu der mythischen Einkleidung rechnen werde; aber aus welchem Grunde läßt er es nun als Thatsache gelten, daß der Name Jesus nicht auch selber mythisch sey, da er alle Kriterien des Mythischen an sich trägt?" Ibid., pp. 301-02. Cf. Strauss, Leben Jesu (1837), 1:247.

[28]Ibid., 1:106.

[29]Mack, "Bericht," p. 62. Courth notes that Mack's methodological criticism at this point compares poorly with the approach taken by his Tübingen colleague, Johannes Kuhn. See Courth, Leben Jesu, p. 275: "So berechtigt auch mancher Einwand Macks sein mag, in der Erfassung der durch Strauß aufgeworfenen Problematik steht er weit hinter seinem Kollegen Kuhn zurück. Dies wird vor allem auch daran deutlich, wie er die Genese des neutestamentlichen Textes beurteilt und welche Bedeutung er der literarischen Form für die Interpretation der einzelnen Perikopen beimißt." Referring to Mack's objection to Strauss's criterion of poetic form (cited above), Courth continues: "Aus dieser Einrede wird offenkundig, welchen Einstieg Mack für seinen Disput mit Strauß wählt; es ist der einer Exegese, die die Interpretation einer Perikope nicht mit der Bestimmung der Form, sondern des überlieferten Inhalts beginnt."

[30]Mack,"Bericht," p. 61. Cf. Strauss, Leben Jesu (1837), 1:108.

[31]Mack, "Bericht," p. 64. Strauss's acceptance of Jesus' messianic self-consciousness serves as a good example of how Strauss's judgments appeared to be arbitrary. It is striking that Strauss had no doubts about the historical truth of Jesus' proclamation of himself as messiah: "Daß Jesus die Überzeugung, der Messias zu sein, gehabt und ausgesprochen habe, steht als unbestreitbare Thatsache fest." (Emphasis mine.) Leben Jesu (1835), 1:469.

[32]Mack, "Bericht," pp. 77-78. Mack discredited Strauss's use of the messianic views of later rabbis as indications of what was believed and accepted by first-century Jews. He rightly argued that Strauss neglected to demonstrate that those later messianic conceptions were also dominant during Jesus' day. "Wollte Strauß in einer Sache, welche von der größten Wichtigkeit für sein ganzes Werk war, weil sie die Quelle betrifft, aus welcher 'der reichste Stoff' zur Mythenbildung geschöpft seyn soll, mit der erforderlichen Umsicht zu Werke gehen, wollte er seiner evangelischen Mythologie irgend eine sichere Grundlage geben: so mußte er die jüdische Christologie von der christlichen Anschauung und Benützung des Alten Testaments unterscheiden, und konnte nur aus jenen evangelischen Stellen, welche die Gesinnung und Erwartung der Juden geben, die Messiasidee entwerfen, welche sagenbildend soll gewirkt haben. Er mußte ferner zuerst nachweisen, daß Ansichten der Juden, wie sie in den jedenfalls erst lange nach den apostolischen Zeiten verfassten Schriften der Rabbinen niedergelegt sind, schon zur Zeit Jesu herrschend waren, bevor er der Gebrauch von ihnen macht, ohne welchen er bei einem großen Theile der evangelischen Berichte keinen Anlauf zur mythologischen Erklärung hätte. Das hat er aber unterlassen, und kann damit dem Vorwurf nicht entgehen, daß er sein Gebäude auf Sand gestellt habe." Ibid., pp. 79-80. For specific examples of Strauss's misrepresentation of messianic expectations, see pp. 79, note; 272-74; 306, note. Cf. also p. 492.

[33]Ibid., pp. 80-81, 309-10.

[34]Mack offered the gospel account of Jesus' childhood, in general, and of his visit to the Temple when he was twelve, in particular, as an example of inferiority to the portrayal of the early lives of Samuel and Moses. Ibid., pp. 317-18. Mack claimed that, if there had been such a proclivity among the early Christians to magnify Jesus' accomplishments, they would not have failed to have Jesus' youth at least measure up to that of a Samuel, Isaiah, Jeremiah, or a David. Mack's conclusion was: "Nein; entweder die Gemeinde wollte nicht dichten, sondern nur, was sie sah und hörte, wissen

und erzählen; oder sie mußte eine reiche und anziehende Jugendgeschichte Jesu produciren." Ibid., pp. 323-24. To bolster his case further against Strauss, Mack appealed to the canonical letters of the New Testament, which he thought offered evidence of the fact that early Christians felt no strong drive to fabricate stories about Jesus, even though they did not know all the details of his life. Ibid., pp. 84-85. Kuhn had made a similar point in his essay, "Von dem schriftstellerischen Charakter."

[35]Mack, "Bericht," p. 666. Cf. Strauss, Leben Jesu (1837), 2:234; (1835), 2:311-24.

[36]Strauss claimed: "Er [i.e., der evangelische Mythenkreis] ist seinem größten Theile nach nicht erst in dieser Zeit (von etlich und dreissig Jahren von dem Tode Jesu bis gegen die Mitte des zweiten Jahrhunderts) entstanden, sondern seine erste Grundlage, die A. T.liche Mythe, schon vor und nach dem babylonischen Exil; die Uebertragung auf den erwarteten Messias und demgemäße Umbildung gieng in den Jahren von da bis auf Jesum vor sich: so daß für die Zeit von der Bildung der ersten Gemeinde bis zur Entstehung der Evangelien nur noch die Uebertragung der größtentheils schon gebildeten messianischen Sagen auf Jesum, sammt der Modification derselben im christlichen Sinne und nach den individuellen Verhältnissen Jesu und seine Umgebung, übrig blieb, während nur verhältnissmäßig wenige erst völlig neu zu bilden waren." Leben Jesu (1837), 1:100. Cf. Mack, "Bericht," p. 83.

[37]Ibid., pp. 274-75, 305, 680.

[38]Ibid., pp. 493-94. Cf. Strauss, Leben Jesu (1837), 2:51-52.

[39]"Wie wir oben gesagt, gesteht H. D. Strauß dem größeren Theil der Reden Jesu in den drei ersten Evangelien historischen Charakter zu. Hierüber kann man sich nicht genug wundern; denn hätte er das Verfahren angewendet, durch welches er bisher seine mythischen Resultate erhielt, so könnte kein unversehrter Fleck auch an diesem Gliede des evangelischen Geschichtskörpers geblieben seyn. Die synoptischen Reden Jesu sollen ein 'höchst originelles Gepräge' tragen. Aber zu einem so bedeutenden Theile derselben führt H. D. Strauß selber die von Andern schon beigebrachten Analogien aus frühern und spätern jüdischen Schriften an, daß seine eigenen Notizen an jener vorgeblichen Originalität mehr als irre machen müssen. Ueberdiess aber enthalten die Schriften des A. T. und die bekannten Spicilegien aus der profanen, namentlich aber der rabbinischen Literatur noch so Vieles, was mit den Reden Jesu verglichen und zu ihnen in Beziehung gesetzt werden kann, daß es mir nicht bange wäre, nach

Strauß'scher Methode den nicht-originellen Charakter sämmtlicher Reden Jesu darzuthun." Mack, "Bericht, " p. 477. See also pp. 473-75, 69, 261-62, 301, 320, and 672. Cf. Strauss, Leben Jesu (1837), 1:635-99, 716; (1835), 1:569-631.

[40]Mack, "Bericht," pp. 427-28, 431.

[41]"Aber gegen eine Behauptung, die selbst ein so kühner Mann, sie H. D. Strauß als ein Vielleicht hinstellt, wäre es thöricht in Ernst zu streiten. Darum genüge ein 'vielleicht nicht.' Genau besehen sind übrigens die Beweismittel, aus welchen H. D. Strauß diesmal nur ein Vielleicht herausgebracht hat, nicht viel schwächer, als die, aus denen er sonst positive Resultate zieht, und mit der größten Zuversicht ausspricht. Ein 'Vielleicht' wäre eigentlich der Schild, welcher an das mythische Gebäude des Lebens Jesu gehörte; aber der Schild müßte sich wie ein freischwebender ausnehmen, man müßte weder Unterlage noch sonst einen Halt wahrnehmen." Ibid., pp. 279-80, note. See also pp. 59, 484-85.

[42]Ibid., p. 64.

[43]Ibid., p. 500. In general, Mack asserted the priority of "experience" over philosophical presuppositions and so-called scientific law. Speaking approvingly of Paul's defense of the reality of resurrection (I Cor. 15), Mack stated: "Aber er [i.e., Paul] hielt der philosophischen Meinung die Thatsache entgegen, daß Christus auferstanden sey, erwies diese Tatsache historisch und ergab sich, daß die philosophische Behauptung auch diessmal, wie immer, wenn sie der Erfahrung widerspricht, ein derber Irrthum sey." (Emphasis mine.) Ibid., p. 676. By "experience" Mack meant either firsthand witness or second-hand testimony from reliable witnesses. Thus, Mack was open to supernaturalism whereas Strauss rejected it. Although Mack accepted reports about angels, the virgin birth, etc., pp. 263, 276, 447-48, he seemed to moderate his supernaturalism at a few points. For example, he said that the critical historian should regard devil-possession as indeed rare, but not impossible. P. 497.

[44]Since he thought there were sufficient and reliable witnesses who encountered Jesus after his death and burial, Mack accepted, for example, the historical objectivity of the resurrection. Ibid., pp. 673-81. Strauss, by contrast, refused, like Hume before him, to accept that the reality of the miraculous could be established by the past testimony of alleged witnesses.

[45]Ibid., p. 470. For Mack's defense of Jesus' early messianic self-consciousness, see p. 319; for his exposition of the relationship of Jesus' divine consciousness to his human consciousness, see pp. 463-64.

[46]"Up to now, the biblical mythologizers have allowed the exertion on behalf of the moral improvement of the nation to stand as an essential and characteristic side of Jesus' plan. Mr. D. Strauss, however, in his striving to discover the correct median between a political and a purely spiritual plan of Jesus, believed that he could allow the movement towards moral rebirth to drop out as a major characteristic of Jesus' plan." Ibid., pp. 464-65.

[47]"Bei der in der höheren Beglaubigung der Evangelien für den Glauben liegenden Beruhigung ist die schlichte Auffassung ihres Inhaltes, nach welcher man jene möglichen oder wirklichen Zuthaten, Auslassungen, Modificationen, Umstellungen, Abweichungen etc. gar nicht in Anschlag bringt, die nächste und ihrem Wesen nach auch die sicherste, da, wie die Geschichte der Kritik, zeigt alle Auffassungsarten, welche einen wesentlichen Theil der evangelischen Geschichte fallen lassen, sich früher oder später als unhaltbar zeigen." (Emphasis mine.) Ibid., pp. 487-88. Mack offered Anton Günther's incarnation theory as an example of how specualtion and history could be properly correlated.

[48]Courth, Leben Jesu, p. 278, agrees: "Zur Wertung des Mackschen Diskussionsbeitrages wird man hervorheben müssen, daß es ihm gelungen ist, die eine oder andere schwache Stelle in der Grundlegung der Straußschen These kenntlich zu machen."

[49]Mack, "Bericht," pp. 486-87.

[50]One such example was Jesus' cry of desperation from the cross (Matt. 27:46; Mk. 15:34). Ibid., p. 661.

[51]Hagel, Standpunkt, p. 99. See also pp. 3-4.

[52]Hagel viewed Strauss' brief christological statement at the end of his book as the justification for Strauss's new interpretation of the gospels. Ibid., p. 82. Hagel regretted that Strauss had not made his theological motivation evident at the very beginning of his work: "Schade, daß Dr. Strauß diese Erklärung nicht gleich zu Anfang seines Buches gesetzt hat; dann hätte man dasselbe gewiß bald aus der Hand gelegt, und auf seine Polemik gegen die Wahrheit der evangelischen Geschichte kein so großes Gewicht gelegt, als diess wirklich geschehen ist; eine Christologie nämlich, wie die Straußische, ist nicht jedermanns Sache, und dürfte selbst jene nicht

aussprechen, denen sonst alles willkommen ist, was dem positiven Christenthum thut." Ibid., p. 85.

[53]Ibid., p. 3.

[54]Ibid., p. 86.

[55]Ibid., p. 102.

[56]Ibid., p. 103. See also pp. 100–01.

[57]Note the mixture of theological and exegetical argument in the following: "Dieses Individuum kann aber kein bloßer Mensch sein; denn ein solcher kann uns nicht die Kräftigkeit seines Gottesbewußtseins mittheilen, noch auch von der Knechtschaft der Sinnlichkeit und Sünde uns befreien. Ist aber das Individuum, das diese Wirkungen hervorbringt, mehr, als ein Mensch, so weiß ich nicht, warum es nicht auch auf übernatürliche Weise gezeugt worden, leiblich auferstanden sein, und zum Himmel sich erhoben haben sollte; und warum man diese Dinge nicht auch darum glauben sollte, weil sie in den heiligen Schriften stehen. Die übernatürliche Erzeugung, die Auferstehung und Himmelfahrt Christi sind nicht unbegreiflicher, als das, was er im Innern des Menschen bewirkt." Ibid.

[58]"Wer Jesus gewesen ist; woher er gekommen ist; was er geredt und gethan hat, läßt sich nicht durch die Philosophie, sondern einzig durch die Geschichte ermitteln; es kömmt hier auf glaubwürdige Zeugnisse an." Ibid., p. 86. The last phrase of this statement signals that Hagel's agreement with Strauss was, indeed, only partial for the two disagreed sharply concerning the principles of historical criticism. Cf. Strauss, Streitschriften, 3:61, 126.

[59]"Nach ihm [i.e., Strauss] sind die neutestamentlichen Mythen geschichtartige Einkleidung urchristlicher Ideen, gebildet in der absichtslos dichtenden Sage; allein dadurch wird der mythischen Auslegungsweise das Anstössige nicht benommen, weil die Geschichte Jesu mit seiner Person zusammenhängt, so daß beide stehen oder fallen." Hagel, Standpunkt, p. 7.

[60]The uncritical nature of many of Hagel's judgments is revealed in the following, characteristic statement: "As long as Jesus was with his disciples, a deception could not gain a foothold among them because Jesus could not permit, much less cause, such a thing. After his departure, a deception was equally impossible according to the character of the disciples. These

[disciples] were, namely, too honest for passing off legends as historical facts." Ibid., p. 90.

61"Keine Biographie eines großen Mannes aus dem Alterthume ist von so vielen und so bewährten Schriftstellern geschrieben worden, als die Geschichte Jesu. Die Verfasser der Evangelien gränzen an den Ort und die Zeit der Geschichte, und sind entweder unmittelbare Zeugen, oder doch mittelbare, die aber ihre Nachrichten aus der ersten Hand erhalten haben, sie standen in der nächsten Verbindung mit den Begebenheiten, und waren völlig im Stande, sich zuverlässige Kenntnisse von den Begebenheiten zu verschaffen. Die Evangelisten hätten also die wahren Begebenheiten umgehen, und absichtlich nach ungewissen Sagen haschen müssen." Ibid., pp. 89-90. Hagel's jump from asserting that the authors of the gospels were able to get reliable information about Jesus' life to suggesting that they had to report accurate and reliable information is characteristic of Hagel's judgments and inferences.

62Ibid., p. 40. See also p. 94.

63"...von dem aber, was einmal geschehen ist, schließt man mit Recht auf das, was geschehen kann." Ibid., p. 13. Similarly: "Hat aber Jesus wirklich Wunder gethan, so ist dieses auch der beste Beweis, daß Wunder möglich sind; denn von der Wirklichkeit schließt man mit Recht auf die Möglichkeit." P. 40. Hagel thought that at least one, unmediated divine intervention into the course of human history was needed for the advancement of the rational education of humanity: "Der erste Mensch brachte eben so, wie wir, nur die Anlage zur Vernünftigkeit mit zur Welt, die also erst entwickelt werden mußte. Dazu war aber äußere Einwirkung nothwendig; und woher kann diese anders gekommen sein, als von Gott? Das Göttliche ist also wenigstens einmal unvermittelt in das Menschliche hereingetreten; ohne dieses Hereintreten würde die Vernunftbildung unter dem Menschengeschlecht nicht einmal angefangen haben, viel weniger fortgeschritten sein." Ibid., p. 5. See also p. 7, where Hagel states: "Daß die Urgeschichte wunderbar ist, liegt in der Natur der Sache; denn der Ursprung und die Erziehung des ersten Menschen lassen sich ohne Wunder nicht begreifen; einmal, wie gesagt, muß das Göttliche unvermittelt in das Menschliche eingetreten sein." Strauss, by contrast, rejected the idea of direct divine intervention into history. Cf. Gotthold Ephraim Lessing, The Education of the Human Race (1780), paragraphs 1-4, 77, to whose view Hagel's bears some structural similarity.

64"Hier stehen wir bei dem leidigen Pantheismus, der, weil er die Freiheit der Individuen und mit dieser die Tugend und Glückseligkeit aufhebt, auf

den Beifall der gesunden Vernunft nicht Anspruch machen kann. Es ist
also nichts weniger, als ausgemacht, daß das Subject jener Prädicate,
welche die Kirche Christo beilegt, eine Idee sein muß. Ist aber Gott ein
Wesen außer und über der Welt, ein Besserer, als der Mensch, ein Anderer,
wie man vernünftiger Weise voraussetzen muß, so kann derselbe eben so
gut Mensch werden, als der endliche Geist sich mit einem Körper vereinigt
und als menschliches Individuum erscheint." Hagel, Standpunkt, p. 85.

[65]Speaking of the apparition of spirits, Hagel said: "Ich weiß wohl, daß man
Geistererscheinungen gleich von vornherein verwirft; indess hat die Un-
möglichkeit noch Niemand erwiesen, und wenn nur Eine von den vielen Er-
scheinungen dieser Art, die man sich erzählt, erweislich stattgefunden hat,
so sind alle Einwendungen dagegen unnütz." Ibid, p. 71. And: "Wo Thatsachen sprechen, müssen alle Einwürfe verstummen." P. 47. Cf. Mack,
"Bericht," p. 676.

[66]Hagel, Standpunkt, pp. 98-99.

[67]Speaking of the miracle at Cana, Hagel stated: "Bei dieser Verwandlung
hatte Jesus nicht etwa die Absicht, den armen Leuten aus der Verlegenheit
zu helfen; überhaupt war Wohltun nur untergeordneter Zweck der Wunder
Jesu . . . Alle Wunder Jesu, also auch die Verwandlung des Wassers in
Wein, hatten zunächst nur den Zweck, ihn als den Messias zu legitimiren,
und diesen Zweck hat Jesus durch jene Verwandlung auch erreicht; denn
der Evangelist bemerkt ausdrücklich, daß von da an seine Brüder an ihn
glaubten." Ibid., p. 40. See also pp. 46, 105.

[68]Ibid., p. 42.

[69]"Um an den Messias, wenn er erscheinen würde, glauben zu können
mußten Weissagungen vorausgehen. Nichts beweist die Vorsehung besser,
als wenn gewiße Begebenheiten vorhergesagt werden, und der
Vorhersagung gemäß erfolgen; denn da Gott allein die Zukunft kennt, so
weiß jedermann, daß eine solche Begebenheit nicht das Werk des Zufalles,
sondern Veranstaltung Gottes ist. Natürlich mußte Jesus erst erschienen
sein und messianische Werke verrichtet haben, ehe man die Weissagungen
auf ihn übertragen konnte; in so fern mage man immerhin sagen, man
habe sie aus dem Erfolge auf ihn übertragen." Ibid., p. 50.

[70]Ibid., pp. 50-51, 54.

[71]Ibid., p. 99. See also p. 102.

[72]Ibid., pp. 89-92.

[73]"Wollte man jeden Widerspruch, der einmal gegen die evangelische Geschichte eingelegt worden, schon als einen Beweis gelten lassen, daß die widersprochene Sache falsch ist, so dürfte davon wenig mehr übrig bleiben; denn es gibt kaum mehr einen Punkt, der nicht schon bestritten worden ist. Es kommt nur darauf an, wie der Widerspruch aufgenommen wird; wenn die Kirche ihn zurückweist, so gibt sie eben dadurch zu verstehen, daß sie nicht desselben Glaubens ist, und es kann Niemand einfallen, den Widerspruch eines Einzelnen gegen den allgemeinen Glauben geltend machen zu wollen." Ibid., p. 97. This line of argument was also characteristic of the replies to Strauss from the conservative Catholic journals. See Chapter 5 below.

[74]Ibid., p. 18. Cf. Mack, "Bericht," pp. 322-24. Concerning Jesus' early years, Hagel noted: "Sie [i.e., Erzählungen der Evangelisten] wissen vom zwölften Jahre bis zum dreissigsten nichts von Jesus zu berichten; was hätte da die Sage für ein weites Feld gehabt? Was wissen nicht aus dieser Zeit die Verfasser der Apokryphen alles zu berichten?" Standpunkt, p. 91.

[75]Ibid., p. 95. Referring to those speeches in which Jesus seems to apply messianic dignity to himself, Hagel says: "Waren die Apostel fähig, solche Reden zu erfinden, und für Reden Jesu auszugeben, so darf man ihnen auch so viel Consequenz zutrauen, daß sie alles verschwiegen, was der höhern Natur ihres Meisters zuwiderläuft. Allein sie erzählen ganz unbefangen auch seine menschlichen Thaten und Schicksale,—ein deutlicher Beweis, daß sie die Reden Jesu treu wiedergegeben haben, ohne von dem Ihrigen dazu oder davon zu thun." P. 26.

[76]Ibid., pp. 25, 62, 97.

[77]Ibid., p. 96.

[78]Ibid., pp. 13-14, 33, 50.

[79]As a result, Jesus' speeches were not always presented in their original form. See ibid., pp. 38, 45. This did not mean, however, that the evangelists fabricated the speeches any more than they falsified the basic story line of Jesus' life.

[80]Ibid. pp. 36, 63.

[81]"Was Johannes erzählt, finden wir zwar bei den übrigen Evangelisten nicht; oder wenigstens anders erzählt; allein es war nicht die Absicht der Evangelisten überhaupt, sich wechselseitig zu controlliren, sondern zu ergänzen; daher erzählt der Eine, was der Andere wegläßt; der Eine erzählt dieselbe Sache mit mehr, der Andere mit weniger Umständen. Es wäre sehr unrecht, wenn man dieses für Widersprüche halten, und darum die Wahrheit der evangelischen Erzählungen bezweifeln wollte." Ibid., p. 29. See also pp. 33-36, 39, 45.

[82]Ibid., p. 59.

[83]See ibid., pp. 21-23, for Hagel's use of John's gospel and pp. 16, 96 for his acceptance of the historical character of Luke's gospel. Typical of Hagel's judgments is his claim that if Jesus had not really raised Lazarus from the dead, the excitement of the crowd at Jesus' entry into Jerusalem could not be explained. Ibid., p. 56.

[84]Hagel expressed his view succinctly: "Die Wissenschaft der Zeit kann dem Christenthume nichts anhaben. Der Stifter desselben ist der Voraussetzung gemäß Gottmensch, und seine Lehre folglich eine göttliche; eine göttliche Lehre aber ist schon an sich vollkommen, und kann durch menschliche Wissenschaft nicht bereichert werden." (Emphasis mine.) Ibid., p. 106.

[85]For example: "Hätten hingegen die Christen Jesu Wunder andichten wollen, so müßte es nur geschehen sein, um sich selbst zu belügen, weil sie ja nicht hoffen durften, solche, die noch nicht Christen waren, durch bloße Erzählungen von Wundern zu bekehren." Ibid., pp. 97-98.

[86]Hagel, however, did not carefully differentiate between using the historical experience of Christians as the locus for an analysis of the adequacy of the Christian view of existence and simply asseverating that that historical experience demonstrated Christianity's adequacy, if not superiority. Consider the following claim: "Die Erfahrung von achtzehnhundert Jahren lehrt, daß es bei dem Christenthume geblieben ist, obschon es nicht an Widersprüchen und Kämpfen gefehlt hat. Diese achtzehnhundertjährige Dauer des Christenthumes berechtiget uns zu dem Schluße, daß es auch noch ferner, wenn schon nicht gerade in Teutschland, dabei bleiben werde. Ein Lehrer, der im Besitze der Wahrheit und dem Irrthume nicht unterworfen ist, muß ja den Menschen zu jeder Zeit erwünscht sein. Daher kommt man früher oder später wieder zum Christenthum zurück, und wir wollten nicht wetten, daß nicht auch Dr. Strauß sich eines Anderen besinnen werde." Ibid., p. 107.

CHAPTER 4

A VETERAN EXEGETE RESPONDS: J. L. HUG

Unlike Kuhn and Mack, Johann Leonhard Hug (1765-1846) joined the debate with Strauss as a veteran exegete in the twilight years of life. He had
already crossed professional swords with J. S. Semler, H. E. G. Paulus, and
the proponents of rationalistic biblical exegesis. In the various editions of
his Introduction to the Writings of the New Testament (1808-1847) as well
as in other writings, he challenged the conclusions of those he regarded as
hypercritical interpreters of Scripture.[1] Now at the age of 74, Hug turned
his apologetic skills against Strauss's Life of Jesus.

Hug's Assessment of The Life of Jesus Critically Examined by David
Friedrich Strauss was originally published in installments in the Freiburg
Journal for Theology from 1839 to 1843, but it was also published as a
book in 1841-42 and then released in a new edition posthumously in
1854.[2] In structure, Hug's response to Strauss was quite like Mack's; it
followed Strauss's exposition carefully, focusing upon the philological and
exegetical points of contention. And like the works of both Mack and
Kuhn, Hug's was a critical, academic assessment of Strauss, not a piece of
personal diatribe or anti-Protestant polemic.[3] It won respect from com-
petent contemporary scholars for having "shaken the scaffolding of hy-
potheses of Strauss's mythicism to the point of toppling it."[4] Although Hug
was very critical of Strauss's exegesis, he was not opposed in principle to
the hermeneutical insights of modern biblical scholarship. In fact, he had
learned for himself the historical-critical method by studying the work of
Protestant scholars Johann David Michaelis (1717-1791) and Johann Jakob
Griesbach (1745-1812).[5]

Although he was familiar with the previous editions of Strauss's Life of
Jesus, Hug chose the latest, i.e., the third, edition as the direct target of his
criticism. Even though this edition made the most concessions to the
traditional views concerning the historical reliability of the gospels and Jesus' uniqueness, Hug found it no less objectionable than the earlier ones.
He strongly criticized it since the possibility of mythical intrusion or the

slightest trace of redactional distortion had no place in a "proper conception" of the gospel narratives.

Hug is an unknown figure today, but his work was well-known in the
nineteenth century.[6] He taught during the age of Enlightenment theology
and had completed most of his professional career before a decisively new
age in biblical scholarship had irrupted.[7] Hug was nonetheless open to the
principles of this movement. His attempts at historical, yet moderate study
of the Bible gained for him recognition as a "constitutive authority" in the
field. His most important work, Introduction to the Writings of the New
Testament, was hailed as epoch-making in Catholic scholarship.[8]

Positive evaluation, however, was not confined to the Catholic world.
Frederic Lichtenberger, a nineteenth-century Protestant historian, observed that, although not many scientific works were produced by
Catholics, some had indeed profited from the new methods of critical
scholarship. To this group, "distinguished by solid erudition and a liberal
spirit, while maintaining a complete accordance with the ecclesiastical tradition," Hug was counted.[9] Others even credited Hug's work with lasting
value.[10] Despite his forgottenness today, the fact that Hug was "the most
influential Catholic Biblical scholar of his time" makes his response to
Strauss worthy of attention.[11]

Hug's Evaluation of Strauss

Hug at first hesitated to respond to Strauss's Life of Jesus due to the many
treatises already written against it by 1839. He finally decided to write
since he thought the exegetical competency of his criticism could contribute to the total rout of Strauss's mythical reading of the gospels, which
had not yet been accomplished.[12] Hug's criticism focused on method, external evidence of the gospels' historical character, and internal evidence
of a mythicization process at work in the gospels. Although he conceived
his contribution to the debate about Strauss's book to be exegetical, Hug's
arguments are colored by his theological presuppositions about the nature
of faith. Those arguments reveal that he conceived of Christianity as a
moral system whose superiority depends upon Jesus' divinity as its warrant.

Hug's evaluation of Strauss's method consisted of a consideration of what constituted true criticism and an exposition of what qualified as historical material. With regard to the first question, Hug refused to acknowledge Strauss's work as truly critical for two reasons. First, Strauss neglected to undertake a literary–critical examination of the gospels and, therefore, was not in a position to make a judicious assessment of their historical worth. Already in his Introduction to the Writings of the New Testament, Hug had criticized those scholars like Strauss who asked the question about the credibility of the gospels' content too early, that is, "before we are at all informed as to the historical character of the writers, the sources from which they drew, and their relation to each other."[13] In this regard, Strauss was yet another representative of the unsatisfactory and destructive biblical criticism that had been spreading in Germany since the end of the eighteenth century.

> Today one is little concerned about it [i.e., a proper critical investigation]. Disinclined towards every procedure that orders and balances [the various gospels], one posits the occupation and task of criticism in assailing them--if perhaps one evangelist has more than the other, one is richer in details while the other is shorter, or if one gives a different placement to a story--and accusing one of ignorance, the other of ineptitude without taking into consideration the progress of the story, the character of the authors, and their relationship to the whole. One will return from this uncritical activity, which is now called criticism, when that agitation will have abated and the gigantism will have been assuaged. For it is impossible to oppose the laws of historical research for ever.[14]

Second, Strauss falsely assumed that he had established the supremacy of the mythological viewpoint once he had pointed out the reasons for being suspicious of the historical credibility of various gospel stories. Hug retorted that mere suspicion was insufficient to overturn a story as historical.[15] He viewed Strauss's accumulation of one small suspicion upon another, by which means "he finally reaches the fairyland of myth," to be insufficient for establishing the general incredibility of the gospels.[16]

The wide disparity of their judgments concerning what constituted balanced criticism becomes even more apparent in Strauss's and Hug's discussion of historical criteria. The central issue here was whether the miraculous could be accorded a place in historical exposition. Whereas Strauss categorically denied the possibility of miracles and of direct divine intervention into human affairs, Hug not only affirmed their metaphysical possibility, but also accepted them as historical causes.[17] Hence, Hug defended the ancient Jews and Christians against Strauss's charge that they were incapable of historical writing because of their mythopoeic outlook.[18] With the exception of Matthew, the early Christian authors lived and wrote outside of Palestine, in an environment in which "a scientific and historical consciousness had dawned long ago."[19] Their gospels displayed the effect of this influence and, consequently, were historical narratives, even if not all of them corresponded exactly to the ideal of Greek and Roman historiography. Hug reminded Strauss that, as the case of Tacitus indicates, the occasional inclusion of a fabulous event did not automatically strip an author of the title "historian."[20]

The issue for Hug was not whether a reported event was fabulous or not, but whether the event was attested by a sufficient number of reliable witnesses. Hug identified as the chief rule in historical criticism "that when I was not myself at the scene of the occurrences ... I must refer for a knowledge of them to the perception of another who was a spectator, to the eye-witness, and with him all further question in respect to historical phenomena, considered as such, is to be discontinued."[21] Hug was clearly not persuaded by David Hume's celebrated argument, that no human testimony can have such force as to establish the probability of a miracle, much less to prove one.[22] On the contrary, Hug confessed that he was a supernaturalist, albeit a moderate one. Consequently, Hug criticized the "rationalists" for not admitting the limits of their knowledge as well as for their strained attempts to transform an apparently supernatural event into a misperceived natural occurrence.[23]

Hug's theological convictions become visible at this point. Theologically, he asserted the divinity of Jesus, which affirmation he thought was warranted. For how else could one explain Jesus's peculiar uniqueness, in regard to the other great religious leaders of antiquity, or explain how Christianity came to be so firmly established in such a short time?[24] Upon the basis of this presumption, Hug argued that it was reasonable to accept Jesus' miracles as historical facts. Hug's exegetical task, therefore, became the task of elucidating the purpose behind the miracles Jesus performed. Their chief purpose, he claimed, was to establish, within the short period of his public ministry, Jesus' divine authority.

> Now everything comes down to the question, how he [i.e., Jesus] would establish his authorization for introducing into the world a new religious legislation. Unruffled about this, he averred that he received the authority directly from God. ...But exactly this, upon which the entire matter ultimately rests, was least capable of being proven a priori and by means of a series of deductions. The proofs of such great power, bestowed by God, had to be exhibited sensibly since they were not to be attained in a discursive way. The people, like the apostles, had to see facts, which no human power sufficed to accomplish, acts of God, which certified the authorization of the new law-giver. If the preceding propositions are correct, then all the philosophical objections, with which one intends to intimidate us, are not sufficient to invalidate the credibility of the Lord's miracles. Or let one show us another way in which he could prove to the people his power to introduce a new law of God.[25]

Jesus' divine authority was the theological warrant for acknowledging his message, and the heart of his message was a moral vision of life. As Hug stated elsewhere, the proof that Jesus was the messiah "was only introductory and preparatory to his doctrines," and the main doctrines comprised "his system for ennobling human life and reforming the nations of the earth."[26] Hug therefore integrated his supernaturalistic exegesis with a moral construal of Christian faith.

Hug defended both of these elements in his position by differentiating Jesus' miracles from the fabulous events reported in the literature of antiquity. Whereas the latter were often nothing more than the demonstration of magical powers for the amazement of their audience, Jesus' miracles were acts of compassion and love. His "deeds of power" were markedly different from "mythical miracles," those extravagant shows that appeared to benefit no one, but only aggrandized the performer.[27] The quality of Jesus' miracles further highlighted the moral nature of his mission.

Hug ultimately rejected what Strauss (and most critical historians after him) regarded as a central canon of critical historiography, i.e., the application of the same principles, in the same critical manner, to all historical documents. Strauss's use of the principle of the uniformity of all events led to the disqualification of Jesus' resurrection as an historical event. Hug, by contrast, refusing to yield either to Strauss's philosophical argumentation or to scholarly embarrassment, insisted that the usual presuppositions did not apply in the case of Jesus.

> We leave aside the extent to which the philosophizing presuppositions, with which the author introduces the discussion of the reality of Jesus' death and resurrection, have general value. Even if they were generally valid, still they are not applicable here, where the point at issue is not a human being like us, but a human being in whom a higher essence is present. His death happens in a human way because he is a human being. But who could know how the divine in him brings back again the sparks of life that have withdrawn? The disciples saw him thus, Jesus, the human being, effecting something superhuman; thus he is historically given to us. By contrast, Mr. Strauss and his successors, in their declaration of war against Jesus, assume as indubitable the proposition: he can only have been a human being like one of us; insofar as he is different, the story lies. Nevertheless, if these men wanted to give a foundation to their governing proposition, it would have to probe somewhat deeper for information and prove that such a meeting of the human and the divine is impossible.[28]

Again, Hug's theological presumption of Jesus' divinity established the boundaries within which his criticism of the gospels had to operate.

Hug's critique of Strauss's mythical reading of the gospels, however, was by no means restricted to methodological considerations. It also addressed Strauss's use of external evidence to demonstrate the (un)historical character of the gospels. Hug introduced two arguments to counter Strauss's judgment. One was characteristic of Hug and his conception of antiquity; the other had already been employed by Kuhn and other respondents to Strauss.

The former argument asserted that myths occur only in the childhood of the human race. This claim, with which he commenced his response to Strauss, was Hug's principal bulwark against the mythical point of view. Hug sought to demonstrate that myths occurred in prehistoric and mythopoeic cultures, but not in an historical age. To this end, he sketched the progressive development of culture and literature from myth to legend to history. Hug concluded that, among the Jews, the historical age began to dawn with Samuel. Since that historical age did not come to full bloom until centuries later, it was still possible to find a few myths included in the writing of Samuel. Nevertheless, that fact had no bearing on the kind of writing of which early Christians were capable.[29] Unlike Strauss, Hug saw the first century as significantly different from preceding ages in cultural achievements and intellectual sophistication. Whereas Strauss, using a particular philosophy of religion, argued on behalf of expecting to find myths in the Christian story with the warrant that picture language and myth were unavoidable components of all religions; Hug, adopting a particular philosophy of history, argued against this view on the basis of the progressive development of human cultures. Humanity has traversed several ages, he said, and has finally arrived in the age of history. In this age, the historians might "commit oversights" or be guilty of "inaccuracies or misstatements," but "there are no myths." This is so since successive ages mean progressive intellectual cultivation. Consequently, the "first age can produce no works like the last; and the last disdains to fantasize like the first."[30]

The second argument that Hug used to combat Strauss's view of the gospels was that the external evidence for the antiquity and apostolic character of the gospels is greater than Strauss admitted.[31] Whereas Strauss saw the period between the death of the apostles (end of the first century) and the earliest testimony for the gospels (middle of the second century) as sufficient for a host of rumors and legends about Jesus to come into circulation, Hug saw the age of the Apostolic Fathers as passionately concerned to preserve apostolic teaching and to prevent the entry of false teaching into the articles of faith.[32] Consequently, Strauss expected to discover myths and untruths in the gospels, while Hug was predisposed to the opposite conclusion. Hug contested Strauss's disparagement of the ancient authors, e.g., Papias, who confirmed the antiquity and apostolicity of the gospels. And, like some of the other respondents to Strauss, he laid the greatest weight upon the testimony of ancient heretics, who acknowledged the gospels as authentic, apostolic compositions.[33]

The third area of Hug's critique of Strauss's Life of Jesus was the internal evidence of a mythicization process at work in the gospels. Hug asserted that Strauss' position stood or fell with the proper determination of the effect of the Old Testament and the messianic expectations of Jesus' contemporaries upon the New Testament portrait of Jesus. Hug observed that not only did Jesus not fit the powerful, military messianic expectations of the people, but also his suffering and ignominious death sharply contradicted them. Even Matthew, who was most interested in proving that Jesus was the messiah, could not ignore the fact that Jesus was not a powerful, magnificent messiah, but rather a spiritual and humble one.[34] Thus, Hug concluded, Strauss had misconceived the role of the Old Testament in the formation of the New Testament picture of Jesus: it did not have a creative, but merely a confirmatory function. The gospels "reported what they knew" and only "afterwards sought the prophetic passages, in which they found the life and suffering of Jesus presaged." Instead of constructing their narratives according to an ideal they had lifted from Hebrew scriptures, the evangelists "looked around for characteristics in the Old Testament that, as prophecies, befitted a mistreated messiah."[35]

Realizing the insufficiency of opposing Strauss's claim in general terms, Hug addressed the specific parallels Strauss alleged to find between the Old Testament messianic prophecies and the gospel narrative.[36] In each case, Hug refused to let general similarities count for imitative correspondence. His critique of Strauss's explication of Jesus' calming of the sea (Matt. 8:23-27, par.) as the mythical imitation of Moses' leading the Israelites through the Red Sea is a good example of Hug's response.

> From this event the myth of Jesus' miraculous voyage is
> formed: Because Moses had a powerful effect on the
> watery element there, then all the more must water sto-
> ries of the messiah be invented.--What should one say
> about such a combination, in which everything is unsuit-

> able: there a sea, here an inland lake; there dry passage
> between towering waves, here the calming of a storm;
> there Moses, here the messiah and Son of God, who did
> not attain to Moses' deeds.[37]

In short, whereas Strauss's explanation of gospel allusions to the Old Testament, as indications of a mythicization process which had its source in the Old Testament stories of the great prophets, was consonant with his devaluation of the historical Jesus for Christian faith; Hug's explication of the allusions, as the attempt by the evangelists to find some scriptural confirmation of Jesus' style of messiahship, was consonant with his assumption of the importance of the historical Jesus for Christian faith. That is, Hug wanted to use the historical truth of the evangelical portrayal of Jesus to explicate the faith accorded Jesus in the first century and to validate faith in him today. His comment upon Matthew's citations of the Old Testament serves as an illuminating summary of his general view of the minimal effect of the Old Testament conception of the messiah upon the gospels.

> Granted that Matthew was the most unsuccessful of ex-
> egetes. What does exegesis have to do with history? He
> wrote down what he knew; thus his work came to be
> with faithful honesty. It is history; history is experience.
> The citation of prophetic passages is automatically distin-
> guished from it; if they [i.e., the passages] were misun-
> derstood in this respect, still the factual, the empirically
> given, remains untouched. From that to want to attack
> the history itself means to mix up what is dissimilar and
> to abolish the boundaries of the disciplines.[38]

Hug's own view of the gospels, which corresponded to his theological construal of Christian faith, was diametrically opposed to Strauss's. Whereas the latter asserted that the gospels were thoroughly permeated by myth, the former insisted that they were generally historical. By this Hug did not mean to say that the gospels were complete biographies. But he did maintain that the gospels accurately presented the major features of Jesus' life. Hug was consistently reticent to allow much of a creative role to the evangelists in the composition of the gospels. He was only prepared to admit that Matthew had subordinated history to the task of portraying Jesus as the messiah.[39] Hug found that apologetic motive less prevalent and the historical interest more evident in the other synoptics. And although John exhibited some creativity in providing the transitions between Jesus' speeches in his gospels, even he was considered by Hug to be a careful historian.[40] In short, the individuality or creativity of the evangelists was largely confined to the phraseology each used to report the events of Jesus' life; it did not include the fabrication of those events.[41]

Strauss had pointed to two facts about the gospels which challenged this view. On the one hand, not all of the gospels reported the same events; one or the other was occasionally silent about the deeds reported by the others. On the other hand, there were not only discrepancies, but also contradictions in the gospels' reporting of the same events. In order to deal with these two serious problems, Hug developed what might be called a theory of sufficient coverage and a theory of progressive development. Cumulatively, they constituted a thorough harmonization of the four gospel narratives.

Hug responded to the first problem with a double rebuttal. He first noted that the evangelists respected a geographical division of labor: the synoptics were concerned chiefly with the events that transpired in Galilee; John, with those in Judea and Jerusalem. To Strauss's query as to why this was so, Hug replied that the personal responsibilities and circumstances of the disciples prevented some of them from witnessing Jesus' full Judean ministry in addition to his Galilean activity.[42]

Hug's second line of rebuttal asserted that an evangelist sometimes remained quiet about an event if others had adequately reported it.[43] John, for example, was silent about Jesus' baptism and the Last Supper because he "could absolve himself from the obligation he had as an historian, to pass over no fact of significance, if he knew that it was already treated satisfactorily by others."[44] Passing over "a detail which changes nothing in the main matter" or making a mistake in reporting some aspect of his story did not take away from the fundamental, historical accuracy of the evangelist.[45]

The transfiguration, however, directly questioned the credibility of this hypothesis of sufficient coverage. Strauss had highlighted the curious fact that all of the synoptic gospels reported the event, even though none of the authors was an eyewitness of it, whereas John, who was supposedly such a witness, did not mention it in his gospel.[46] Hug refused to renounce his view as inapplicable in this case, and he appealed to his former rebuttal, the geographical division of labor, to rescue it.[47]

Hug's chief instrument in combatting the second major problem facing the historical view of the gospel narratives was his theory of the narrative's progressive development. The objection based upon the disparity in the gospels' exposition of circumstances is resolved, said Hug, by perceiving "the progressive accomplishments of the historians."[48] Matthew provided the foundation for the evangelical narrative, while Mark, by including the circumstances omitted by the former and correcting some of his historical inaccuracies, provided a text that critically clarified Matthew's story.[49] Luke's story offered the most complete coverage of events outside of Judea; in comparison with it, the other synoptics appeared to be "more an outline than a history that makes a claim to completeness."[50] Wherever Strauss claimed to detect contradiction, Hug perceived supplementation.[51]

Harmonization was the required hermeneutical correlate of accepting Hug's theory about the progressive development of the gospel story. One gospel could correct or supplement, but never contradict, another; otherwise, the gospels could not be regarded as generally reliable history. But if the gospels, despite the diversity of their organization, "readily allow themselves to be erected into one body ...without disruption, ...then this harmonious historical life is an irrefutable proof of the soundness of the elements which are its foundation."[52] Hug accepted Strauss's challenge to demonstrate that the synoptic material could be fitted into the Johannine chronology.[53]

Although he claimed that his reconciliation of the disparities between the gospels was not strained, Hug did have to presuppose certain points for his exposition to be tenable. For example, he required four marriages of obligation in the course of a millennium in order to harmonize the genealogies of Matthew and Luke. With some comparable adjustments, Hug reconciled the different stories of Jesus' birth and of his crucifixion.[54] His harmonization of the post-resurrection stories, however, reveals the creative lengths to which he went to preserve the historical integrity of the gospels. Presupposing the greater accuracy of Luke's presentation and presupposing his own theory of the progressive development of the gospels, Hug harmonized the various contradictions of the gospel stories. Strauss, by contrast, had rejected a harmonized sequence of events, such as Hug presented, as ridiculous.[55]

In the end, Hug believed that he had disclosed the faultiness of Strauss' method and had refuted the substance of the latter's charge about the unhistorical character of the gospels. In fact, Hug had opposed Strauss's methodical presuppositions with a set of his own, which was vulnerable to criticism for its dogmatic bias.

Hug's Theological Motivation

Hug responded to Strauss's _Life of Jesus_ ostensibly because he saw its exegesis to be flawed. What alarmed him most, however, was that Strauss's work undermined belief in the gospels as historically accurate accounts of Jesus' life. If the gospels were thus undermined, Hug's conception of Christian faith was put into jeopardy.

The theological foundation of Hug's exegetical enterprise was his conception of Christianity as a moral vision and code of conduct. He announced this view in the Preface to his _Introduction to the New Testament_, which contained his basic critique of the inadequacies of naturalistic and rationalistic biblical interpretation and which articulated his defense of Christianity as the supreme moral system. Hug's argument was that supernaturalism established Christianity as the ideal model for a virtuous life. Rationalism, as well as any other human philosophical construct, would have been unable to achieve this.

> The greatest philosopher can be no more than a virtuous man; what illiberality, then, in forbidding one to travel in any reputable road, except that of Rationalism! They [i.e., the Naturalists] separate Religion and Morals, because the Greeks and Romans did so. But without any reason. Christianity in its very nature is _practical_; and pure virtue, in its perfect state, is the Christian religion. All the doctrines which respect God, a future state, etc., tend only to produce a virtuous life; which is the highest end

of man. The edifice of Christianity was built in a few
years by using the scaffolding of Supernaturalism, and
was in a short time filled with many inmates from different countries. But if Christianity had been only a school
of philosophy, instructing and arguing on the grounds of
mere reason, it would have attracted but a narrow circle
of inquirers, like other schools, e.g. the Academy, and the
Porch, and the Peripaton, and would never have been a
popular Institute.[56]

Hug, therefore, saw the purpose of the incarnation to be the introduction of a new moral conception into the world. Jesus was incontestably
more important than other world-historical figures because he had
"influenced the progress of the moral formation and refinement of our race
in a lasting way." Hug presented him as "a colossus of moral power and
glory in the middle of the nations, which owe their moral improvement to
him."[57] Correlatively, the evangelists were chiefly concerned to further
the establishment of this moral-religious vision. The messiahship and divinity of Jesus, which Matthew and John specially highlighted in their
gospels, was not their ultimate message. Rather, it was only "the divine
warrant" for authorizing the new moral conception Jesus delivered.[58]

Within this context, the historical veracity of the gospel narrative was
necessary to establish factually the highest authorization for Jesus' moral
doctrines. If the Christian code were to be regarded as the uniquely
superior one, then its founder had to be presented as uniquely superior
among human beings. Hug, therefore, took great pains, on the one hand, to
defend Jesus against Strauss's claim that his views sometimes did not rise
above those of the masses and to establish, on the other, the perfection of
Jesus' knowledge and personality.[59] The most decisive proof of Jesus' exalted status, of course, was his performance of miracles.

Hug held that everything came down to the question how Jesus was to
"establish his authorization for introducing a new religious legislation into
the world." Jesus could do that, Hug argued, only by proving that his
authority came from God.[60] The performance of miracles was the absolutely essential means to that end.

All of the Lord's miracles had only one major purpose,
namely, to convince his age that he has not taken hold of
his agency as a merely human teacher, but has received
it from God, who sent him with perfect power to bring
forth a new creation in the moral world. He established
this firm faith among his contemporaries through works,
the likes of which to perform is not given to human beings. He had to do that. For in two years and some
months, which he filled up in the occupation of teaching,
it was impossible to convince the masses, in theoretical
ways, of the divine origin of his teaching and to establish
this higher teaching reputation so firmly that it perse-
vered unshaken.[61]

As Hug saw it, the legitimation of Jesus' moral message was so important
that compassion and the desire to help those in need was only a subordinate reason for the performance of his miracles.[62]

The backing for Hug's entire argument was the historical truth of the
gospels' claim that Jesus did perform miracles and did exhibit himself as a
truly divine personality. Hence, Hug's construal of Christian faith induced
him hermeneutically to uphold, as far as possible, a supernaturalistic exegesis of the gospels. His entire evaluation of Strauss's work, just like his
earlier evaluation of Paulus's Life of Jesus, aimed at exposing the mythical
and naturalistic interpretations as unproven dogmatism or flawed exegesis,
while simultaneously displaying the supernaturalistic interpretation as the
truly "natural" and adequate mode of interpretation.

They [i.e., the objections against the historical truth of the
gospels] are collectively based upon a single principle,
which the majority of naturalistic exegetes have in common with Mr. Strauss, namely, the dogma which they
have revealed to themselves: Jesus was, so it says, a
mere human being as all of us are. On the one side, their
dogma; on the other, history with indelible features,
which knew him as the messenger of God to humanity,
different from all human beings by virtue of superhuman
deeds and fate. This history they cannot sweep away or
invalidate by means of accusation, when its statements
contradict each other. Still, they have not succeeded in
bringing into play contradictions for which there would

be no solution. Here is historical faith, there an assumed
tenet. Our position, the supernaturalistic one, on the
contrary, is at bottom the natural position. An enemy to
artificial methods, it despises the travestied Christ and
the Straussian-mythological absurdity altogether. It hon-
ors the Christ, as he is given, and only this [Christ] bene-
fits the world.[63]

Hug's supernaturalism, however, was modified by his adoption of some
principles of historical criticism. A curious amalgam of tenable critical
theory and flawed critical practice was the consequence of seeking to
balance his understanding of Christian faith with the demands of historical
criticism. For example, Hug declared that he could presuppose neither the
inspiration of Scripture nor the credibility of the evangelists.[64] Yet he, unlike Strauss, always gave tradition and the evangelists the benefit of the
doubt, even when the case against them was considerable.[65] Hug also recognized that a literary-critical investigation of the gospels had to precede a
definitive statement on their character and reliability. And in his own investigation, he noticed the interdependence of the synoptics and acknowledged that Luke and Mark generally agreed in the order of their narrative
against Matthew.[66] Yet the soundness of this part of Hug's theory was undermined elsewhere by his uncritical judgments.[67]

Hug could have maintained his moral construal of Christianity, while
becoming more critical of the alleged historical character of the gospels, if
only he had not also wanted to maintain the superiority of Christianity. Its
superiority was established for Hug by the uniqueness of its founder, Jesus
the Christ. Whereas Strauss's surrender of Jesus' uniqueness allowed him
to apply historical criticism to the gospels in its most radical form, Hug's
dogged belief in the insurpassability of Jesus ultimately subverted his
critical judgment on the gospels. If he had been satisfied, on the contrary,
with asserting that, upon the basis of historical effects and intrinsic value,
Jesus had founded an admirable and most influential vision of life, he
would not have had to cling to the alleged historicity of Jesus' miracles as a
warrant for his adoption of that same vision. As it was, Hug could accept
neither Strauss's specification of the content of Christian faith nor his approach to the validation of its truth. For Hug, belief in Jesus' divinity and
insurpassability constituted a central part of faith, in that Jesus' divinity

validated the truth of Christian moral and religious doctrine. The Christian, according to Hug, believed that Jesus was the way to a redeemed life not merely insofar as he revealed that life, but, more importantly, insofar as he lived it in a way that empowered others to take it up. For Strauss, it was not Jesus, but the idea he represented, that constituted the integral part of Christian faith; and the truth of that faith was validated by a philosophy of religion, not by history.

In short, Hug's response to Strauss not only exhibits the conflict between two different conceptions of the content of faith, but it also discloses the tension Hug experienced between the demand for his book to be appropriate to the Christian tradition and to be adequate in terms of modern historical consciousness. Hug's understanding of Christian faith did not allow him to endorse a mythical interpretation of Scripture, yet his desire to examine Scripture critically did not allow him to embrace extreme supernaturalism. Wherever possible, he adopted a natural interpretation of the events reported by the evangelists, thus hoping to limit the number of supernatural events requiring belief.[68] Similarly, Hug recognized that he could not always save all aspects of a gospel story from Strauss's corrosive criticism. In those cases, his theological convictions compelled him to preserve as much of the historical core of the story as possible, surrendering the details surrounding it to Strauss's attack.[69] In the end, Hug could moderate his historical, supernaturalistic reading of the gospels, but he could not abandon it without simultaneously abandoning his understanding of Christian faith.

NOTES

[1]Walter Drum observed around the turn of the century: "In Germany no Biblical scholar had more influence in stemming that destructive tide than had Hug. Not only his books but numerous articles by Hug, especially in the Freiburg 'Zeitschrift,' kept up a constant attack on the arbitrary method and questionable tactics of the negative critics. Even today the historical studies that Hug made in the New Testament are of value to the thorough student of Holy Writ." The Catholic Encyclopedia (1910), 7:515. See also Adalbert Maier, Gedächtnissrede auf Joh. Leonh. Hug, bei dessen akademischer Todtenfeier in der Universitäts-Kirche zu Freiburg am 11. März 1847 (Freiburg: Universitäts-Buchdruckerei von Hermann M. Poppen, 1847), p. 33. Hermann Gunkel and Leopold Zscharnack, eds., Die Religion in Geschichte und Gegenwart, 2d ed. (Tübingen: Mohr, 1927-31), 2:2037. Erwin Keller, "Johann Leonhard Hug (1765-1846)," in Katholische Theologen Deutschlands im 19. Jahrhundert, 1:266-67.

[2]Werner, p. 528. References in this chapter to Hug's Gutachten über das Leben Jesu, kritisch bearbeitet von David Friedrich Strauss will be to the 1854 edition published by the Friedrich Wagner Buchhandlung.

[3]Hug suffered rare lapses. See Gutachten, 2:202-03, where Hug attributes bad motives to Strauss. See also 2:210.

[4]Werner, p. 528.

[5]See Maier, p. 9; Keller, p. 256.

[6]Hug remains unknown for two principal reasons. First, contemporary biblical scholarship has advanced far beyond the state of biblical studies in the first half of the nineteenth century, and it shows little interest in those opinions that are no longer tenable. Second, Catholic biblical scholarship, from the sixteenth through the nineteenth century, generally lagged behind the Protestant in critical rigor and in the scope of its insight. As a result, the best of Catholic scholarship in this period rarely measured up to the achievements of the Protestant vanguard. Correlatively, little attention is paid to nineteenth-century Catholic biblical studies when one wants to uncover the seminal impulses for the promotion of the critical study of the Bible.

[7]Kümmel suggests 1820 as a dividing line between the age of the after-effects of Enlightenment theology and the age of advanced historical-

critical study of the Bible. Werner Georg Kümmel, "Das Erbe des 19. Jahrhunderts für die neutestamentliche Wissenschaft von heute," in: Wilhelm Schneemelcher, ed., Das Erbe des 19. Jahrhunderts: Referate vom Deutschen Evangelischen Theologentag, 7.-11. Juni 1960 in Berlin (Berlin: Alfred Töpelmann, 1960), pp. 67-68.

[8] Maier, p. 12. Maier highlights the difficult challenge that faced Hug in rising to this height: Hug had to acquire on his own much of the critical, linguistic, and philological skills needed since he had not been formally instructed in biblische Einleitungswissenschaft during his university studies. Concerning Hug's Introduction, Keller, p. 257, observes: "Was die Einleitungswissenschaft des Neuen Testaments betrifft, so war Hugs Werk unstreitig auf diesem Gebiet eine bahnbrechende Leistung auf katholischer Seite. Hier wurden bisher in der sogenannten Hermeneutik lediglich einige leichtere Einleitungsfragen behandelt. Den schwierigen Fragen, die sich von der historisch-kritischen Forschung her ergaben, hat erstmals Hug sich in vollem Umfang gestellt." That Hug's work was important is reflected in the fact that the book went through four editions, was translated into French and English (twice each), and was used as a basic text at several major European universities, including Budapest, Copenhagen, and Uppsala. See Maier, pp. 32-33. The Theologische Quartalschrift, moreover, called it "the classical work" for Catholics. Keller, p. 261.

[9] F[rederic Auguste] Lichtenberger, History of German Theology in the Nineteenth Century, trans. and ed. W. Hastie (Edinburgh: T. & T. Clark 1889), p. 589.

[10] See Johann Jakob Herzog, ed., Real-Enzyklopädie für protestantische Theologie und Kirche, 3d expanded ed., (Leipzig: J.C. Hinrichs, 1896-1913), 8:429-31, which attributed much of the value of Hug's work to its "critical acumen and the relative impartiality of its procedure." The Encyclopaedia Britannica (1891) recognized the acuteness of Hug's arguments against Eichhorn and concluded that Hug's Introduction was "specially valuable in the portion relating to the history of the text ... and in its discussion of the ancient version." Although Protestant scholarship tended to find Hug's academic work constricted by his Catholicism, some, by contrast, regarded his work as quite "Protestant," i.e., critical. See Moses Stuart's Prefatory Remarks: "He [i.e., the reader] must know, then, that Hug is a Roman Catholic with a kind of Protestant heart. He wears, rather impatiently, if I discern aright, the chains which his profession imposes upon him, and when he comes to critical conclusions which he apprehends may be construed as being included under the banns of Mother-Church, he

143

endeavours to make a separation between his <u>critical</u> and his <u>Catholic</u>
conscience. His critical conscience is at liberty, while his Catholic
conscience is permitted to go along with the multitude." <u>Hug's Introduction</u>
<u>to the New Testament</u>, trans. from the third German edition by David
Fosdick, Jr., with notes by M. Stuart (Andover: Gould and Newman, 1836),
p. vi. Cf. Keller, pp. 262-63, who contests the opinion of those Protestants
who asserted that Hug was not truly serious in all his Catholic-sounding
asseverations.

[11] <u>The New Catholic Encyclopedia</u> (1967), 7:187.

[12] Hug, <u>Gutachten</u>, 1:4. Elsewhere Hug made it clear that he did not
conceive his task as being theological. See pp. 174, 181.

[13] <u>Hug's Introduction</u>, p. 64.

[14] Hug, <u>Gutachten</u>, 1:164.

[15] Hug thought that Strauss's treatment of the three cases in which Jesus
was said to have raised someone from the dead provided a good example
of Strauss's faulty method. Borrowing some objections from Thomas
Woolston (1670-1733), Strauss had claimed that there exists an
unmistakable gradation in the three stories: Jesus raised Jairus' daughter
on her deathbed, the youth of Nain as he was being taken on a litter to his
grave, and Lazarus after he had already been buried. Such climax-building
raised Strauss's suspicion about the historical truth of the stories. <u>Leben</u>
<u>Jesu</u> (1838), 2:166. Hug replied that suspicion about the gospel narrative
by itself did not establish the truth of Strauss's view. He asserted,
moreover, that the correct sequence of events involved the reversal of the
placement of the Jairus and Nain stories. This meant that the gradual
intensification of effect had been eliminated. Hug, <u>Gutachten</u>, 2:49.

[16] Ibid., 2:58-59. See also 2:150 and 1:36.

[17] Hug accepted the existence of higher beings, such as angels, admitted
the possibility of their intervention into human affairs, and conceived the
"natural" in the widest possible terms. See his <u>Gutachten</u>, 1:60-61, 107;
2:100, 146, 189-90. Although even Strauss accepted some of Jesus'
"miraculous" cures as historical, Hug also accepted as historical all those
which his Protestant contemporary rejected. Strauss accepted those cures
that could be explained as the results of influence from animal magnetism.
See his <u>Leben Jesu</u> (1838), 2:7-9. Cf. Hug, <u>Gutachten</u>, 2:8.

[18]Strauss insisted that "ein rein historisches Bewußtsein ist dem hebräischen Volke während der ganzen Zeit seines politischen Bestehens eigentlich niemals aufgegangen, da selbst seine spätesten Geschichtswerke, wie die Bücher der Makkabäer, und sogar die Schriften des Josephus nicht frei von wunderhaften und abentheuerlichen Erzählungen sind." Leben Jesu (1838), 1:85–86. Hug began his reply: "Es war also eine historische Zeit in der gesammten Umgebung von Palästina, von welcher die Juden nicht unberührt blieben." Gutachten, 1:52–53.

[19]Ibid., 1:54–55.

[20]Ibid., 1:46. Hug felt that the gospel of Matthew least measured up to the ideals of Roman historiography. See 2:255.

[21]Hug's Introduction, p. 369.

[22]David Hume, An Enquiry Concerning Human Understanding (1777), Section X, Parts 1 and 2. Concerning Strauss's handling of the miracles at sea, Hug commented: "After the author dismissed the attempts at naturalistic exegesis, he concludes on p. 190: 'Thus the matter remains: as the evangelists report the event to us, we must acknowledge a miracle in it. But to elevate that from an exegetical result to a real fact is extremely difficult, whence suspicion against the historical character of the story arises.' I accept the first part of this statement for myself with pleasure. As regards the other part, it is well known that the reality of a fact is ascertained through witnesses. Their statements lie here before us, and to the charges which Mr. Strauss, in the Introduction to his Life of Jesus, has brought against their credibility, sections 11, 12 and 13 of our evaluation make a sufficient reply." Gutachten, 2:57–58. In sections 11–13 of his work, Hug marshalled the external evidence in support of the age and reliability of the gospels. The acceptance of the gospel narrative as authentic by heretics was for Hug a specially strong confirmation of the evangelists' credibility as witnesses to the events of Jesus' life. See 1:37–44, especially p. 40.

[23]Ibid, 1:192–93. See also 2:57–58.

[24]See Hug's Introduction, p. 65.

[25]Hug, Gutachten, 2:4–5. See also 2:48–49, 56, 79.

[26] Hug's Introduction, p. 366.

[27] Hug used an example from Muslim literature to highlight the contrast. Gutachten, 2:5. He further remarked that the Pharisees' request for a sign from Jesus also gave the evangelists the opportunity to exaggerate Jesus' power and stature. That they did not avail themselves of this opportunity attests to their fidelity to the historical given. Ibid., p. 7.

[28] Ibid., 2:232. Cf. Hug's criticism of H. E. G. Paulus's handling of the resurrection story: "[Recension über] Das Leben Jesu, als Grundlage einer reinen Geschichte des Urchristenthums (1828)," Zeitschrift für die Geistlichkeit des Erzbisthums Freiburg, Drittes Heft (1829):185-87.

[29] Hug, Gutachten, 1:5-10. See also pp. 46-50. Cf. his specious argument in defense of the "unadorned simplicity" and historical character of Jewish writing, Hug's Introduction, p. 65.

[30] Hug, Gutachten, 1:7. Hug, however, did not mean to say that myths, construed in a broader sense, were impossible in a so-called historical era. He readily admitted that fairy tales, fables, and the like occur in historical ages, but he claimed that they do not belong to the genre of history. Ibid., note 1. Gospels, by contrast, did belong in the historical genre. Consequently, one might find inaccuracies or false assertions in them, but not myths. It is interesting to note that whereas Strauss castigated some of his predecessors for finding in the gospels more historical than philosophical myths, Hug did not regard the latter as myths at all, but viewed them rather as parables. Ibid., 1:8.

[31] Other theologians, both Catholic and Protestant, had used this argument against Strauss. Hug seems to have focused upon the external evidence in his Gutachten because Strauss had treated it cursorily and he himself had already evaluated the internal evidence in his Introduction, whose conclusions he presupposed here. Hug had adduced there the corrupted style of Greek, the frequent resemblance to Hebrew in the use of words and grammar, and the uncommonly accurate knowledge of the geographical, social, ethnic, and political situations as proof of the genuineness of the gospels. See Hug's Introduction, pp. 12-24.

[32] Hug, Gutachten, 1:27-30, especially pp. 29-30. See also p. 45.

[33] Ibid., 1:30-40. Cf. Hug's Introduction, pp. 28-29.

[34] Hug, Gutachten, 1:19-24. The only elements that were usable from the common conception of the messiah were the idea of entering Jerusalem on an ass and the messiah's healing power. See 1:25-26.

[35] Ibid., 1:45.

[36] Concerning the birth of Immanuel from a maiden (Isa. 7:14), for example, Hug argued that the Jewish scribes had not referred that Isaianic passage to the messiah, but understood it as referring to Hezekiah, son of Ahaz. Therefore, the Jews of Jesus' day "lacked the material to form a myth out of these words and to pass it on to the Christians." Ibid., 1:90. To Strauss's claim that Jesus' cure of the man with the withered hand (Matt. 12:9-14) was a mythicizing imitation of the cure of Jeroboam's withered hand by the man of God (I Kings 13:1-10), Hug replied that the dissimilarity of details in the two stories destroyed Strauss's claim. Ibid., 2:41. Although the evidence Hug marshalled against Strauss was, in the case of John the Baptist (1:65-67), more impressive than the counter-arguments cited here, it still did not eliminate the basic force of Strauss's general point, namely, that there is sufficient evidence in the gospels that the evangelists' portrayal of Jesus, at least in certain regards, may have been influenced by something other than the factual course of events.

[37] Ibid., 2:58. See Hug's refutation of the alternative naturalistic interpretation of this passage by Paulus and by another defender of naturalistic exegesis, Johannes Schulthess, in his "Zugabe zur Erklärung der Abschnitte, Joh. II. 1-12. Die Hochzeit zu Kana, und Matth. VIII. 23-27. Jesus gebeut Ruhe dem Sturme," Zeitschrift für die Geistlichkeit des Erzbisthums Freiburg, Fünftes Heft (1830):47-48.

[38] Hug, Gutachten, 1:110. Cf. Hug's Introduction, pp. 342-44.

[39] "Die Schrift des Matthäus beabsichtigt, eine Idee durchzuführen, der er den Geschichtsstoff untergeordnet hat. Der vorwaltende Gedanke: Jesu von Nazaret ist der Messias, zieht sich durchs Ganze hindurch, und wird mittelst der Vergleichung seiner Thaten und Geschichte mit Stellen der Propheten, an denen sie die Eigenschaften des Messias vorbedeutet haben, bewahrheitet. Die Geschichten werden nur in Grundlinien dargelegt, so weit es aber nöthig war, ihre Aehnlichkeit mit den prophetischen Vorsagungen bemerklich zu machen." Ibid., 2:19. See also p. 28. Although he admitted, 1:76, that Matthew was quite free at times in his treatment of history, Hug maintained that Matthew was faithful to the basic history of Jesus' life. Ibid., 1:110, 156.

147

[40] Ibid., 1:199. Cf. Hug's Introduction, pp. 420-21, where Hug says: "This Evangelist proceeds on a plan of his own, resembling Matthew so far as this, that he aims throughout the history to prove certain positions, making everything tend to this object; but he differs from him in this respect, that he never loses the thread of the narrative or deviates from the real succession of events, and, with a very complicated and artificial plan, is notwithstanding careful to preserve historical order." Hug praised him for not putting anything in Jesus' mouth that was not attributable to him and for keeping his private opinion of Jesus' speeches separate from what the latter actually said. Gutachten, 2:127. Hug, moreover, argued that John's detailed description of such stories as the man born blind (9:1-41) and Lazarus' resurrection (11:1-54) was proof of his status as a well-informed and trustworthy historian, who had recorded Jesus' speeches with the same accuracy and fidelity. Ibid., 1:201-02. Cf. 2:222. Here, as in many other cases, Hug is building upon the results of his investigations in his Introduction. Of the synoptics, Hug preferred Luke's account since it was more complete and generally more precise in its chronology. Gutachten, 1:161-62, 169; 2:48, 198. Luke was, in Hug's estimation, simply a better historian. See 2:211,217.

[41] Hug's Introduction, p. 407.

[42] Matthew, for example, belonged to this group. He was least able to be absent from his home in Galilee because of his daily collection of taxes; John and James, by contrast, had more freedom to accompany Jesus on his several trips to the great religious feasts in Jerusalem. Gutachten, 1:149, 152, 156, 168.

[43] Applying these dual lines of response to the two alleged eyewitnesses of Jesus' ministry, Hug had Matthew retort: "I have kept nothing silent, I have only not said more than I knew and that was serviceable for illuminating and strengthening the principal tenet of my book: Namely, Jesus is the messiah. John would reply: I have kept nothing silent, I have only not repeated what was already said." Ibid., 1:150.

[44] Ibid., 2:147.

[45] Ibid., 2:172, 216-17.

[46] Strauss, Leben Jesu (1838), 2:281-82.

[47] In his Introduction, p. 427, Hug had stated that one was compelled to adopt his view since the alternative was absurd: "Now did he [i.e., John] leave unnoticed these forcible facts, with which circumstances made him better acquainted than either of the Evangelists, in the hope that in time there would appear historians who would record them, and bring forward what would have been his best arguments? or is it certain that he would not and could not have omitted them, had not others already made use of these materials, which would have been so much to his purpose, so that he could not use them without going over beaten ground? If the first conclusion be, as it is, absurd, we must adopt this second. There remained, therefore, for the Apostle, to be employed for his purposes, only what had been omitted by previous writers. These omitted portions of the history were all which he could treat of, even tough they might not be by any means so important as those which had been already presented. He was thus, not only able, but compelled, to proceed as he has done, in the execution of his plan." Cf. his Gutachten, 2:85.

[48] Ibid., 2:40.

[49] Ibid., 2:19, 28, 43. Cf. Hug's Introduction, pp. 378-80, 384-85.

[50] Hug, Gutachten, 2:169. See also pp. 129-30. Cf. 1:163-64, 169.

[51] See, for example, Hug's handling of the story of Jesus' trial before the high priests, ibid., 2:155-56, and of his post-resurrection appearances, 2:218-20. Cf. Hug's Introduction, pp. 381-82. And for a summary statement of how the alleged contradictions are resolved, see p. 414.

[52] Hug, Gutachten, 1:163. Hug further claimed that a smooth harmonization of stories would be impossible if the individual elements in the stories had no historical basis, but were the discrete creations of different authors. See 2:169.

[53] According to Strauss, harmonization was conceivable only if this could be achieved. See his Leben Jesu (1838), 1:520-25. Cf. Hug, Gutachten, 1:164-65. For a sketch of Hug's comprehensive harmonization of John's gospel with the synoptics, see Hug's Introduction, pp. 450-54.

[54] Concerning the genealogies, see Hug's Gutachten, 1:78. For his harmonization of the stories of Jesus' birth, see 1:108, and see 2:172-73 for his handling of the accounts of Jesus' crucifixion.

[55] Ibid., 2:210-12, 219-22. Cf. Strauss, Leben Jesu (1838), 2: 654-55.

[56] Hug's Introduction, p. vii. Hug espouses a kind of accommodation theory: God realized that the way to direct people's attention to Christianity was not through the use of philosophical argumentation, but through the sensible demonstration of Christianity's divine origin. Rationalistic naturalism was incapable of convincing the masses of the moral superiority of Christianity; miracles, however, were quite persuasive: "The first [i.e., the Naturalists] have made pure Theism their aim; and acknowledge nothing as appropriate in the way of investigation respecting morals and theology, excepting a philosophy, into which the common people can never make any deep researches. This last class of men need the positive in religion, and always will need it. This is given to them in a manner so noble, so perfect, so intelligible, that the simpleton becomes as good and virtuous, or even more so than the most learned, and more so than learning can make them. Why should we substitute, then, the commands of philosophy for those of the God of heaven?" Ibid.

[57] Hug, Gutachten, 1:4. See also 2:232-33: "Ihn [Jesus], der gegeben ist, in Wechsel und Veränderung als das Stätige und Bleibende an dem Höhepunct unseres Gesichtkreises wie eine Leuchte zu stehen, wohin jeweils die Welt blicke, daß sie nicht die Pfade sittlicher Würde verliere, und in Thorheit versinke."

[58] "It [Jesus' messiahship] was not itself the doctrine, but was the seal of the sacredness and obligatory nature of the doctrine, and it was only from accidental circumstances that it became the main idea of Matthew's book, as the prevailing idea in John's is that Jesus was the Son of God." Hug's Introduction, p. 366.

[59] See Gutachten, 2:24-25, where Hug seeks to deflect Strauss's charge that Jesus shared the common conception of illness as a consequence of sin. See also 2:34, where Hug insists upon Jesus' perfect knowledge. He asserts there that Jesus knew who had touched him in the story of the woman with the hemorrhage (Mark 5:25-34; Luke 8:43-48), but asked "Who touched me?" to move the woman to a public confession of her cure by Jesus. To the rebuttal, that such an intent was anomalous in view of the times Jesus commanded silence of those whom he cured, Hug replied: "Wenn Jesus hie und da den Geheilten verbot, von dem, was mit ihnen vorgegangen ist, zu reden, so hatte er besondere Ursachen dazu; im Ganzen aber waren die Wunderheilungen eben so viele Beweise seiner Macht, den Menschen ein neues von Gott gekommenes Gesetz zu überbringen."

[60] Philosophical theory and logical argument would be inadequate to establish such authority. Jesus needed to certify it in a sensible way. "Das Volk wie die Apostel mußte Thatsachen sehen, die zu verbringen kein menschliches Vermögen zureicht, Werke Gottes, welche die Ermächtigung des neuen Gesetzgebers bezeugten." Ibid., 2:4-5.

[61] Ibid., 2:56. Hug expounds at length his argument for the necessity of such divine authorization in his article, "Ist das Entstehen des Christenthums auf natürliche Weise erklärbar?" Zeitschrift für die Geistlichkeit des Erzbisthums Freiburg, Heft 7 (1834):176-244.

[62] "Gewiß waren dem Herrn die Gefühle des Wohlwollens, der Theilnahme und des Mitleidens nicht fremde, die er so oft kund gegeben hat; aber die ihm beiwohnende Wunderkraft hatte zunächst den Zweck, die göttliche Vollmacht seiner Sendung an die Menschen zur Begründung einer neuen Ordnung der Dinge darzuthun; diesem untergeordnet war die Wohlthätigkeit . . ." Hug, Gutachten, 2:48-49. See also 2:79: "Der erste Zweck aller Wunder Jesu war . . . die ihm von Gott übertragene Gewalt zur Gründung einer neuen Weltordnung auf eine für Jedermann begreifliche Weise darzuthun."

[63] Ibid., 2:250.

[64] "As the first question is, whether these books have any historical value, we naturally cannot take their inspiration into account, which can only be proved when this point is decided." Hug's Introduction, p. 349 and note 1. In his actual exposition of inspiration, Hug distanced himself from the narrow, traditionalist view. See Gutachten, 2:229-30.

[65] See ibid., 1:105, 200-01.

[66] Hug's Introduction, p. 415. Hug perceived some of the elements which later led to the formulation of the two-source theory, but he assembled them in a different configuration. See pp. 418-19.

[67] Hug, like Paulus and Kuhn before him, accepted uncritically Luke's asseveration, in the Prologue of his gospel, that he was going to present a careful, ordered account of the major events of Jesus' life. See his Gutachten, 1:56 and 74. He, therefore, mistook Luke for a careful historian. And although Hug admitted that both a rigorous internal and external analysis of the gospels was required and that the results of each had to be

critically correlated, in practice he seemed to derive the historical
credibility of the evangelical accounts from their apostolic genuineness.
See Hug's Introduction, p. 64.

68 "Obschon entschiedener Supranaturalist und Gegner aller
Travestirungen der Evangelien, verschmähe ich es, Wunder anzunehmen,
wo die natürliche Deutung, ohne Zwang und exegetische Gewalthätigkeit,
sich mir selbst in die Hände legt." Hug, Gutachten, 1:113. See also 1:192-
93 and 2:226-27. In the process of attacking rationalistic and naturalistic
exegesis, Hug was himself accused of being a "closet" rationalist. Cf. Die
Religion in Geschichte und Gegenwart (1928), 2:2037; Lexikon für
Theologie und Kirche (1960), 5:507.

69 Hug, Gutachten, 1:157; 2:30, 143.

CHAPTER 5

THE RESPONSE IN THE CATHOLIC JOURNALS

In the years immediately following the publication of The Life of Jesus Critically Examined, a number of critiques and reviews were published in Catholic journals. Many of the reviews were polemical and superficial, such as the ones that appeared in The Catholic and Historical-political Newspaper for Catholic Germany. A few were negative, but not quite as polemical, such as the brief reviews by Johann Adam Möhler and Franz von Baader. On rare occasion, such as in the review by Joseph Sprissler, there was positive appreciation of Strauss's work. As a whole, these essays of the 1830s and 1840s contribute to a fuller picture of both the unity and the diversity of Catholic thought with regard to historical criticism and its consequences for faith.

The Response of The Catholic

The full title of this journal enunciates its aim, which was the "instruction and warning" of the Catholic public. Begun in 1821, The Catholic's editorship was ultimately taken over in the 1840s by professors appointed by Bishop Ketteler of Mainz.[1] Their approach to the preservation and defense of Catholicism stressed traditional discipline, unswerving obedience to the pope, the removal of Catholic students from public universities (the vast majority of whose faculty was Protestant), and the greater importance of "having good priests than educated ones."[2]

The three articles published in The Catholic in response to Strauss avoided detailed refutation of Strauss's exegesis, but confined themselves to a categorization of his chief errors and the situating of Strauss within Protestantism. Although the articles indulged in isolated ad hominem attacks, they focused most of their polemical criticism on the Protestantism that had produced Strauss. The anonymous author of "Dr. Strauss and His Position on Protestant Theology" claimed that Strauss, by pulling together in his work the various strands of the Protestant tradition, revealed the true nature of Protestantism.[3] Stated in the starkest terms, Protestantism was the grave of Christianity. Stated somewhat less negatively, Protestantism's essence was deviation and division. Whereas Catholicism's failure to change exhibited its unwavering possession of the truth, Protestantism demonstrated its falsity by its internal opposition and its constant change.[4]

Strauss's opponents in The Catholic identified three problematic characteristics of his Life of Jesus. First, they observed that Strauss's work intemperately imbibed the spirit of the age, which transformed everything historical into something ideal. More specifically, they identified Strauss's Life of Jesus as the culmination of the rationalistic biblical criticism promoted by Reimarus and others.[5]

Second, the critics faulted Strauss's Life of Jesus for its hypercriticism. Although they thought the Protestant approach in general was unduly critical, Strauss's work struck them as especially destructive in that it doubted the authenticity of the gospel texts.[6] Strauss's skepticism vis-à-vis the gospel stories resulted from a failure to recognize and respect the distinction between divine and secular science. Although Mack and Kuhn had already called into question the scientific character of Strauss's work, Schütz's call for a proper scientific method entailed the refusal to admit that the objects of theology were to be examined by the same tools used in studying other objects of knowledge.[7] Another Catholic critic made an appeal for fideism, noting that the peace which faith bestows on a questioning mind is "higher than all reason."[8]

Third, these critics identified pantheism as a root flaw in The Life of Jesus Critically Examined. Strauss's view was in this respect symptomatic of the prevalent philosophy, against which, one critic insisted, traditional orthodoxy (as expressed in Catholicism) had to be posited.[9]

For their part, these opponents offered Catholicism as the antidote for the poison Strauss was spreading. All three respondents identified the objective tradition and authority of the Church as the safeguard against the destructive subjectivity of Strauss's work. One author explained that Catholics, unlike their Protestant counterparts, could remain undisturbed by Strauss's Life of Jesus because they believed that the Christ had promised to keep "both channels for spreading and preserving his eternal word" free from falsification. Even if the worst were to happen, that is, "something human were to be encountered in Scripture," then that human addition could easily be corrected "through the living spirit of tradition."[10]

Catholics such as these clearly were not disposed to accept the higher criticism of the Bible.[11]

Two of the critics who wrote for The Catholic identified authority as the issue distinguishing Protestant from Catholic. Although granting that Strauss was not altogether incorrect to observe that an orthodox Protestant was closer to a Catholic than to a Protestant rationalist, the author of "Dr. Strauss" insisted that, in principle, both parties in Protestantism were blood-related. Both agreed on the primary authority and "the self-discretion of the individual." In this they differed sharply from the Catholic, who located primary authority in the Church.[12] Even Schütz, who sometimes praised the work of Schleiermacher and other Protestants, pointed out that Protestantism had embarked on a wrong direction with Luther. The latter, "instead of receiving the faith of Christ through the Church," had placed the principle of faith in his own subjectivity.[13]

With regard to the substance of the position they wanted upheld, these Catholic critics insisted upon the necessity of an historical basis for faith. They observed that Strauss minimized the importance of historical knowledge about Jesus, which was, in their opinion, tantamount to undermining Christianity's very foundation. One critic argued that Christianity must be based on God's historical revelation in Jesus because "people everywhere base their religious faith upon external revelation," and faith "rests ultimately upon an historical basis."[14] The other two authors in The Catholic identified Strauss's failure to give Jesus an essential place in his conception of Christian faith as evidence of his attempt to de-historicize it. Schütz, for example, explained Strauss's attack on the gospel sources as the consequence of his distaste for their constant reference to Jesus and their attempt to maintain an essential link between him and those who wished to be redeemed.[15] Schütz, by contrast, held that the redemptive quality of Christian faith presupposed the divinity of Jesus the Christ, which the sacraments claimed to mediate and which tradition affirmed by labelling the scriptural portrayal of Jesus true and accurate.

In the end, it is difficult to avoid drawing the conclusion that Strauss's critics in The Catholic wanted to use, either explicitly or implicitly, historical information about Jesus to establish his divinity and to validate their own faith. They could not conceive that Christian faith might still be possible and meaningful without the total historical veracity of the evangelical narrative. Thus, they could only condemn Strauss (and the Protestantism that produced him) for daring to challenge the authority of their traditional beliefs.

The Response of the Historical-political Newspaper

Like The Catholic, the Historical-political Newspaper for Catholic Germany supported the defeat of liberalism and a return to scholasticism within Catholicism.[16] Founded in 1838 at Munich by the jurist and convert George Phillips (1804-1872) and Guido Görres (1805-1852), the journal remained throughout the nineteenth century the leader among Catholic journals advocating a conservative political agenda.[17] In the 1830s and 1840s the journal published four articles critical of Strauss's theology. Three of the articles were anonymous; the fourth was authored by Johann Adam Möhler, but was published posthumously.[18] Except for Möhler's truncated response, the articles do not attempt an explicit rebuttal of Strauss's interpretation of the gospels. Instead, they seek to situate Strauss's book within the history of Protestant theology and to demonstrate that the direction taken by modern Protestant theology is ultimately destructive of Christian faith.

This point was made in a number of ways. The author of "Historical and Mythical Christ" declared:

> We can set out here in advance the general proposition that should be proven true in the following demonstration: 'All characteristically Protestant doctrinal statements are directed towards and have achieved their goal in the undermining of the historicity of the person Jesus Christ—as the gospels present him—and in handing over positive Christianity to myth.'[19]

And the author of "The Veteran Soldiers of Negation," although he claimed that his purpose was not the polemical refutation of Strauss, Feuerbach, or Bauer, sought to persuade the reader that the critical philosophy of these three men aimed at the destruction of all religion and that it had its origin in Protestantism.[20] The principal point the anonymous critics repeated was that Strauss was a true son of the Reformation.[21]

The _Historical-political_ _Newspaper_ claimed that the sixteenth-century Reformers began the defection from Christianity by defying the traditional authority of the Church and by replacing the objective givenness of tradition with subjective evaluations of the conformity of Church teaching with Scripture. Strauss's mythicization of the Jesus story was merely the inevitable outcome of the move towards subjectivism initiated by Luther.[22] Whereas Luther separated Scripture from Tradition, Strauss removed history from Scripture. One critic went so far as to say that, although Strauss did bad things to Christian faith, other Protestants did worse. Strauss thoroughly undermined the historical basis of Christianity by means of his destructive biblical criticism; still, he could appreciate Christianity as a great, albeit "incomplete, stage in spiritual development." By contrast, Ludwig Feuerbach held Christianity to be a "sick" worldview; Bruno Bauer, an "unnatural" worldview.[23]

In addition to identifying the lineage of his views, Strauss's critics in the _Historical-political_ _Newspaper_ specified what they thought to be the salient errors of Strauss's book. The errors were both formal (or methodological) and material. Among the formal problems, two were outstanding.

First, Strauss's work displayed antipathy, representative of radical Hegelianism, to the world of feeling and intuition. The journal saw Hegelianism as a philosophy of concepts, and it perceived in Strauss's work a Hegelian "tyranny of reason." Such an orientation was unacceptable to the journal because it established a fundamental bifurcation in the human person between reason and feeling; it mistakenly assumed that reason was the only source of knowledge and truth; and it failed to realize that faith was a response of the whole person—reason, will, and feeling.[24]

Second, Strauss's work exemplified a fault characteristic of all forms of Protestant theology, namely, the use of criticism free from the guidance of ecclesial authority. Such license inevitably ends up, so the argument went, in a false spiritualism or a false rationalism.[25] In Strauss's case, rationalism was the sin. His exegetical and dogmatic works were the products of subjective skepticism. Thus, the refrain of the _Historical-political_ _Newspaper_ was sounded again: Protestantism could not disown Strauss for having gone too far, since it had embraced subjectivism already in the sixteenth century.

> Protestantism has only the alternative: either to recog-
> nize an authority of the Church over academic freedom
> and to acknowledge as binding the faith of the Fathers
> and the creeds of the genuine church councils, or, since it
> gives free rein to subjectivity, to be quiet and to endure. .
> . . For its continued existence, the Christian Church has
> need of an authority. Also in this respect, the principle is
> justified: outside the Church there is no salvation![26]

Strauss's subjective skepticism was so severe, however, that his critical principles could make every history uncertain.[27]

Among the material flaws of Strauss's book, the journal singled out radical divine immanence as the chief problem, from which a number of other deficiencies derived. The Catholic critics suggested that the doctrine of radical immanence entailed pantheism, which, in turn, led ultimately to atheism.[28] This position, therefore, was seen to be objectionable not only for its distortion of the traditional understanding of God, but also for its ethical consequences. Once the hereafter was collapsed into the now and once personal immortality was denied, the blurring of the distinction between good and evil was inevitable.[29] Moreover, in such a "pantheistic" system there was no need for a perfect mediator between God and humanity. The idea of a single incarnation of God had to be denied. What Strauss proposed as an adequate reformulation of Christian faith was, in reality, the destruction of faith. One critic admitted that people who adopt Strauss's perspective might still regard themselves as Christian, but, he added, "it is illusion, not truth."[30]

The central problem in Strauss's christology was its unhistorical rendering of the gospels' Jesus story. But this trend toward de-historicizing Christian faith, one Catholic critic claimed, had its roots in spiritualizing interpretations of the sacraments. Strauss's "mythical Christ developed out of the docetic Christ in the Protestant doctrine of the Lord's Supper."[31] The connection between a spiritualizing interpretation of the Eucharist and an idealistic construal of Christian faith was by no means accidental. The author of "Historical and Mythical Christ" explained the connection this way: If a person did not believe that there was something "truly divine in the sacraments," then "no further, real intercourse with the incarnate son of

God" was possible; no living contact with God's son over time entailed that "even faith in the divinity of Christ himself disappeared."[32]

The Catholic Christ, by contrast, had a definite form, namely, the form that resulted from an uncritical, composite reading of the canonical gospels. This Christ was "historical," in contrast to the "mythical" Christ of the Protestants. By "Christ" Strauss's critics meant the person Jesus as depicted in the canonical gospels, who died for the reconciliation of God and humankind, and who was now really present in the sacramental life of the Church.[33] Just as there were several different conceptions of Christ in Protestantism (Petrine, Pauline, or Johannine), corresponding to the divisions within Protestantism, there was in Catholicism only one conception of the Christ, indicative of the unity of the Catholic Church in the possession of the essential Christian truths.

To defend taking the canonical gospels at face value, Strauss's critics asserted that the historical truth of the gospel stories was confirmed in and through the life of the Church. In short, the history of its effects established the truth of Christian faith. On the one hand, the fact that Jesus' followers were eventually successful in getting the Roman Empire to pay homage to Jesus testified to the strength of the impression Jesus' historical life had made upon them. On the other hand, willing martyrdom provided similar testimony to the reality of the Christ's remarkable deeds. As one respondent to Strauss argued, people would not have suffered and died willingly for their faith unless they were absolutely convinced, either through first-hand experience or through the reliable testimony of others, that Jesus was indeed the wonder-working Christ of God.[34]

The Church itself, however, was the final guarantor of the gospels' veracity. In the eyes of the anonymous Catholic authors, the Church was the product of Christ's miracles, and in its proclamation, action, and sacrament, the Church gave living embodiment to all the aspects of Christ's life. Contrary to the sola scriptura of the Protestants, living tradition was the ultimate authority in the Roman Church.

> The Catholic Church alone has handed on the sacred
> books as she received and collected them in time from
> the hands of their authors. The evidence concerning the
> canon of the Bible, its authenticity, integrity, authority,
> and inspiration--nothing but presuppositions upon which

> dogmatic use is based--rests purely and simply upon the
> living tradition alone, just as the canon itself forms an
> integrating component of the entire traditional content.
> Therefore, whoever, like Luther, simply rejected the au-
> thority of ecclesial tradition had renounced thereby all
> right to these books. For each and every tenable basis
> had been withdrawn at the outset from faith in the Bible,
> which now hung, so to speak, in the air freely and emp-
> tily.[35]

This critic in particular believed that the Hegelian-Straussian movement demonstrated more clearly than any other that "the rationalistic Christ" was the logical result of Protestantism's defective ecclesiology. Quoting Schelling, this critic averred: "Without the pope, the historical Christ would have been lost long ago."[36]

Many of the themes that surfaced in the anonymous critiques of Strauss had been sounded earlier by Johann Adam Möhler (1796-1838), one of the bright lights of the Catholic Tübingen School. In fact, whatever truly theological content the articles against Strauss in the Historical-political Newspaper possess probably derived from Möhler.[37] The impor- tance of positive religion over a timeless natural one, the possibility and significance of Jesus' miracles, and the connection between a mythological approach to Scripture and a faulty ecclesiology and sacramental theology are all alluded to in Möhler's brief essay, which appeared in the very first volume of the Historical-political Newspaper.[38] Despite its brevity, Möhler's article is significant for it sets forth quite concisely and forcefully an understanding of Christian faith that resonated at least with the editors of this journal, and probably with many other Catholics as well. The chief point upon which Möhler insisted was that the person Jesus belonged in- extricably to the content of faith and could not, therefore, be replaced by the abstract idea of the unity of humanity and divinity. Moreover, the Church, which proceeded from Jesus' historical ministry, had become the guarantor and preserver of that ministry.

> Jesus Christ our Lord, during his life on earth, did not
> merely teach our religion, such that his history and our
> religion are only externally connected. Rather, his history
> is our religion, his person is our faith and our love. The

mass of the faithful and the Church have proceeded living from this particular person, who is circumscribed by a series of facts and separated from everything else. Engendered from his history, the Church also certifies his history, as in word, so in its cult--whose essential components, which were already present in its beginning, have taken up the facts of his life and make them present eternally--and finally also in its history and, thereby, throughout its entire existence.--Now if the faith of the Church is one with the history of Jesus Christ, then it is indeed clear that the faith of the Church can never be exposed to a doubt as long as the history of its founder is not, even gradually, called into question. As the teaching of the Church is somehow suspected of being arbitrary, then the seed is therewith planted for transforming the historical Christ into a mythical one.[39]

According to Möhler, the Church's teaching about Jesus was not arbitrary, but rather the directed work of the Holy Spirit. And in the Church's structure and sacraments, the divine presence of its founder was objectively manifest.[40] The continued life of the Church and its faith, therefore, was irrevocably tied up with the divinity of the Christ and his continuing presence in the world.

Möhler's consistent maintenance of the objective reality of God's presence in Jesus included defending the objective reality of Jesus' miracles reported in the gospels. Defense of miracles was necessary since, in Möhler's opinion, the miracles demonstrated the special power and authority of Jesus, upon which certain other aspects of Christian faith depended. To dismiss Jesus' miracles, as Strauss did, was to bring to a culmination the reductionistic construal of Christian faith. Speaking of those who have consistently "reduced" faith, Möhler stated:

It is, therefore, comprehensible from this point of view when finally the opinion, that the miracles have been added externally to the story of Jesus, is defended. For a long time they showed a Jesus without Christ, a Christ without God's Son, a son of God without a church, a church without a cult, a cult without priesthood, a priesthood without a victim, a victim without representation, representation without love, love without faith, faith

> without works. No wonder if now even life itself is sup-
> posed to be without life. . . . Everything dissolved into
> nothing, and the entire, great historical reality of the
> Church proceeded from a dream and now disappears
> again into a dream![41]

Möhler went beyond the other critics of Strauss who published in the
Historical-political Newspaper by explicitly trying to refute Strauss's case.
Möhler's rebuttal comprised two major points. First, he countered
Strauss's mythological interpretation of the miracles with the assertion
that there existed "the clearest historical evidence" to support the reality
not only of Jesus' miracles, but also of the subsequent miracles by Jesus'
disciples; conversely, he alleged that the denial of the historical possibility
of miracles rested upon a dubious, "torpid logic and metaphysics."[42] Second, Möhler offered three, not entirely novel, arguments in refutation of
Strauss's explanation of how the myths about Jesus formed.

He argued, on the one hand, that extensive myth-production was inconceivable on account of the hostile environment in which Jesus and his
disciples lived and on account of the suspicious scrutiny to which their
deeds and words were subjected. These hostile circumstances did not dis-
suade Jesus' followers from acclaiming him as the wonder-worker and
from dying for him. All of this suggested to Möhler that the Jesus story of
the gospels was not mythical. On the other hand, Möhler pointed out that
there was not sufficient time between Jesus' death and the composition of
the gospels for elaborate myths about Jesus to be created.[43] It is Möhler's
third argument, however, which is most significant.

Möhler claimed that Strauss's view was untenable for it could not explain the success of Christian missionary activity outside of Palestine. As
Möhler saw it, the Gentiles came to believe in Jesus as the Christ either
without any help from the miraculous stories told about him or precisely
on account of the stories. Möhler argued that the first assumption was
untenable since it was self-evident that "Jesus separated from his miracles
could not ever have been an object of faith." If the first assumption were
true, only Jesus' doctrines, not he himself, would have been the object of
faith.[44]

Möhler's discounting of the possibility that Jesus' teaching could have
been sufficient to convert people to Christianity illuminates the contrast

between Strauss's and this characteristically Catholic way of construing the content and motive for faith. Strauss could dismiss Jesus' miracles without harm to his understanding of Christian faith because he placed faith not in the person of Jesus, but in the idea that Jesus symbolized (and perhaps embodied). Möhler's understanding of faith, by contrast, made historical knowledge about Jesus essential since the primary object of faith was a person, not a doctrine or idea. Faith was a matter of intellectual assent to the special status of Jesus, as defined by the Church, as well as a matter of experience of the Christ in the sacraments of the Church.

Although this construal of faith accorded well with orthodoxy, there were problems in it which Möhler's essay reveals. First, Möhler used history in this essay as a warrant validating his faith in Jesus as the Christ. Second, he mistakenly believed that the gospels yielded the historical evidence he needed to defend his faith stance. Strauss challenged both assumptions, and critical scholarship has followed Strauss's lead.

Other Responses: Hafen, Baader, and Sprissler

Johann Baptist Hafen (1807-1870) wrote several reports on Strauss's Life of Jesus for the General Church Newspaper for Germany and Switzerland.[45] Consonant with his priestly vocation and the practical demands of pastoral care, Hafen discussed Strauss's work in the Lucerne weekly not to counter Strauss's position with his own sophisticated interpretation, but to calm those people upset by Strauss's interpretation of the gospels.[46] Thus, Hafen's reports were primarily critical summaries of the various works written by others both against and in support of Strauss since 1835. The negative responses overwhelmingly predominated, and Hafen probably listed them all to convince the reader that Strauss's view was easily refuted.[47]

As far as his own interpretation of Strauss's work is concerned, Hafen admitted that Strauss's book had had some positive effects, among which were the challenge to strengthen one's faith by examining it critically and the encouragement to delve more deeply into Scripture. By and large, however, Hafen's evaluation was negative. His comments, interspersed between his summaries of other respondents, make clear that Hafen thought that Strauss replaced religion with philosophy, that he undervalued the role of Jesus in faith, and that he eliminated the essential content of Christian faith.[48] To that content belonged a personal, transcendent God and the divinity of God's Son Jesus, which Strauss's immanentist view jeopardized. In this regard, Strauss represented for Hafen that branch of Protestantism that led to atheism.[49] Like some of Strauss's other critics, Hafen thought the the effects of Christianity supported the historical truth of the gospel depiction of Jesus. To Strauss's rebuttal of this contention, Hafen replied:

> Above all Strauss has to provide the proof that he has not yet given, that lies—like the most beautiful facts of the gospel are, according to him--that lies could be capable of raising those bent down, strengthening the weak, comforting the unhappy, and leading sinners to repentance-- yes, that lies have a power within themselves which causes totally sensible people to sacrifice health, wealth, and life for the honor of God and the well-being of others.[50]

Like Möhler, Hafen could not imagine that one could truly be a Christian unless he/she were convinced that the divine authority of Jesus was truly such as described by the gospels. Strauss, on the other hand, appreciated the religious power of the gospel story as story. The contrast between his and Hafen's understanding of the motives of faith is sharp in the following exchange.

> Against one and another of these weighty rebuttals and also against Steudel's sentence, 'that a crucified Jew never could have transformed the pagan world,' Strauss summons up all his dialectical power and says namely: 'Jesus' extraordinary personality, his relation to the messianic idea, his speeches, his tragic end explain perfectly the riddle of the origin of Christianity. To believe that Jesus would not have been able to find a following with speeches alone and without miracles presupposes poor trust in the power of truth. Or was the Jewish people so crude and obtuse that one could affect them only with miracles?'[51]

Strauss then asked how one could explain the rejection of Jesus by the Jews if Jesus had done all the things reported of him by the gospels. To stave off Strauss's challenge, Hafen appealed to the traditional, worn arguments of orthodoxy. He observed that the people of the age expected a political messiah, and he suggested that many were misled by the Pharisees. Moreover, providence sent Jesus "precisely to this sinful race, which would kill him for the redemption of the world."[52]

In the end, Hafen did not really engage Strauss in a theological debate on the nature of faith, but simply offered an alternative view of faith (traditional orthodoxy), confident that the number of Christians opposed to Strauss's view signified that truth was on their side.

Franz von Baader's (1765–1841) commentary on Strauss's Life of Jesus took a different tack and form. Written in January of 1836, this response was part of Baader's open letter to Dr. von Malfatti of Vienna upon the occasion of an article published in the General Newspaper, which contended that there was nothing to object to Strauss's book from the academic side.[53] Baader, a leading member of the Munich Circle of Romantic Catholics, welcomed the opportunity to comment on Strauss's book because it gave him the chance to state his conclusions about the "radical errors" of which philosophy had been guilty for a long time.[54] One of the chief errors was a "false, dualistic view concerning the behavior of the ideal to the real." Baader thought that Strauss had severed the connection between the two, the consequence of which was that Strauss evacuated the "historical content" of Christian faith.[55]

This charge, as we have seen, was made by other critics of Strauss. Like some of them, Baader did not specify what the historical content was. Furthermore, he did not deal explicitly with Strauss's mythical reading of the gospels or make specific references to Strauss's text. Instead, he discussed in general terms what he thought were the pertinent philosophical issues involved in Strauss's work. And he did that at a high level of abstraction. Consequently, the judgment of fellow Catholic Hafen on the quality of Baader's reply is not wide of the mark:

> Certainly everyone who honors Mr. Baader as the father
> of theological speculation puts down these few pages with
> surprise and astonishment. For here there are only mys-

tical formulas, numbers and ciphers of spirit, soul, and nature; but nothing is refuted, explained, or said.[56]

Joseph Sprissler's review, which appeared in 1835–36 in the Candid Press Concerning Theology and Church, stands in remarkable contrast to Baader's and, in fact, to all the other reviews of Strauss's Life of Jesus published in Catholic journals.[57] Its remarkable quality consists primarily in Sprissler's partial acceptance of the legitimacy of a mythological approach to the New Testament. This acceptance, quite extraordinary for a nineteenth-century Catholic, was not out of character for Sprissler (1795–1879). He was suspended from his post as pastor in Empfingen in 1849 by the Freiburg Archdiocese on account of his political activity and unconventional church views.[58]

In contrast to the diatribes against Strauss and Protestantism in The Catholic and the Historical-political Newspaper, Sprissler's review exhibited a scholarly and objective approach to Strauss's work reminiscent of the responses of Kuhn and Mack.[59] Sprissler noted that The Life of Jesus Critically Examined was worthy of the attention of the general Christian public. In fact, he praised the book for inaugurating "a new period in the theological world."[60] Although he found some points to criticize in Strauss's book, Sprissler advanced his criticism in a measured way.

Sprissler's principal objection was directed against the philosophical underpinnings of Strauss's work. Like other respondents to Strauss, Sprissler thought that the mythological interpretation of Scripture was the necessary consequence of Strauss's adoption of a philosophical perspective derived from Schelling and Hegel. Sprissler, much clearer on this point than Baader, regarded Strauss merely as the "flank-man" for the philosophical direction that dominated the nineteenth century, namely, pantheism.[61] Sprissler called for the rejection of this trend because it conflated the two fundamental realities, God and nature, into one. A proper philosophical understanding, by contrast, distinguished "two realities, metaphysics and physics, God and nature; the former as the first, unconditional reality, the latter as secondary, conditioned reality."[62]

The detrimental consequence of this philosophy of identity was the denial of the possibility of supernatural revelation and the elimination of history as the record of the spiritual intercourse between God and human beings (as distinct entities). Sprissler, echoing the convictions of other nineteenth-century Catholics, averred that history was the form in which divine revelation occurred. Myth, he insisted, "cannot be the essence of history and cannot be the form of revelation." Therefore, he refused to follow Strauss in comprehensively applying a mythological interpretation to the gospels.[63]

One argument Sprissler used to challenge the tenability of Strauss's theory was the claim that the conditions necessary for producing comprehensive, detailed myths about Jesus did not exist. Although he admitted that it was possible for the early Christian community to make additions "to the real, historical course of events" and even to generate "many a legend," Sprissler, like Hug, found it inconceivable that a myth could be produced "without historical foundation" in an age that was as sophisticated as the first century and that had produced educated historians such as Josephus.[64] Even if the sophistication of the age was discounted as a fact contradictory to wide-scale myth-production, Sprissler still thought that the disparity between the spirit of the times and Jesus' preaching established the basic historical truth of the gospels' portrayal of Jesus. The spirit of the age in first-century Palestine was so "full of grave presentiments of woe, flight, and ruin" that "the myth should have proclaimed in the coming of the messiah not 'peace' to people on earth, but rather the 'sword.'"[65]

Another argument Sprissler advanced against Strauss's theory was based upon the tremendous spiritual and social effects of the early Christian movement. Sprissler asked how the foolish myth of the cross could conquer the world or how Christianity could have accomplished so much unless something other than the power of myth was its driving force. There were other great figures in human history, Sprissler noted, but no other had accomplished what the carpenter from Nazareth had.[66]

Despite these objections, Sprissler still acknowledged the service Strauss performed for contemporary theology. Strauss was to be commended for destroying the plausibility of rationalistic exegesis. In Sprissler's opinion, it was better to have a Jesus who did not perform all the miracles that the gospels reported of him than the Jesus of the rationalists, who pretended to be a miracle-worker.[67] Strauss was also to be commended for destroying the supernaturalistic interpretation of certain parts of the gospel, e.g., the story of Jesus' birth at Bethlehem. Similarly,

Sprissler approved of Strauss's critique of those who tried to harmonize the synoptic accounts of Jesus' miraculous deeds.[68] Sprissler, however, distinguished his position from Strauss's by insisting that the gospel story about Jesus was basically historical, to which legendary features were often added, whereas Strauss held the story to be essentially mythical.

> Not as if we deny every myth, but history precedes it and is its bearer, on and next to which the former is cultivated. Even Jesus of Nazareth has a history, and we ask where is it if we don't find it in the gospels?[69]

Sprissler maintained that the true approach to the gospels lay between the supernaturalism of traditionalist Catholics and the mythological theory of Strauss. Convinced that the mythical reading was appropriate to parts of the gospels, Sprissler optimistically--and naively--predicted that even the supernaturalists would come to acknowledge this within the next decade. Moreover, he claimed that Catholicism was better able than Protestantism to accept a mythical interpretation of Scripture.[70] Although subsequent history proved Sprissler's prediction wrong, his own openness to the mythological approach to Scripture is noteworthy.[71]

On the other hand, Sprissler was also convinced that Strauss had overextended his case. He, therefore, expressed the hope that Strauss would moderate his position. If he did, Sprissler thought that ecumenical accord on the Bible and its inspiration was possible between the Roman Catholic and Protestant churches.[72] In the end, Sprissler kept ranks with other Catholic critics of Strauss by refusing to give unequivocal approbation to The Life of Jesus Critically Examined, which undervalued historical knowledge about Jesus. Impressive and learned as it was, Strauss's position was worth less than the historical one it had wanted to replace.[73] Faith, as Sprissler understood it, required belief in the special authority and extraordinary nature of Jesus and not merely the adoption of a particular ("Christian") way of living in the world. For this reason, the historical accuracy of the gospels was a matter of theological concern for Sprissler. Although he could concede legendary accretions to the story about Jesus, he could not accept the comprehensive mythicization suggested by Strauss's Life of Jesus.

Concluding Remark

Most of the replies to Strauss from the Catholic journals contributed little to the theological debate of the specific issues Strauss's Life of Jesus raised. Instead, they situated Strauss within the history of Protestantism and attempted to demonstrate that Strauss was the genuine offspring of Luther. To the subjectivity of faith represented by Protestantism, the critics opposed the objectivity of faith in Catholicism; to Strauss's emphasis on idea, they opposed an emphasis on history. When these Catholic critics did attend explicitly to the actual content of Strauss's book, they tended to focus on its philosophical deficiencies, highlighting the problems entailed by the "pantheism" of Strauss's viewpoint. The critiques rarely went beyond criticism to theological construction. Nonetheless, the replies of Möhler and Sprissler were specially noteworthy; Möhler for enunciating most clearly the role of Jesus in a Catholic conception of faith, Sprissler for admitting the partial validity of a mythical reading of the gospels.

In the end, all of these Catholic critics were united in insisting that faith has an historical referent, namely, the person of Jesus now acclaimed as the Christ. They resisted Strauss's construal of faith for they correctly saw that it could easily lead to dismissing Jesus from any significant role in the origin or content of faith. But, in opposing Strauss, they did not present persuasive arguments sufficient to refute his basic point about the mythological character of the gospels or his contention that faith was not primarily a matter of historical affirmations. In opposing Strauss, they tended to misuse history and (alleged) historical knowledge about Jesus to validate and confirm their present faith. Thus, despite the inadequacy of Strauss's position, the alternative offered by these Catholic authors was no more acceptable.

NOTES

[1] Concerning the move of the journal from Mainz to Strasbourg and Speyer and then back to Mainz, see Hubert Jedin and John Dolan, eds., History of the Church, 10 vols. (New York: Crossroad, 1981), 8:54. For an informative sketch of the "Mainz Circle," see Franz Schnabel, Deutsche Geschichte im Neunzehnten Jahrhundert, 2d ed., 5 vols. (Freiburg: Herder, 1951), 4:74-92. See pp. 76 and 80 for specific information about Der Katholik.

[2] Jedin and Dolan, 8:240.

[3] The author asserted that Strauss used a bit of Hegelianism to complete the direction taken by Protestant rationalism. And this critic used Strauss's own admission of fidelity to contemporary Protestantism against him: "Strauss glaubt sich also selber in seinem guten Rechte, wenn er die evangelische Geschichte in einen Mythus, in eine Fabel umwandelte, und der Menschheit ihren Erlöser raubte; denn er sagte damit 'nicht Eigenes,' sondern 'er faßte nur zusammen,' was ihm durch die protestantische Theologie stückweise 'gegeben' war. Das also wäre das köstliche Besitzthum des Protestantismus, auf welches sie so hoffärtig sind, mit Luther sprechend: 'Das Wort sollen sie uns lassen stehen,' daß sie ein Buch besitzen, dessen historischer Theil, wo er Uebernatürliches, durch gottliche [sic] Kraft Gewirktes, berichtet, in das Gebiet 'der absichtslosen Dichtung' gehört." "Dr. Strauss und seine Stellung zur protestantischen Theologie," Der Katholik 79 (1841):47.

[4] Ibid., p. 49. A. von Schütz, "Die Stellung der protestantischen Theologie zu des Dr. Strauss Leben Jesu," Der Katholik 65 (1837):60-61: "Und der Protestantismus war von Anbeginn an eine Abweichung, so sehr Abweichung, daß es ihm weniger darum zu thun war, ein höchstes und letztes Ziel zu erreichen, welches sein Streben aufsuchte, als nur abzuweichen, nur die Opposition zu bilden und nöthigen Falls sie zu erhalten. ...Unter den vielen Merkmalen der Wahrheit und des Irrthums ist est vielleicht eins der sprechendsten, daß jene sich immer mehr in ihrem Centrum befestigt, und gerade in Folge der Opposition; während diese letztere, welche der Irrthum zu seinem Vehikel macht, sich dadurch charakterisirt, daß kein sich opponirender Irrthum auftreten kann, ohne die Opposition gegen sich selbst mit zur Welt zu bringen."

[5] "Reflexionen aus dem Standpunkte eines christlichen Weltbürgers über das Leben Jesu von Dr. D. F. Strauss," Der Katholik 63 (1837):279-83. See also Schütz, pp. 155, 164, and "Dr. Strauss," p. 45.

[6] "Reflexionen," p. 282; Schütz, pp. 72, 74-75, 164.

[7] Ibid., pp. 154-55.

[8] "Reflexionen," p. 294.

[9] Ibid., pp. 289-90, 292.

[10] Ibid., p. 296.

[11] "Befässen wir auch einen dem Dr. Strauss gleichen Scharfsinn, eine gleiche Divinationsgabe, eine gleiche gewandte Kunst der Auslegung, nein! uns würde es doch anwidern, die Sonde der Kritik an jeden Nerv, an jede Muskelfasser des biblischen Jesu zu halten, um zu prüfen, ob auch ihr die Pulse des Lebens entgegen schlügen." Ibid., p. 282. It should be noted that Schütz, by contrast, believed that Strauss could be refuted by making use of biblical criticism. He mentioned Richard Rothe, among the Protestants, and M. J. Mack, among the Catholics, as just two of the several scholars he thought capable of refuting Strauss with critical tools. See Schütz, pp. 158-59.

[12] "Dr. Strauss," p. 52.

[13] Schütz, p. 70.

[14] "Reflexionen," pp. 287, 295.

[15] "Es muß folglich der Widersacher, will er sein Extrem erreichen, im Protestantismus, und will er den Abfall von Christus hier bis zu dem Punkt vollziehen, wo dieser Protestantismus sein letztes von Religionseigenschaft verliert, nothwendig den Angriff auf die Quellen richten, aus denen allein hier die Wissenschaft von der Gottheit Christi und von seinem Erlösungsberuf sich will schöpfen lassen." Schütz, p. 73.

[16] See Jedin and Dolan, 8:105, 241.

[17] Schnabel, pp. 147-48. There is some confusion concerning the original founders of the journal. Although Roger Aubert credits Karl E. Jarcke and George Phillips (see Jedin and Dolan, 8:32, 54), von Schulte, H. Holland, and Franz Schnabel all cite Görres and Phillips as the men responsible for be-

ginning the journal. See <u>Allgemeine</u> <u>Deutsche</u> <u>Biographie</u>, 1st ed. (1879–88); reprint ed. (1968–71), s. v. "Phillips, George" and "Görres, Guido." At any rate, there is no dispute that the journal had a conservative Catholic orientation. Von Schulte observes, in his article on Phillips, that one's name upon the pages of the journal was "the identity card of purest Catholicity." The journal helped to make Munich a center of ultramontanism and of the fight against Prussia.

[18] The articles are: "Historischer und mythischer Christus," <u>Historisch-politische Blätter</u> 9 (1842):401–27, 529–41, 673–84; 10 (1842):175–89; "Ein Straußisches Curiosum," ibid. 11 (1843);491–92; and "Die Triarier der Negation," ibid. 14 (1844):673–703. Möhler's incomplete commentary on Strauss's <u>Life of Jesus</u> was published as "Erinnerung an Möhler," ibid. 1 (1838):131–40.

[19] "Historischer," p. 674.

[20] "Triarier," pp. 674, 689, 699. Cf. "Curiosum," p. 492.

[21] "Die 'Historisch-Politischen Blätter' . . . erinnerten an die romantische Geschichtsphilosophie, die zuerst gelehrt hatte, daß die Aufklärung und die politische und soziale Revolution nur die Folgen der mit der Reformation begonnenen Bewegung seien. Die Empörung--so führte man aus--begann mit dem Angriff auf die Kirche, dann richtete sie sich auch gegen die weltliche Obrigkeit, um schließlich gegen Familie und Eigentum vorzugehen. In der Glaubensspaltung sah man den Keim aller politischen Verirrungen ..." Schnabel, p. 147.

[22] "Seine [i.e., Strauss's] Theorie des Christenthums, wenn man es noch so nennen will, ist die natürlichste Blüthe jenes Keimes, den jener Reformator [i.e., Luther] seiner Kirche einerzeugte, und welcher in der Tradition zur Reife sich vollendet. ...Luther hat die kirchliche Autorität zernichtet, den lebendigen Christus aus seinem Werk hinweggedrängt, aus der sichtbaren Kirche weggestossen, und in die Dämmerung des individuellen 'Ich' zurückgebannt, die Offenbarung seiner Gottesherrlichkeit in seinem Reich--der Kirche, eingestellt. ...Irrthum ist es darum, zu meinen, Strauß habe den biblischen oder historischen Christus von seinem Sitz verdrängt; die Reformatoren haben in dem ihnen zugefallenen Theil der Menschheit ihn entthront, das Christenthum gestürzt." "Historischer," p. 410. See also pp. 184–87, 536, 538.

173

23 "Triarier," pp. 688 and 699. See also pp. 678-79, 683. For the author's description of Feuerbach's views, see pp. 684-85; concerning Bauer, whose Kritik der evangelischen Geschichte der Synoptiker the author considered to be the zenith of modern philosophical critiques of Christianity, see p. 686.

24 Ibid., pp. 694-95.

25 That is the alleged fate of all heresies: "Das Zweite, allen Häresien Gemeinsame, ist das Ueberwiegen der Subjectivität über das Objective, die gegebene Geschichte, und zwar entweder in der Form einer falschen Innerlichkeit, eines falschen Spiritualismus, der die äußere Welt in sich zu absorbiren sucht; oder eines falschen Rationalismus, der das Göttliche durch das Menschliche begränzt und verflacht." "Historischer," p. 532.

26 "Triarier," p. 692. See also pp. 691 and 700. Cf. "Historischer," pp. 534-35.

27 "Triarier," p. 698.

28 The journal primarily blamed Hegel for the tendency of modern philosophy towards pantheism and atheism. Strauss was culpable insofar as he had assumed the Hegelian superstructure into his theology. See ibid., pp. 678, 693-96. Cf. "Historischer," pp. 401-06. Immanence was probably singled out for special criticism because Strauss's Glaubenslehre, in which this doctrine was highlighted, had recently been published. See "Triarier," p. 680.

29 "Historischer," pp. 405-06; "Triarier," pp. 696-97.

30 "In a word, the principle of transcendence, upon which the old worldview rested, has been transformed into the principle of immanence. . . . The identity of the primitive Christian faith and modern religious knowledge and science is, according to the principle, abolished and torn to pieces. Expressed more elementarily, the defection from primitive Christianity has become, in the clear and well-conceived consciousness of these most educated Protestants, an undeniable fact, about which one is to be happy and not sad, since it constitutes not a retreat, but an advance of spirit. When the matter is viewed honestly in the light, Christianity has thus actually ceased to rule. Whoever--to speak with these 'evangelical theologians'--regards him/herself still a Christian may do so, but it is illusion, not truth." "Historischer," pp. 402-03. Although the critics in this journal found the

christological consequences of Strauss's perspective objectionable, they did
not censure them more strongly than the other limitations of Strauss's
book. In this regard, they differed from Mack and Kuhn. The difference
can be accounted for by the fact that the critics who responded to Strauss
through the journals in the 1840s included his Glaubenslehre in their critiques, and by the fact that the journal articles did not intend to provide
detailed refutations of Strauss's theology, but rather to summarize the
general problems inherent in it.

[31] "...the formlessness of the Protestant Christ of the Lord's Supper represents the formlessness of their biblical faith in general. And were someone
to be tempted to draw a conclusion backwards from the present confessional doctrine of the Lord's Supper of the Protestant theologians and
preachers to the person of Christ himself, then he/she would be able to de-
cipher scarcely anything more than the Christ of Strauss, which has been
shaped many ways and is, therefore, without form. The mythical Christ
developed out of the docetic Christ in the Protestant doctrine of the Lord's
Supper." Ibid., p. 182.

[32] Ibid., p. 178.

[33] Ibid., pp. 424-26.

[34] Ibid., pp. 415, 417, 531.

[35] Ibid., p. 539.

[36] Ibid., p. 189.

[37] See Franz Courth, "Evangelienkritik," pp. 79-80. Paul-Werner Scheele
offers a good introduction to Möhler's life and work in Johann Adam
Möhler, Wegbereiter heutiger Theologie (Graz: Styria, 1969), especially pp.
10-71. Cf. Scheele's essay on Möhler in Fries and Schwaiger, 2:70-98. In
view of Möhler's engagement with Protestantism, see also Joseph Fitzer,
Moehler and Baur in Controversy,1832-38: Romantic-Idealist Assessment
of the Reformation and Counter-Reformation, AAR Studies in Religion 7
(Tallahassee: American Academy of Religion, 1974).

[38] Concerning the importance of the historical, see Möhler, pp. 132-33; concerning Jesus' miracles, pp. 134, 139-40; concerning the relationship of the
mythological theory and ecclesiology, pp. 133-34, 139. This essay exhibits

the concern of the later Möhler for the objectivity of revelation over against his earlier mystical and "evolutionist" approach to theology.

[39] Ibid., p. 133.

[40] "So ist dann auch das Wunder ein immerwährendes, die Kirche und ihre Erhaltung ist Wunder, besonders ist der wesentliche Theil des Kultus (das Sacrament) Wunder. Wenn das Wunder jemals in der Kirche aufhören könnte, so ist niemals in ihr ein Wunder gewesen; weshalb es sich uns wieder nur als ganz folgerichtig darstellt, das wundervolle Leben des Herrn zu läugnen, wenn die Kirche als Menschenwerk, der heil. Geist als abwesend, und das Sacrament als ein inhaltleeres Zeichen betrachtet wird. Sätze wie diese: Die sichtbare Kirche ist ein kühner, poetischer Versuch, die unsichtbare Gemeinschaft der Geister darzustellen--das Sacrament ist ein leeres oder doch nur halb erfülltes Symbol--sind nur ein anderer Ausdruck für den Satz: Christus ist eine Mythe." Ibid., pp. 133-34.

[41] Ibid., p. 139.

[42] Ibid., pp. 134-35.

[43] Ibid., pp. 135-36, 139-40.

[44] Möhler continued: "Not only not as an object of faith, but also not even as an accredited warrantor of his doctrines could he have been proclaimed, with the result that no one would have believed him, let alone believe in him." Ibid., p. 137.

[45] Hafen filed three reports on Strauss's book. The first report was a brief notice concerning the publication and general content of Strauss's book; the second and third reports are more important since they contain Hafen's evaluative comments on the various responses to Strauss. These reports were published as: "Zweiter Bericht über 'das Leben Jesu,' kritisch bearbeitet von Dr. Strauss, oder ausführliche Anzeige der für und gegen das genannte Werk bisher erschienenen Schriften," Allgemeine Kirchen-Zeitung für Deutschland und die Schweiz (Lucerne), 6 January 1837, pp. 1-5; 13 January 1837, pp. 9-15; 20 January 1837, pp. 19-21; 4 February 1837, pp. 35-37; 18 February 1837, pp. 51-55. "Dritter Bericht über das Straußische Leben Jesu oder die Kritiker u. der Antikritiker," ibid., 22 July 1837, pp. 233-38; 29 July 1837, pp. 241-45; 12 August 1837, pp. 257-60.

[46]Concerning Hafen's life and work, see Allgemeine Deutsche Biographie, 1st ed. (1879); reprint ed. (1968), s.v. "Hafen, Joh. Baptist."

[47]Hence, after a lengthy survey of the works, Hafen concluded: "Wir haben an dem Bisherigen jetzt genug und glauben den Stand des Kampfes hinlänglich bezeichnet zu haben, auch glauben wir, es sei genügend dargethan, daß Str. von den gewaltigen, gegen ihn bisher vorgebrachten Gegenreden noch keine eigentlich widerlegt habe und auch keine widerlegen werde." (Emphasis mine.) "Dritter Bericht," p. 257.

[48]Hafen strung together a number of Strauss's statements in defense against his opponents; Hafen then added his own comments in parentheses. Thus: "[Strauss:] 'Habe ich denn in einer populären Schrift dem Volke seinen Glauben zu nehmen gesucht?' (Stürzen denn seine Grundsätze, die schnell verbreitet wurden den Glauben an Christum bei Unbefestigten nicht um?)--'Habe ich denn den Geistlichen den Rath ertheilt, statt Christum Schleiermacher oder Hegel zu predigen?' (Er weiß nach dem Schluß seines Werkes wenigstens keinen bessern Rath.)-- ...'Ist der, welcher in gefährlichen Zeitumständen mit Preisgebung des Unwesentlichen das Wesentliche zu retten sucht, als ein Feind eben dieser Sache zu bezeichnen?' (Ist der Glaube an einen persönlichen, freien, liebevollen, außerweltlichen Vater und an seinen Sohn Jesus Christus etwas Außerwesentliches? Und will uns Strauß diesen Glauben nicht entwinden? Giebt es ohne diesen noch ein Christenthum?)" Ibid., p. 242.

[49]The other branch of Protestantism, represented by the supernaturalists, converged with Catholicism. See ibid., p. 244.

[50]Ibid.

[51]Ibid., p. 245.

[52]Ibid.

[53]The brief response, "Ueber das Leben Jesu von Strauss auf Veranlassung einer in der Allgemeinen Zeitung (10. Jänner 1836) Anzeige dieser Schrift aus einem Sendschreiben an Hrn. Doctor von Malfatti in Wien" (Munich: Georg Franz, 1836), can be found in Franz von Baader's Sämmtliche Werke, Erste Hauptabtheilung (Leipzig: Hermann Bethmann, 1850-1860), 7:261-70.

54 Thus Baader, like many of the other Catholic critics, saw its philosophical presuppositions as the chief problem in Strauss's Life of Jesus. Baader identified Strauss as a student of Hegel. See Baader, pp. 261, 265-66. But it is not clear to what extent Baader held Hegelian philosophy totally responsible for Strauss's "errors." The editor of "Ueber das Leben Jesu" rightly regretted that Baader did not discuss more precisely the Strauss-Hegel relationship. See ibid., p. 265, note. Concerning Baader's life and work, see Hans Grassl, "Franz von Baader (1765-1841)" in Fries and Schwaiger, 1:274-302. See also Allgemeine Deutsche Biographie, 1st ed. (1875); reprint ed. (1967) s.v. "Baader, Franz Benedict von." Cf. Theodor Steinbüchel, "Romantisches Denken im Katholizismus mit besonderer Berücksichtigung der romantischen Philosophie Franz von Baaders," in: Theodor Steinbüchel, ed., Romantik: Ein Zyklus Tübingen Vorlesungen (Tübingen: R. Wunderlich, 1948).

55 Baader, pp. 261-62. "Aber dieselbe fasche [sic] idealistische Gnosis hat sich seitdem traditiv ...in mancherlei Gestalten bis auf unsere Zeiten fortgeerbt; wie ich denn z.B. Kunde von einer noch am Ende des vergangenen Jahrhunderts in Paris bestandenen geheimen pietistisch-mystischen Secte erhielt, welche sich es vorzüglich und mit wirksameren Mitteln als unsere Rationalisten angelgen sein ließ, allen Glauben an das Historische des Christenthums als nicht bloß überflüssig sondern auch als eine unmoralische Christolatrie (Idolatrie) begünstigend unter den Menschen zu tilgen.--Derselbe Zweck würde oder sollte nun durch die jüngst erschienene Schrift: Ueber das Leben Jesu, auf wissenschaftlichem Wege erreicht werden, ..." Ibid., p. 265.

56 Hafen, "Zweiter Bericht," p. 3. The Protestant Rosenkranz, moreover, had accused Baader of not even having read Strauss's Life of Jesus. See Baader, p. 261, note.

57 Sprissler's lengthy book review was published in two parts: Freimüthige Blätter über Theologie und Kirchenthum, Neue Folge 6 (1835):306-36; 8 (1836): 77-110. The review will hereafter be referred to simply as Sprissler.

58 An unabashed supporter of the rights of the people, Sprissler was elected to represent the principality of Sigmaringen at the 1848 National Convention in Frankfurt. See "Josef Sprissler, Pfarrer von Empfingen," Hohenzollerische Heimat 13, No. 2 (1963):23. There he not only accused the Catholic hierarchy of a mania for power, but also advocated adoption of the principle of religious freedom, stating: "Niemand darf zur Erfüllung re-

ligiöser Pflichten gezwungen, und niemand kann wegen Nichterfüllung oder Verletzung derselben mit weltlichen Strafen belegt werden." See Adolf Rösch, Das religiöse Leben in Hohenzollern unter dem Einfluße des Wessenbergianismus: 1800-1850 (Cologne: J. P. Bachem, 1908), pp. 32-33. On account of these views, his funeral oration in honor of the revolutionary Robert Blum, and his vocal opposition to celibacy, Sprissler was relieved of his priestly duties. For his oration concerning Blum and his speech to the people of Empfingen concerning his suspension, see Sprissler, Drei Beiträge zu den Vereinsblättern (Hechingen: Georg Egersdorff, 1849).

[59] Sprissler felt that Strauss's book deserved to be treated in a calm, scholarly fashion, free from personal invective, since Strauss had written his book in a calm, academic tone. See Sprissler, pp. 322-24.

[60] Ibid., p. 335. Sprissler's praise did not go unnoticed. In the Foreword to the second edition of his Life of Jesus, Strauss referred to Sprissler's review as one of the few that pleased him. Strauss, Leben Jesu (1837), 1:v. This appreciation notwithstanding, Strauss was also critical of Sprissler's and the other positive reviews for highlighting the areas of their disagreement with Strauss, while neglecting to undertake their own independent investigation of the whole gospel story.

[61] Sprissler, p. 324. Cf. Kuhn, Leben Jesu, pp. v-vii, 117-18; Mack, "Kritische Bearbeitung," Theologische Quartalschrift 19 (1837):46-64, 683-86; Hagel, Standpunkt, pp. 82-86. Bantle suggests a difference between Mack and Sprissler concerning the influence of philosophy on the development of Strauss's mythical reading of the gospels. Whereas Sprissler saw the mythological theory as the necessary consequence, Mack did not think that Hegelian philosophy necessarily required a mythical reading of the gospels. Franz Xaver Bantle, "Evangelienkritik und Glaube eines führenden Wessenbergianers--Pfarrer Joseph Sprissler und das 'Leben Jesu' des Dav. Fr. Strauß," Münchener Theologische Zeitschrift 28 (1977):372. Cf. Courth, "Evangelienkritik," pp. 90-91.

[62] Sprissler, pp. 324-25. Such a distinction was necessary for moral reasons as well: "Aber auch die Philosophie muß eine andere Richtung einschlagen, sie muß eine monotheistische vor Allem werden, einen persönlichen Gott und eine persönliche Fortdauer anerkennen; ihre pantheistische Richtung löst die Kraft der Sittlichkeit auf; ihr Gott als Macht und Denken begunstigt Despotie und schlaues Pfaffenthum, ohne es zu wollen. Ist das Wirkliche immer auch eben darum vernünftig, so ist das Unrecht heilig

und Widerspruch ein Verbrechen, und die Gesellschaft muß im Fatalismus des Orients zusammenfallen." Ibid., p. 109.

[63] In this regard, Sprissler's opposition to Strauss was the same as that of other Catholic critics. Courth rightly corrects Bantle's claims about Sprissler on this point. See Bantle, p. 373. Cf. Courth, "Evangelienkritik," p. 88.

[64] Sprissler, p. 326. And if there was as much myth in the gospels as Strauss alleged, Sprissler wondered why or how one could ever draw the line: "Sind die Evangelien eine Mythe, so ist die ganze Bibel nichts anderes, und warum nicht auch gleich Jesus selbst, da sein Name recht absichtlich darauf hinzudeuten scheint, oder sollten wir bei unserem exegetisch ökonomischen Aufräumen nicht begreifen, daß eine wirkliche Person ein wahrer Luxus in einer Mythe sey?" Ibid., p. 328.

[65] Ibid., pp. 326-27.

[66] Ibid., p. 329. Cf. the similar argument in "Historischer und mythischer Christus," pp. 415-17.

[67] Sprissler, pp. 322, 335.

[68] Ibid., pp. 84-85, 91-93. Sprissler, however, did not think that Strauss was justified in interpreting all of Jesus' miracles mythically. See ibid., p. 326. Concerning Sprissler's concept of miracle and its relation to Schleiermacher's, see Bantle, pp. 380-81, especially notes 67 and 68.

[69] Sprissler, p. 325. See also p. 307.

[70] The reason was that Protestant dogma rested solely upon the inspiration of Scripture, whereas Catholic dogma rested upon the authority of tradition, which interpreted and mediated the Word of God in Scripture. Sprissler, pp. 320-21. The editor of the Candid Press disagreed with Sprissler at this point. See his note, ibid. J. B. Hafen also censured Sprissler. See Hafen's "Zweiter Bericht," pp. 3-4.

[71] His admission that legend and myth are mixed into the gospel stories places him in the company of Kuhn. Both men took steps in biblical interpretation that official Catholicism resisted for some time. Bantle, however, overstates his case for Sprissler on p. 379. Cf. Courth, "Evangelienkritik," pp. 90-91.

[72] Sprissler, pp. 335-36.

[73] "Es handelt sich hier gar nicht u m eine oder die andere Thatsache, richtige oder falsche Auffassung derselben, sondern u m den ganzen Standpunkt. Herr Strauß hat unstreitig den bisherigen evangelischen und christkirchlichen erschüttert: aber sein eigener ist doch in der That weniger werth, als der erschütterte, von welcher Seite wir ihn betrachten." Ibid., pp. 108-09.

CONCLUSION

The preceding chapters have shown Strauss's Catholic respondents resist-
ing his attempt to remove Jesus from the core of Christian faith and correlatively insisting that historical knowledge about Jesus was both obtainable
and theologically important. These chapters also have shown that, although the focus of these responses--like the bulk of Strauss's project it-
self--was the articulating of the proper hermeneutical theory and exegetical practice to be applied to the gospel presentation of Jesus' life, the ultimate point of contention was theological. In short, Strauss and his Catholic
critics differed sharply over the appropriate construal of Christian faith
and the place therein of christological assertions about Jesus.

Chapter 1 argued that Strauss used the tools of historical criticism and
Hegelian philosophy for an explicitly theological end. This end required
the undermining of the traditional, historical reading of the gospels so that
the meaning of christology could be reformulated more appropriately for
the modern world. The subsequent chapters demonstrated that the common thread in the Catholic critiques of Strauss was their objection to
Strauss's attempt to transform "historical Christianity" into "idealized
Christianity." Although the Catholics did not always articulate fully the
theological reasons they had for finding Strauss's attempt unacceptable,
chapters 2 to 5 suggested that the primary reason was the failure of
Strauss's reformulation of the content of Christian faith to be appropriate
to the Church's tradition of personal faith in Jesus as the Christ.

The purpose of this concluding section is twofold: to summarize the
noteworthy historical-critical and theological points of the respective cases
made by Strauss and his Catholic critics, and to pinpoint the interest that
debate has for contemporary theology. We begin with the summary evaluation.

Contemporary biblical scholarship has validated the relative superiority of Strauss's understanding and application of historical criticism to the
gospels. Strauss not only demanded, as did Kuhn, that the gospels be examined according to the same method and with the same tools used with
regard to other historical documents, but also insisted, unlike Kuhn, that
the starting point of true criticism could not be the assumption of the
apostolic authenticity or historical credibility of the gospels. Similarly,

contemporary historical scholarship has approved Strauss's refusal to use the miraculous as a category of historical explanation.

In general, contemporary biblical scholarship has also found Strauss's material conclusions about the gospels to be more adequate than that of his Catholic respondents. Strauss cast doubt upon the apostolic origin of the gospels and the use of John's gospel as an historical source. Moreover, he perceived the influence of the Old Testament and of messianic expectations upon the evangelical portrait of Jesus. And although Strauss's Catholic critics detected some weaknesses in his interpretation of the gospels, their criticisms were ultimately ineffective in dismissing the major point of Strauss's exegesis, namely, that there was much more myth in the gospels than his Catholic critics could admit.

Theologically, Strauss argued that Christian faith does not merely comprise christological assertions about the actual or historical Jesus.[1] The truth of Christian faith for Strauss was not entirely dependent upon historical inquiry. Strauss recognized that the religious meaning of christological assertions was not limited solely to what the actual or historical Jesus understood himself to be or what the evangelists intended to say about him, but rather included the way of perceiving reality and of living in the world that is disclosed by those christological assertions.[2] The reality disclosed by the gospel's christological assertions about Jesus was, for Strauss, the fundamental unity of God and the human race. The meaning of Christian faith, therefore, was not belief in an exalted savior figure of the past, but the raising of one's consciousness to recognize one's own divine potential as a bearer of truth and meaning and as an agent of historical change. In other words, Strauss was suggesting that faith is the acceptance of a certain vision of the world (and of the interrelationship of God, self, and world); its "salvific" effect (Strauss would prefer to say "liberating" quality) is established as "eternally true" by a philosophical analysis of present experience, not by historical knowledge.

Strauss's Catholic critics perceived the radical nature of Strauss's reformulation of Christian faith. They noted that it so emphasized the idea represented by the biblical Christ that it became largely irrelevant whether the actual Jesus had said or done what the gospels reported. The Catholics agreed with Strauss that historical analysis alone could establish the tenability of the claim that the actual Jesus had done miraculous deeds and that, therefore, God was active in him, but they disagreed sharply with him concerning the amount of historical evidence available to support that claim. More importantly, the two sides did not agree on the extent to which the actual Jesus or the historical Jesus constituted a referent of faith.

The validity of the Catholic critique of Strauss depends upon the accuracy of two fundamental judgments: that Strauss's relocation of the christological focus from Jesus to the human species constituted a proposal for a Christianity without Jesus, and that the apostolic testimony of the gospels made christological assertions about the empirical-historical Jesus.[3]

Although the later editions of Strauss's Life of Jesus offered conflicting data, the first edition did contain evidence supportive of the Catholics' judgment that Strauss's position eventually culminated in a Christianity without Jesus.[4] The Catholic critics rejected this proposal for failing to demonstrate persuasively its appropriateness to the tradition's confession of faith in Jesus of Nazareth (and not merely faith in the idea he represented or in his message).

The second issue, whether the earliest witnesses made christological assertions about the empirical-historical Jesus, was and remains difficult to determine. Strauss's Catholic critics thought that such assertions had been made. Even Kuhn, who clearly recognized the confessional context of the gospel narratives, insisted that the gospels contained historical reminiscences of the actual Jesus. The extent to which that is the case and the extent to which the apostolic witnesses made christological assertions about the empirical-historical Jesus continues to be contested today.

At any rate, Strauss's Catholic critics declared that Christian faith was not a general philosophy of religion, but an articulation of the meaning of the person, deeds, and words of the actual Jesus as remembered, interpreted, and reported by the authors of the New Testament. By positing the actual Jesus merely as the occasion by means of which the Christian community made explicit the understanding of existence it already unconsciously possessed, Strauss seemed to his Catholic critics to have undervalued the connection between this particular understanding of reality and the person who was held to have authorized it.[5] This is what the Catholic critics meant when they referred to the destructive consequence of Strauss's book as the "idealization" of Christianity.[6]

Insofar as Strauss's Catholic respondents were convinced that the empirical-historical Jesus was a referent of faith's christological assertions, their concern for finding authentic historical material in the gospels is intelligible. But the dangers inherent in such a concern become immediately apparent. Knowing that retrieval of the empirical-historical Jesus was necessary for their theological program, the Catholics could not execute the task of a critical analysis of Scripture with due rigor. Moreover, their fervor to maintain the view that faith entails christological assertions about the empirical-historical Jesus misled them into undervaluing the existential aspect of faith and into using historical knowledge about Jesus, often in a veiled or indirect way, to validate the truth of the existential referent (i.e., the Christian understanding of reality). Hug, Mack, Hagel, and Kuhn, therefore, were vulnerable primarily in their historical judgment (that the gospel portrait of Jesus is more reliable historically than it actually was) and secondarily in their theological judgment (not giving the existential referent of christological assertions sufficient weight).[7]

The common strength of the Catholic replies to Strauss was the recognition that, if they were to be faithful to the gospel and to the Christian tradition, "Jesus" could not be removed from the core of Christian faith. The value of this contribution, however, was formal rather than material in nature. That is, the Catholics properly identified "Jesus" as belonging to the core of Christian faith, but they did not adequately specify the material identity of that Jesus. Thus, they inappropriately suggested that the retrieval of the empirical-historical Jesus was absolutely necessary for Christian faith, whereas their concern for specifying their understanding of reality as Christian only required them to maintain a necessary place for the existential-historical Jesus.[8] It was "Jesus in his meaning for us" whom the Catholics wanted to preserve, but it does not follow that his significance for us can be firmly established only to the extent that we can confidently confirm that the actual Jesus is substantially and accurately portrayed in the gospels.[9]

In light of the advances made in biblical scholarship and in theological reflection with the past 150 years, what interest can the Strauss-Catholic debate have for theology today? I submit that that nineteenth-century debate illustrates paradigmatically that different construals of faith result in significantly different functions and varying importance being assigned to historical knowledge about Jesus. More importantly, I submit that the validity of the reciprocal criticism of Strauss and his nineteenth-century Catholic opponents suggests the need for a reading of the gospels and a construal of faith that goes beyond those two alternatives. That need is evident in the recent christological discussion between Hans Küng and Edward Schillebeeckx, on the one hand, and Schubert Ogden and Van Harvey, on the other.

Like their nineteenth-century predecessors, Küng and Schillebeeckx assert that "the person of Jesus" belongs to the core of Christian faith, and they resist any attempt to transform "historical Christianity" into "idealized Christianity."[10] Although they are not always precise about the material identity of the Jesus whom they declare to be essential to faith,[11] they seem ultimately to mean that the empirical-historical Jesus is the norm and criterion of what believers may responsibly say about Jesus.[12] By arguing that "Jesus" occupies the central core of Christian faith and by assigning theological importance to historical knowledge about Jesus, Küng and Schillebeeckx maintain considerable continuity with Strauss's Catholic critics of the nineteenth century.

Just as Hug and Mack in the nineteenth century thought that the traditional christology of orthodoxy was correct since it was based on the solid historical evidence of the gospels, Küng and Schillebeeckx today continue to base the legitimacy of their christologies upon the historical evidence of the gospels, even though they recognize that the historical base is much narrower than their predecessors had imagined. Despite the steady paring down of that base, Küng and Schillebeeckx are confident that "the typical basic features and outlines of Jesus' proclamation, behavior and fate" can be historically reconstructed.[13] Thus, they reflect the confidence of their predecessor Kuhn, who thought that even if historical criticism significantly reduced the amount of historical material in the gospels, the Church's tradition still was sufficiently trustworthy to account for the remainder of a minimal historical core. Küng and Schillebeeckx distinguish themselves, however, from their Catholic predecessors by recognizing that the historical material about Jesus recoverable from the gospels cannot establish the broad claims of orthodox christology.

This fact notwithstanding, Küng and Schillebeeckx appear to be vulnerable to the same charge that was directed at Strauss's nineteenth-century Catholic critics, namely, that they exaggerate the importance of the historical quest of Jesus. Whether the charge is valid depends, as we have seen, upon one's understanding of faith. Insofar as faith is construed as entailing a christological assertion about the empirical-historical Jesus, there is theoretical legitimacy to Küng's claim that historical knowledge about the actual Jesus is relevant to faith.[14] But historical retrieval cannot establish as historical fact that the empirical-historical Jesus was the Christ or that the christological interpretation of the existential-historical Jesus is not "a projection of faith."[15] Thus, the significance of the historical quest is considerably less than the claims for its necessity might lead one to believe.

Van Harvey and Schubert Ogden challenge this contemporary Catholic proposal at two of the points where Strauss had challenged his Catholic critics in the nineteenth century. First, they ask whether the quantity and quality of information obtainable about the empirical-historical Jesus is sufficient to make it theologically important. Second, they suggest that historical knowledge about Jesus is not necessary for the christological assertions of faith. As in the nineteenth century, the divergence in perspective with regard to these questions reflects disparate conceptions of faith. The ultimate question Harvey and Ogden raise for Küng and Schillebeeckx is whether faith must be construed as entailing christological assertions about the empirical-historical Jesus.

Harvey articulates the theological issue at stake by distinguishing two kinds of belief: "the belief that the actual Jesus was as the perspectival image pictures him, and the belief that the perspectival image does illumine our experience and our relationship to that upon which we are absolutely dependent."[16] The former is a belief about a contingent fact whereas the latter is a belief about the adequacy of an image for interpreting the structure and character of reality itself. Like Strauss, Harvey emphasizes the value of the latter belief. Although Harvey asserts, especially in his earlier work, that the existential judgment involved in Christian faith is related, indeed is "indissolubly and powerfully wedded," to the person in the historical past who mediated this understanding of human existence (i.e., Jesus of Nazareth), he ultimately lets the decisive weight in Christian faith fall to the existential evaluation.[17] For him, no historical event can be the basis for religious confidence about the present. In his later work, Harvey emphasizes this point more strongly and clearly.[18]

Ogden concurs in this judgment that historical knowledge about Jesus is insignificant for faith. Like Harvey, he thus challenges the adequacy of both the historical and the theological judgments inherent in the cases of Küng and Schillebeeckx. Whereas Küng and Schillebeeckx follow their Catholic predecessors in believing that the quest of the historical Jesus is possible, convinced that the road in the gospels runs from history to myth and not from myth to history,[19] Ogden avers that form criticism has rendered the quest impossible.[20] More importantly, he argues that even if the quest were historically possible, it would still be theologically unnecessary.[21] This is so, he suggests, because the existential-historical, not the empirical-historical, Jesus is the real object of faith's christological assertions. And to affirm the existential-historical Jesus as the object of faith does not require that we know more about the actual Jesus than that he lived and was believed by the earliest witnesses to him to be of decisive significance for humanity.[22]

Schillebeeckx, by contrast, demands that we pare away at the existential-historical Jesus presented in the gospels until we arrive at the empirical-historical Jesus, who can then serve as the theological norm of appropriateness for the claims of faith. Like Ogden, Schillebeeckx justifies his demand with an appeal to the earliest strata of witness contained in the gospels. But unlike Ogden, he perceives in the earliest strata various credal trends, all of which enshrine an historical interest in the person of Jesus. This perceived interest in and reference to the empirical-historical Jesus authorizes the theologian, according to Schillebeeckx, to make normative use of historical knowledge about Jesus.[23]

Without denying the possibility of retrieving the empirical-historical Jesus, Tracy objects to Schillebeeckx's argument. Like Ogden, he holds that the apostolic profession of faith, rather than the empirical-historical Jesus, is the true norm and standard for christology. According to Tracy, the theologian need not go behind the scriptural witness itself in search of the primary norm of faith. To want to do so is to confuse the theologian's question of appropriateness with the historian's question of intelligibility.[24]

As this reference to the christological proposals of a few contemporary theologians indicates, the discussion initiated by Strauss and his Catholic critics continues today. Strauss continues to serve theology today by challenging it to refute his claim that faith is of such a nature that the supernatural birth, miracles, and resurrection of the Christ remain "eternal truths regardless of how much their reality as historical facts may be doubted."[25] Moreover, he warns of the ways critical biblical scholarship is impeded by the theological presuppositions of Christian orthodoxy, and he demands that we soberly face the question whether the only kind of faith possible today is the faith of Barabbas, who affirms the Christian community's basic understanding of life but declines to comment on the empirical-historical Jesus.[26]

The critique of Strauss by his nineteenth-century Catholic opponents, on the other hand, can, despite its weaknesses, continue to serve theology today by asking whether faith can be described as Christian if it fails to have "Jesus" as its core. Negatively, it illustrates that we cannot use dogmatic presuppositions to decide historical-critical questions. Positively, it insists that, although we cannot speak about God's own intentions concerning the actual Jesus or about the actual Jesus' self-understanding,[27] "the Christ-principle without Jesus is always in danger of captivity to a personal or cultural mood."[28]

In short, the Strauss-Catholic debate of the nineteenth century serves theology today by forcing us to consider a third alternative to its opposing positions. In this third alternative, "Jesus" is held to belong to the core of Christian faith. He is identified, however, neither as the _idea_ represented by the actual person of Jesus nor as the _empirical_-historical Jesus recovered by historians, but rather as the _existential_-historical Jesus. By demonstrating the need for a more adequate and appropriate conception of faith, the nineteenth-century debate is worthy of our attention today.

NOTES

[1] The terminology is derived from Van Harvey who distinguishes between 1) the actual Jesus, 2) the historical Jesus, 3) the perspectival image of Jesus, and 4) the biblical Christ. See his _Historian_, pp. 265-68. I use these terms, where they occur in the text, in the sense defined by Harvey.

[2] As we saw in Chapter 1, Strauss understood the evangelical portrayal of Jesus as the Christ to be the result of unconscious, unintentional myth-formation by the Christian community. That suggested for Strauss that the meaning of that portrayal was not to be found in grasping the intent of the authors of that portrayal, but rather in perceiving the idea that the Jesus of the gospels represented. That idea was the unity of divinity and the human race. To the extent that he saw the meaning of the gospel text as distinct from both the historical reconstruction of the text and the sense of the text, Strauss was advocating a kind of revisionist understanding of the hermeneutical task. Concerning the revisionist model, see David Tracy, _Blessed Rage for Order: The New Pluralism in Theology_ (New York: Seabury Press, A Crossroad Book, 1975), pp. 49-52, 73-79. Cf. Ogden, pp. 27-29. Ogden argues that the christological assertion about Jesus also intends to answer the fundamental questions, Who is God? and Who am I?

[3] Ogden's distinction between the empirical-historical Jesus and the existential-historical Jesus is helpful at this point in that it allows the historical person Jesus to be a reference point for faith without claiming that specific historical knowledge about this person is necessary for christological assertions. By empirical-historical Jesus, Ogden means "Jesus in his being in himself;" by existential-historical Jesus, "Jesus in his meaning for us." See his _Point_, pp. 55-62.

[4] Despite the historical sketch of Jesus' life that he provided in his book, Strauss seemed to hold that historical knowledge about Jesus was irrelevant to faith. This is most clear in the first edition and least clear in the third edition of _The Life of Jesus Critically Examined_. In the first edition, Strauss stated that Jesus was merely the occasion for raising the idea of the _Gottmenschlichkeit_ of the human species into general consciousness. A modern reformulation of faith declared that this "reference to an individual belongs only to the temporal and popular form of this doctrine." _Leben Jesu_ (1835), 2:735-36. Strauss asserted that Christianity had to choose between "the holy history in its biblical form" and "the concept which is true in and for itself." Strauss's choice was clear: "What is essential in Christianity, for the philosophical point of view, are the idea

and its eternal realization in humanity." <u>Streitschriften</u>, 3:65. This view, however, contrasts sharply with Strauss's later portrayal of Jesus as a religious genius and his assertion that religion was unthinkable without Jesus. Cf. <u>Zwei Friedliche Blätter</u>, pp. 116-17, 132. In the fourth edition of his book, Strauss returned to the original conclusions of the first two editions. See above, pp. 25-26.

[5] See Strauss, <u>Leben Jesu</u> (1835), 2:736: "Wie der Gott des Plato auf die Ideen hinschauend die Welt bildete: so hat der Gemeinde, indem sie, veranlaßt durch die Person und Schicksale Jesu, das Bild ihres Christus entwarf, unbewußt die Idee der Menschheit in ihrem Verhältniss zu Gottheit vorgeschwebt."

[6] Kuhn stated the common Catholic conviction in opposition to Strauss most forcefully when he said: "It is a thoroughly futile attempt to dissolve historical Christianity into an ideal one and to want to cover the loss of the former with the magnificent appearance of the latter. The former exists no more as soon as it ceases to be historical; and that which is substituted for it is something completely different, which bears the name of Christianity with grave injustice." "Hermeneutik," p. 35. And Möhler specified the place of Jesus in the core of faith for his fellow Catholics most clearly when he asserted: "Jesus Christ our Lord, during his life on earth did not merely teach our religion, such that his history and our religion are only externally connected. Rather, his history is our religion, his person is our faith and our love . . ." "Erinnerung an Möhler," <u>Historisch-politische Blätter</u> 1,1 (1838):133.

[7] Kuhn, for example, was mistaken when he suggested that Christian faith disappears if it no longer possesses clear historical evidence that God was active in the empirical-historical Jesus. What is rendered uncertain or disappears in that case is one part of the traditional core of Christian faith, namely, the belief that the actual Jesus of Nazareth manifested clear evidence of God's presence within him. But the meaning this Jesus had for early Christians is nonetheless preserved in the gospel, and the truth of the understanding of God and of neighbor disclosed by the gospel story about Jesus can be established by a transcendental analysis of the religious dimension of common human experience. See Tracy, <u>Blessed Rage</u>, pp. 52-56. Conversely, Hug is mistaken to think that considerable historical information about the actual Jesus was available or that it could be used to validate the truth of the Christian understanding of self with regard to the neighbor in the world.

[8] Historical information about the actual Jesus would thus be historically interesting and theologically important in a restricted sense (i.e., insofar as it helped to inform responsible Jesus images adopted by the Church). Norman Perrin makes this point well when he refers to the tradition's juxtaposition of the two names "Jesus" and "Christ" as the warrant, in shorthand form, for the theological legitimacy of the historical question. See Erich Grässer, "Norman Perrin's Contribution to the Question of the Historical Jesus," Journal of Religion 64 (1984):493.

[9] The Catholics overemphasized the value of historical confirmation because they held to a correspondence theory of truth, which required them to demonstrate a correspondence between belief statements and historical facts. A coherence theory of truth, by contrast, would only require them to show a correlation between belief statements and present human experience. For a discussion of the two alternative theories, see Francis Schüssler Fiorenza, Foundational Theology (New York: Crossroad, 1984), pp. 270-84.

[10] Küng argues that Christianity "cannot in the last resort be reduced to any kind of eternal ideas, abstract principles, human attitudes. The whole of Christianity is left hanging in mid-air if it is detached from the foundation on which it is built: this Christ. An abstract Christianity is of no importance to its followers or to the world." Hans Küng, On Being a Christian, trans. Edward Quinn (Garden City: Doubleday and Co., 1976), p. 124. See also pp. 145-46: "The Christ of Christianity--this cannot be sufficiently stressed against all old or new syncretism--is not simply a timeless idea, an eternally valid principle, a profoundly significant myth. ...The Christ of the Christians is no other than Jesus of Nazareth. And in this sense Christianity is essentially based on history, Christian faith is essentially historical faith." Schillebeeckx concurs, exhibiting a passion about this point that is reminiscent of Kuhn: "For me, therefore, a Christianity or kerygma minus the historical Jesus of Nazareth is ultimately vacuous--not Christianity at all, in fact. If the very heart of the Christian faith consists of an affirmation, in faith, of God's saving action in history--and that decisively in the life-history of Jesus of Nazareth--for the liberation of human beings ... then the personal history of this Jesus cannot be lost sight of, nor our speaking of it in the language of faith degenerate into ideology." Edward Schillebeeckx, Jesus: An Experiment in Theology, trans. Hubert Hoskins (New York: Seabury Press, A Crossroad Book, 1979), p. 76.

[11] Küng and Schillebeeckx speak at times of "the living Jesus of history" or "the very person of Jesus" as the source and criterion of Christian faith. This "living Jesus," however, is not necessarily identical with the empirical-

historical Jesus, whom they seem to mean when they insist upon the indispensability of the historical-critical method for Christianity. See Küng, "Toward a New Consensus in Catholic (and Ecumenical) Theology," in Consensus in Theology?, ed. Leonard Swidler (Philadelphia: Westminster Press, 1980), p. 6: "The source, standard and criterion of Christian faith is the living Jesus of history. Through historical-critical research into the life of Jesus the Christian faith is historically responsible in the light of the contemporary consciousness of problems and is protected from faulty interpretations arising from within or outside the Church." See Schillebeeckx, Interim Report on the Books "Jesus" and "Christ" (New York: Crossroad, 1981), p. 33: "It is not the historical picture of Jesus but the living Jesus of history who stands at the beginning and is the source, norm and criterion of the interpretative experience which the first Christians had of him." See Jesus, p. 65, where Schillebeeckx speaks of "the real Jesus of Nazareth" as the "corrective and directive" criterion of Jesus-images in the Church. See pp. 73, 76-77, 440. These statements need to be compared with Schillebeeckx's insistence that the question "whether or not to absorb the historico-critical method" is a matter "of life or death for Christianity." Ibid., p. 70.

[12] See ibid., p. 73: "When Jesus of Nazareth ... is the norm and criterion of what believers in Jesus say about him within their own cultural and religious milieu, ...then a view of Jesus based on the approach through historical criticism is of essentially theological importance." Cf. Kasper's critique of Küng's and Schillebeeckx's position as illegitimate attempts to make a pre-dogmatic or undogmatic Jesus the criterion of orthodoxy. Walter Kasper, "Christologie von unten? Kritik und Neuansatz gegenwärtiger Christologie," pp. 162-63, and "Für eine Christologie in geschichtlicher Perspektive," p. 180, both of which are in Grundfragen der Christologie Heute, ed. Leo Scheffczyk (Freiburg: Herder, 1975). Also see his acerbic review of Schillebeeckx's Jesus: "Liberale Christologie," Evangelische Kommentare 6 (1976):357-60.

[13] See Küng, On Being Christian, p. 159. His following statement, p. 157, demonstrates both the similarity of outlook with the nineteenth-century Catholics (the first sentence) and the extent of the dissimilarity because of the advance in biblical scholarship (the second sentence): "If we examine the state of the New Testament sources without prejudice, we shall describe the Jesus tradition historically as relatively reliable. This means when we come to interpret it that the transformations, developments and contrarieties of the New Testament tradition exclude the smooth assumption that Jesus himself or the Holy Spirit made provision for an exact re-

tention and transmission of his words and deeds." Although Schillebeeckx concedes that an historical reconstruction can only yield "a Jesus image, never the real Jesus of Nazareth," he insists that "the Jesus whom the gospels present resembles—not of course in every detail but substantially--the historically 'real thing,' in spite of all the Church's updating activities." Jesus, pp. 34, 71-72. See also Interim Report, pp. 27-28.

[14] "Despite all difficulties then we can uphold the historical possibility and the theological legitimacy of a recourse to the Jesus of history." After stating why that recourse is possible, Küng says: "Why is it also justified? Because the primitive Christian proclamation of Christ could have emerged and can be understood only in the light of the history of Jesus. Why is it even necessary? Because it is only in this way that the primitive Christian and thus too the modern proclamation of Christ can be protected from the suspicion that it is not founded on a historical fact, but is merely an asser- tion, a projection of faith, or even a pure myth, an apotheosis." On Being Christian, p. 159. See also his Menschwerdung Gottes: Eine Einführung in Hegels Theologisches Denken als Prolegomena zu einer künftigen Christologie, Ökumenische Forschungen, Soteriologische Abteilung, vol. 1 (Freiburg: Herder, 1970), p. 593. Cf. Schillebeeckx, Jesus, pp. 73, 270; Interim Report, pp. 27, 31-32. The question remains whether this claim is materially significant in light of the paucity of knowledge actually obtain- able by an historical retrieval. Küng's claim that the proclamation of Christ must be founded upon "historical fact," is, therefore, ambiguous. Insofar as it suggests that it must be shown that the actual Jesus existed and that his actual life and teaching does not conclusively falsify traditional Christian claims about his significance, the claim is intelligible. In this case, histori- cal retrieval provides a negative or corrective, rather than a materially constitutive, service. It establishes the basis upon which Christian faith builds, but it does not supply the essential content of that faith, which con- sists in the statement of the decisive significance of the vision of reality and mode of living disclosed by the existential-historical Jesus. If, on the other hand, Küng's claim means that the Christian interpretation of Jesus must be shown not to be a "projection of faith," it is not at all clear how historical retrieval could successfully accomplish that task. In this case, one could easily fall into the same trap of the nineteenth-century Catholics, i.e., making historical research subject to theological presuppositions and using historical information about Jesus to verify faith claims about the Christ.

[15] Küng is constrained to admit: "Naturally historical-critical research into the life of Jesus neither desires nor has the capacity to prove that the man

Jesus of Nazareth is in reality the Christ of God. . . . However, historical-critical research can aid us in assuring that the Christ in whom we believe is really the man Jesus of Nazareth and not some other person or perhaps no one at all. Our belief in the true Christ can all too easily be distorted into a superstitious attachment to an imaginary Christ or to a mere sign or symbol. . . . The projections of belief as well as unbelief must undergo scrutiny from the perspective of the genuine historical reality of Jesus." "Consensus," p. 7. Cf. Schillebeeckx, Jesus, pp. 73-74: "Historical study of Jesus is extremely important, it gives a concrete content to faith; but it can never be a verification of faith. A historically reconstructed picture of Jesus can never do more than allow for or keep a place for the Christian interpretation; it cannot from its own standpoint make this obligatory." (Emphasis mine.) Schillebeeckx specifies further that "the historian's quest for Jesus is theologically relevant because in its thematic import its aim is to help clarify the continuing 'Opposite Presence' of Jesus of Nazareth, as norm and criterion, vis-à-vis the churches and all who consider that salvation is to be found in Jesus." Ibid., p. 77.

[16] Harvey, Historian, p. 282.

[17] Ibid., p. 287.

[18] See Harvey, "Christology," p. 11. Although this essay represents a modification of his position in The Historian and the Believer, it still affirms a conception of faith consonant with the earlier work. See Historian, pp. 280-81, where Harvey asserts: "Indeed, if we understand properly what is meant by faith, then this faith has no clear relation to any particular set of historical beliefs at all. Faith has to do with one's confidence in God, which is to say, with one's surrender of his attempts to establish his own righteousness and his acceptance of his life and creation as a gift and a responsibility. It is trust and commitment."

[19] Küng, On Being Christian, p. 148; Menschwerdung Gottes, p. 608. Schillebeeckx, Jesus, pp. 21, 482, 484. Küng and Schillebeeckx are much more aware than their nineteenth-century predecessors of the creative and not merely retentive function of the evangelists' faith. They therefore want to occupy a median position, at a distance both from the credulity of their predecessors and from the skepticism represented by Gager. See Küng, On Being Christian, p. 157; Menschwerdung Gottes, pp. 590-91. Schillebeeckx, Jesus, pp. 34-35, 86. Cf. John Gager, "The Gospels and Jesus: Some Doubts about Method," Journal of Religion 54 (1974):272-74.

[20] Ogden, _Point_, p. 51.

[21] "My position, however, is that a quest for Jesus is and would be theologically unnecessary, regardless of any question whether it is also historically possible. This is so, I maintain, because the real subject of the christological assertion is not the historical Jesus, or, as we may now say more precisely, the _empirical_-historical Jesus, for which the earliest stratum of Christian witness must be used as historical source. Rather, the subject of the christological assertion is correctly identified formally as the _existential_-historical Jesus, for which this same earliest stratum of Christian witness plays the very different role of theological norm." _Ibid._, pp. 55-56. See also p. 63. Cf. David Tracy, _The Analogical Imagination: Christian Theology and the Culture of Pluralism_ (New York: Crossroad, 1981), p. 243, note 12; p. 245, note 23. Like Ogden, Tracy regards the quest of the historical Jesus as theologically unnecessary. But unlike Ogden, he admits that the reconstruction of the historical Jesus is possible, though difficult. Tracy further distinguishes his position from Ogden's by making the earliest apostolic witness to Jesus "the major but not sole corrective" of the tradition. See ibid., p. 244, note 13.

[22] Ogden carefully distinguishes between what the earliest witnesses asserted and what they assumed about Jesus. _Point_, pp. 58-61.

[23] See Schillebeeckx, _Jesus_, pp. 81-85, 440. Schillebeeckx and Küng reject the radical Bultmannian disjunction between Jesus the proclaimer and Christ the proclaimed. See ibid., pp. 66, 72, and Küng, _On Being Christian_, p. 157. For this reason they find the alternative of regarding the earliest stratum of Jesus-tradition exclusively either as the witness of faith or as historical report to be unacceptable. Cf. Elizabeth A. Johnson, "The Theological Relevance of the Historical Jesus: A Debate and a Thesis," _The Thomist_ 48 (1984):18-19, where she states: "The very existence of the gospel genre, coming chronologically as it did _after_ kerygmatizing and mythologizing tendencies had taken root in Christian consciousness, points to the Christian communities' concern not only for the presence of the glorified Lord but also with the actual history of Jesus of Nazareth, in whom God was believed to have acted, and acted _before_ there ever were believers. In the gospel genre, an historical account of a past event is precisely the form that the Church's word takes. ...Theology is interested in historical information about Jesus of Nazareth because the gospel tradition itself considers this important."

[24] The question of intelligibility is the concern of the person who wants to know "what historians on strictly historical grounds can tell me about the 'historical Jesus.'" But for the theologian, whose primary concern is the appropriateness of christological, not historical, assertions: "The 'historical Jesus' is at best a relatively external and secondary criterion of appropriateness for certain necessary assumptions or presuppositions of that witness to Jesus." Tracy, Analogical Imagination, p. 238. See Schillebeeckx, Interim Report, p. 29, where he engages in an apparent, but not entirely fair, critique of Tracy: "Faith in search of historical understanding is an intrinsic consequence of the fact that Christianity is not just concerned with a decisive message from God, but at the same time with the person of Jesus Christ, someone who appeared in our history and therefore must also be given a place within the whole of the history of God with us. This puts a fundamental question-mark against purely literary-critical exegesis, which is only interested in 'texts', and has an almost self-consciously modern disdain when it comes to asking historical questions about Jesus." Cf. Johnson, p. 21. In the references of both Schillebeeckx and Johnson, the term "historical" is used in an imprecise sense. At this point, Ogden's distinction between an empirical-historical and an existential-historical interest is of considerable help. By stating that faith has an intrinsic interest in the existential-historical Jesus, Schillebeeckx could maintain his concern for the historical character of Christianity and for its personal referent without demanding that retrieval of the empirical-historical Jesus be constitutive of theology's task.

[25] Strauss, Leben Jesu (1835), 1:vii.

[26] See Harvey, "Christology," pp. 12-13. Cf. Schillebeeckx's discussion of the two types of Christianity, which are based upon two different types of christology. Jesus, p. 30.

[27] In his desire to establish the theological necessity of historical knowledge about Jesus, Schillebeeckx seems to fall victim to some of the problems that befell the old and new quests—despite his explicit repudiation of both (Jesus, pp. 34, 68, 70). See Interim Report, p. 28, where in reference to a proper understanding of Christian faith, he says: "It is not just a question of a human event in which people are opened up in Jesus to their own deepest understanding of life—Jesus, as the interpreter of the deepest and most decisive human existential experience—but at the same time of a confession that in Jesus we know ourselves to be addressed by God's own intention concerning Jesus. In that case God does not sanction a cultural and anthropological model or process, but this man Jesus. And therefore it

is important to know who this man really was in history." (Emphasis mine.) Concerning the old quest, see Schweitzer. Concerning the new, see James M. Robinson, A New Quest of the Historical Jesus (London: SCM Press, 1959).

[28] Tracy, Analogical Imagination, p. 243, note 12. Cf. Schillebeeckx, Jesus, p. 65: "The question ... is whether all the Christological patterns are pure projections of our own, time after time prevailing, incessantly changing interpretations of reality. Once somebody has discovered final salvation in Jesus, it is natural (and proper) that he should project his own expectations and ways of envisaging the 'true being' of man on to Jesus. Correlatively, of course, this means that a real facet in Jesus' life must at least point in that particular direction if we are not to turn Jesus into a mere receptacle for our own predilections, an arbitrary 'cipher,' that we are manipulating; in that case, surely, Jesus might very well be left out of it."

SELECTED BIBLIOGRAPHY

Primary Sources: Nineteenth Century

Baader, Franz von. "Ueber das Leben Jesu von Strauß auf Veranlassung
einer in der Allgemeinen Zeitung (10. Jänner 1836) Anzeige dieser
Schrift aus einem Sendschreiben an Herrn Doctor von Malfatti in
Wien." In Franz von Baader's Sämmtliche Werke, Erste
Hauptabtheilung, 7:261-70. Leipzig: Hermann Bethmann, 1850-60.

Baur, Ferdinand Christian. Ausgewählte Werke in Einzelausgaben:
Historisch-kritische Untersuchungen zum neuen Testament. Edited
by Klaus Scholder. Stuttgart: Friedr. Frommann, 1963.

_____. Kritische Untersuchungen über die kanonischen Evangelien, ihr
Verhältniss zu einander, ihren Charakter und Ursprung. Tübingen:
Ludwig Fues, 1847.

_____. Symbolik und Mythologie oder die Naturreligion des Alterthums.
3 vols. Stuttgart: J. B. Metzler, 1824-25.

Hafen, Johann Baptist. "Zweiter Bericht über 'das Leben Jesu,' kritisch
bearbeitet von Dr. Strauß, oder ausführliche Anzeige der für und
gegen das genannte Werk bisher erschienenen Schriften."
Allgemeine Kirchen-Zeitung für Deutschland und die Schweiz
(Lucerne), 6 January 1837, pp. 1-5; 13 January 1837, p. 9-15; 20
January 1837, pp. 19-21; 4 February 1837, pp. 35-37; 18 February
1837, pp. 51-55.

_____. "Dritter Bericht über das Straußische Leben Jesu oder die
Kritiker u. der Antikritiker." Allgemeine Kirchen-Zeitung für
Deutschland und die Schweiz (Lucerne), 22 July 1837, pp. 233-38; 29
July 1837, pp. 241-45; 12 August 1837, pp. 257-60.

Hagel, Maurus. Dr. Strauß' Leben Jesu aus dem Standpunkt des
Katholizismus betrachtet. Kempten: Jos. Kösel'sche Buchhandlung,
1839.

Hegel, Georg Wilhelm Friedrich. Grundlinien der Philosophie des Rechts.
Berlin: Nicolai, 1821.

_____. Lectures on the History of Philosophy. Translated by E. S.
Haldane and F. H. Simpson. New York: Humanities Press, 1963.

_____ . Lectures on the Philosophy of Religion. 3 vols. Translated by E. B. Speirs and J. B. Sanderson. New York: Humanities Press, 1962.

_____ . The Philosophy of History. Translated and with a Preface by J. Sibree. New York: Dover Publications, 1956.

_____ . Sämtliche Werke. 20 vols. Edited by Hermann Glockner. Stuttgart-Bad Canstatt: Friedrich Frommann, 1965.

Historisch-politische Blätter für das katholische Deutschland. "Erinnerung an Möhler." 1 (1838):141-49.

_____ . "Historischer und mythischer Christus." 9 (1842):401-27, 529-41, 673-84; 10 (1842):175-89.

_____ . "Ein Straußisches Curiosum." 11 (1843):491-92.

_____ . "Die Triarier der Negation." 14 (1844):673-703.

Hug, Johann Leonhard. Gutachten über das Leben Jesu kritisch bearbeitet von David Friedrich Strauß. Freiburg: Friedrich Wagner'sche Buchhandlung, 1840; reprint ed., 1854.

_____ . Hug's Introduction to the New Testament. Translated from the 3d German ed. by David Fosdick, Jr., with notes by M. Stuart. Andover: Gould and Newman, 1836.

_____ . "Ist das Entstehen des Christenthums auf natürliche Weise erklärbar?" Zeitschrift für die Geistlichkeit des Erzbisthums Freiburg (1834), pp. 176-244.

Der Katholik. "Reflexionen aus dem Standpunkte eines christlichen Weltbürgers über das Leben Jesu von Dr. D. Fr. Strauß." 63 (1837):279-96.

_____ . "Dr. Strauß und seine Stellung zur protestantischen Theologie." 79 (1841):45-52.

Kuhn, Johannes Evangelist von. "Ueber Apostelgeschichte 5, 36.37." Jahrbücher für Theologie und christliche Philosophie 1 (1834):3-34.

_____ . "Ueber Glauben und Wissen, mit Rücksicht auf extreme Ansichten und Richtungen der Gegenwart." Theologische Quartalschrift 21 (1839):382-503.

_____ . "Hermeneutik und Kritik in ihrer Anwendung auf die evangelische Geschichte." Jahrbücher für Theologie und christliche Philosophie 7 (1836):1-50.

_____ . Das Leben Jesu wissenschaftlich bearbeitet. Mainz: 1838; reprint ed., Frankfurt: Minerva, 1968.

_____ . "Ueber Matthäus 23,35." Jahrbücher für Theologie und christliche Philosophie 1 (1834):339-72.

_____ . "Rezension von David Schulz, Die christliche Lehre vom Glauben (1834)." Jahrbücher für Theologie und christliche Philosophie 4 (1835):109-24.

_____ . "Von dem schriftstellerischen Charakter der Evangelien im Verhältniss zu der apostolischen Predigt und den apostolischen Briefen." Jahrbücher für Theologie und christliche Philosophie 6 (1836):33-91.

_____ . "Selbstanzeige über das Leben Jesu, wissenschaftlich bearbeitet von Dr. Johannes Kuhn." Theologische Quartalschrift 20 (1838):564-75.

Mack, Martin Joseph. "Bericht über die kritische Bearbeitung des Lebens Jesu von Dr. Strauß." Theologische Quartalschrift 19 (1837):35-91, 259-325, 426-505, 633-86.

Möhler, Johann Adam. See "Erinnerung an Möhler," Historisch-politische Blätter für das katholische Deutschland. 1 (1838):141-49.

Schütz, A. von. "Die Stellung der protestantischen Theologie zu des Dr. Strauß Leben Jesu." Der Katholik 65:60-76, 152-66.

Sprissler, Joseph. Drei Beiträge zu den Vereinsblättern. Hechingen: Georg Egersdorff, 1849.

_____ . "Rezension über das Leben Jesu, kritisch bearbeitet von D. Fr. Strauß." Freimüthige Blätter über Theologie und Kirchenthum, N. F. 6 (1835):306-36; 8 (1836):77-110.

Strauss, David Friedrich. Ausgewählte Briefe von David Friedrich Strauß. Edited by Eduard Zeller. Bonn: Emil Strauss, 1895.

_____. Die christliche Glaubenslehre, in ihrer Entwicklung und im Kampfe mit der modernen Wissenschaft. 2 vols. Tübingen: Osiander, 1840.

_____. In Defense of My Life of Jesus Against the Hegelians. Translated by Marilyn Chapin Massey. Hamden: Archon Books, 1983.

_____. Gesammelte Schriften: Nach des Verfassers letztwilligen Bestimmungen zusammengestellt. 12 vols. Edited by Eduard Zeller. Bonn: Emil Strauss, 1876-78.

_____. Das Leben Jesu, kritisch bearbeitet. 1st ed. Tübingen: C. F. Osiander, 1835.

_____. Das Leben Jesu, kritisch bearbeitet. 2d ed. Tübingen: C. F. Osiander, 1837.

_____. Das Leben Jesu, kritisch bearbeitet. 3d ed. Tübingen: C. F. Osiander, 1838.

_____. Das Leben Jesu, kritisch bearbeitet. 4th ed. Tübingen: C. F. Osiander, 1840.

_____. Das Leben Jesu für das deutsche Volk bearbeitet. Leipzig: F. A. Brockhaus, 1864.

_____. The Life of Jesus Critically Examined. The Lives of Jesus Series. Edited and with and Introduction by Peter Hodgson. Translated by George Eliot. Philadelphia: Fortress Press, 1972.

_____. Streitschriften zur Vertheidigung meiner Schrift über das Leben Jesu und zur Charakteristik der gegenwärtigen Theologie. Tübingen: C. F. Osiander, 1838.

_____. Zwei Friedliche Blätter. Altona: J. F. Hammerich, 1839.

Primary Sources: Twentieth Century

Harvey, Van Austin. "A Christology for Barabasses." Perkins Journal of
Theology 29 (1976):1-13.

_____. The Historian and the Believer. New York: Macmillan, 1966.

Küng, Hans. Menschwerdung Gottes: Eine Einführung in Hegels
Theologisches Denken als Prolegomena zu einer künftigen
Christologie. Ökumenische Forschungen, Soteriologische Abteilung,
vol. 1. Freiburg: Herder, 1970.

_____. On Being a Christian. Translated by Edward Quinn. Garden City:
Doubleday, 1976.

Ogden, Schubert M. The Point of Christology. San Francisco: Harper and
Row, 1982.

Scheffczyk, Leo, ed. Grundfragen der Christologie Heute. Freiburg: Herder,
1975.

Schillebeeckx, Edward. Interim Report on the Books "Jesus" and "Christ."
New York: Crossroad, 1981.

_____. Jesus: An Experiment in Theology. Translated by Hubert
Hoskins. New York: Seabury Press, A Crossroad Book, 1979.

Swidler, Leonard, ed. Consensus in Theology? Philadelphia: Westminster
Press, 1980.

Tracy, David. The Analogical Imagination: Christian Theology and the
Culture of Pluralism. New York: Crossroad, 1981.

_____. Blessed Rage for Order: The New Pluralism in Theology. New
York: Seabury Press, A Crossroad Book, 1975.

Secondary Sources

Adam, Karl. Gesammelte Aufsätze zur Dogmengeschichte und Theologie
der Gegenwart. Augsburg: P. Haas, 1936.

Backhaus, Gunther. <u>Kerygma</u> <u>und</u> <u>Mythos</u> <u>bei</u> <u>David</u> <u>Friedrich</u> <u>Strauß</u> <u>und</u> <u>Rudolf</u> <u>Bultmann</u>. Hamburg-Bergstedt: Herbert Reich Evangelischer Verlag, 1956.

Bantle, Franz Xaver. "Evangelienkritik und Glaube eines führenden Wessenbergianers--Pfarrer Joseph Sprißler und das 'Leben Jesu' des Dav. Fr. Strauß." <u>Münchener</u> <u>Theologische</u> <u>Zeitschrift</u> 28 (1977):366-82.

Barnikol, Ernst. "Der Briefwechsel zwischen Strauß und Baur: Ein quellenmäßiger Beitrag zur Strauß-Baur Forschung." <u>Zeitschrift</u> <u>für</u> <u>Kirchengeschichte</u> 73 (1962):74-125.

Brandt, Hans-Jürgen. <u>Eine</u> <u>katholische</u> <u>Universität</u> <u>in</u> <u>Deutschland?</u> <u>Das</u> <u>Ringen</u> <u>der</u> <u>Katholiken</u> <u>in</u> <u>Deutschland</u> <u>um</u> <u>eine</u> <u>Universitätsbildung</u> <u>im</u> <u>Neunzehnten</u> <u>Jahrhundert</u>. Cologne: Böhlau Verlag, 1981.

Burtchaell, James Tunstead. <u>Catholic</u> <u>Theories</u> <u>of</u> <u>Biblical</u> <u>Inspiration</u> <u>Since</u> <u>1810</u>: <u>A</u> <u>Review</u> <u>and</u> <u>Critique</u>. Cambridge: Cambridge University Press, 1969.

Courth, Franz. "Die Evangelienkritik des D. Fr. Strauß im Echo seiner Zeitgenossen." In <u>Historische</u> <u>Kritik</u> <u>in</u> <u>der</u> <u>Theologie</u>, pp. 60-98. Edited by Georg Schwaiger. Göttingen: Vandenhoeck and Ruprecht, 1980.

_____. <u>Das</u> <u>Leben</u> <u>Jesu</u> <u>von</u> <u>David</u> <u>Friedrich</u> <u>Strauss</u> <u>in</u> <u>der</u> <u>Kritik</u> <u>Johann</u> <u>Evangelist</u> <u>Kuhns</u>: <u>Ein</u> <u>Beitrag</u> <u>zur</u> <u>Auseinandersetzung</u> <u>der</u> <u>Katholischen</u> <u>Tübinger</u> <u>Schule</u> <u>mit</u> <u>dem</u> <u>deutschen</u> <u>Idealismus</u>. Göttingen: Vandenhoeck and Ruprecht, 1975.

Cromwell, Richard S. <u>David</u> <u>Friedrich</u> <u>Strauss</u> <u>and</u> <u>His</u> <u>Place</u> <u>in</u> <u>Modern</u> <u>Thought</u>. Foreword by Wilhelm Pauck. Fair Lawn, New Jersey: R. E. Burdick, 1974.

Fitzer, Joseph. <u>Moehler</u> <u>and</u> <u>Baur</u> <u>in</u> <u>Controversy</u>, <u>1832-38</u>: <u>Romantic-Idealist</u> <u>Assessment</u> <u>of</u> <u>the</u> <u>Reformation</u> <u>and</u> <u>Counter-Reformation</u>. AAR Studies in Religion, vol. 7. Tallahassee: American Academy of Religion, 1974.

Fries, Heinrich. <u>Johannes</u> <u>von</u> <u>Kuhn</u>. Wegbereiter heutiger Theologie. Graz: Styria Verlag, 1973.

Fries, Heinrich and Schwaiger, Georg, eds. Katholische Theologen Deutschlands im 19. Jahrhundert. 3 vols. Munich: Kösel Verlag, 1975.

Geiselmann, Josef Rupert. "Der Glaube an Jesus Christus --Mythos oder Geschichte? Zur Auseinandersetzung Joh. Ev. Kuhns mit David Friedrich Strauß." Theologische Quartalschrift 129 (1949):257-77, 418-39.

_____ . Die Katholische Tübinger Schule: Ihre Theologische Eigenart. Freiburg: Herder, 1964.

_____ . Die lebendige Überlieferung als Norm des christlichen Glaubens: Die apostolische Tradition in der kirchlichen Verkündigung--das Formalprinzip des Katholizismus dargestellt im Geiste der Traditionslehre von Ev. Kuhn. Freiburg: Herder, 1959.

Graf, Friedrich Wilhelm. Kritik und Pseudo-Spekulation: David Friedrich Strauß als Dogmatiker im Kontext der positionellen Theologie seiner Zeit. Münchener Monographien zur historischen und systematischen Theologie, vol. 7. Munich: Chr. Kaiser, 1982.

Grassl, Hans. "Franz von Baader (1765-1841)." In Katholische Theologen Deutschlands im 19.Jahrhundert,1:274-302.

Hagen, August. Gestalten aus dem schwäbischen Katholizismus: Zweiter Teil. Stuttgart: Schwabenverlag, 1950.

Harris, Horton. David Friedrich Strauss and His Theology. Cambridge: Cambridge University Press, 1973.

Hartlich, Christian and Sachs, Walter. Der Ursprung des Mythosbegriffs in der modernen Bibelwissenschaft. Tübingen: J. C. B. Mohr (Paul Siebeck), 1952.

Harvey, Van Austin. "D. F. Strauss's Life of Jesus Revisited." Church History 30 (1961):191-211.

Hausrath, Adolf. David Friedrich Strauß und die Theologie seiner Zeit. 2 vols. Heidelberg: Bassermann, 1876-78.

Heyer, Friedrich. The Catholic Church From 1648 to 1870. Translated by D. W. D. Shaw. London: Adam and Charles Black, 1969.

Hillerbrand, Hans J. A Fellowship of Discontent. New York: Harper and Row, 1967.

Hodgson, Peter C. Ferdinand Christian Baur on the Writing of Church History. New York: Oxford University Press, 1968.

Jedin, Hubert and Dolan, John, eds. History of the Church. 10 vols. New York: Crossroad, 1981.

Kahnis, Karl Friedrich August. Der innere Gang des deutschen Protestantismus seit Mitte des vorigen Jahrhunderts. 2d ed. Leipzig: Dörffling and Franke, 1860.

Keller, Erwin. "Johann Leonhard Hug (1765-1846)." In Katholische Theologen Deutschlands im 19.Jahrhundert,1:253-73.

Lang, Wilhelm. "Ferdinand Baur und David Friedrich Strauß: Erster Teil." Preußische Jahrbücher 160 (1915):123-144.

_____ . "Ferdinand Baur und David Friedrich Strauß: Zweiter Teil." Preußische Jahrbücher 161 (1915):123-144.

_____ . "Das Leben Jesu von Strauß." Preußische Jahrbücher 13 (1864):465-84, 587-613.

Lawler, Edwina. "Critical Response to Schleiermacher and Strauss, 1800-1850." Ph.D. dissertation, Drew University, 1980.

Lichtenberger, F[rederic Auguste]. History of German Theology in the Nineteenth Century. Edited and translated by W. Hastie. Edinburgh: T. and T. Clark, 1889.

Lösch, Stephan. Die Anfänge der Tübinger Theologischen Quartalschrift (1819-1831). Rottenburg: Bader'sche Verlagsbuchhandlung, 1938.

_____ . "Die katholisch-theologischen Fakultäten zu Tübingen und Giessen (1830-50)." Theologische Quartalschrift 108 (1927):159-208.

Mackintosh, Hugh R. Types of Modern Theology: Schleiermacher to Barth. 8th ed. London: Nisbet, 1937; reprinted, 1952.

Maier, Adalbert. Gedächtnissrede auf Joh. Leonh. Hug, bei dessen akademischer Todtenfeier in der Universitäts-Kirche zu Freiburg am 11.März 1847. Freiburg: Universitäts-Buchdruckerei von Hermann M. Poppen, 1847.

Massey, Marilyn Chapin. Christ Unmasked: The Meaning of the Life of Jesus in German Politics. Chapel Hill, University of North Carolina Press, 1983.

_____. "David Friedrich Strauss's Christological Thought: The Influence of Friedrich Schleiermacher." Ph.D. dissertation, University of Chicago, 1973.

Müller, Gotthold. Identität und Immanenz: Zur Genese der Theologie von David Friedrich Strauß. Zurich: EVZ-Verlag, 1968.

Nippold, Friedrich. Handbuch der neuesten Kirchengeschichte seit der Restauration von 1814. 2d, revised ed. Elberfeld: R. L. Friderichs, 1868.

Noonan, John T. "Hegel and Strauss: The Dialectic and the Gospel." Catholic Biblical Quarterly 12 (1950):136-52.

Rapp, Adolf. "Baur und Strauß." Blätter für württembergische Kirchengeschichte 54 (1954):182-86.

_____. "Baur und Strauß in ihrer Stellung zueinander und zum Christentum." Blätter für württembergische Kirchengeschichte 52 (1952):95-149.

Reinhardt, Rudolf. Tübinger Theologen und ihre Theologie. Tübingen: J. C. B. Mohr (Paul Siebeck), 1977.

Robertson, J. M. A History of Freethought in the Nineteenth Century. 2 vols. London: Watts and Co., 1929.

Sandberger, Jörg. David Friedrich Strauß als theologischer Hegelianer. Studien zur Theologie und Geistesgeschichte des Neunzehnten Jahrhunderts, vol. 5. Göttingen: Vandenhoeck and Ruprecht, 1972.

Scheele, Paul-Werner. Johann Adam Möhler. Wegbereiter heutiger Theologie. Graz: Styria Verlag, 1969.

Schnabel, Franz. _Deutsche Geschichte im Neunzehnten Jahrhundert_. Vol. 4: _Die religiösen Kräfte_. 2d ed. Freiburg: Herder, 1951.

Schwaiger, Georg, ed. _Historische Kritik in der Theologie_. Göttingen: Vandenhoeck and Ruprecht, 1975.

Schweitzer, Albert. _The Quest of the Historical Jesus_. Translated by W. Montgomery with a Preface by F. C. Burkitt. London: A. and C. Black, 1910.

Slenczka, Reinhard. _Geschichtlichkeit und Personsein Jesu Christi_. Studien zur christologischen Problematik der historischen Jesusfrage. Göttingen: Vandenhoeck and Ruprecht, 1967.

Smart, Ninian; Clayton, John; Katz, Steven T.; and Sherry, Patrick, eds. _Nineteenth Century Religious Thought in the West_. 3 vols. Cambridge: Cambridge University Press, 1985.

Specht, Thomas. _Geschichte des Kgl. Lyceums Dillingen (1804-1904): Festschrift zur Feier seines 100jährigen Bestehens_. Regensburg: G. J. Manz, 1904.

Stempfle, Laurentius. _Erinnerung an Dr. Maurus Hagel_. Dillingen: Joseph Friedrich, 1843.

Traub, D. "Die Stiftsakten über David Friedrich Strauß." _Blätter für württembergische Kirchengeschichte,_ N. F. 27 (1923):48-64.

_____ . "Die Stiftsakten über David Friedrich Strauß, Nachtrag." _Blätter für württembergische Kirchengeschichte,_ N. F. 28 (1924):15-22.

Türk, Hans Günther. _Der philosophisch-theologische Ansatz bei Johann Evangelist Kuhn_. Theologie im Übergang, vol. 5. Frankfurt: Peter D. Lang, 1979.

Weizsäcker, Carl. "David Friedrich Strauß und der württembergische Kirchendienst." _Jahrbücher für deutsche Theologie_ 20 (1875):641-60.

Werner, Karl. _Geschichte der katholischen Theologie: Seit dem Trienter Concil bis zur Gegenwart_. Munich: J. G. Cotta'sche Buchhandlung, 1866.

Wolf, Ernst. "Die Verlegenheit der Theologie: David Friedrich Strauß und die Bibelkritik." In Libertas Christiana: Festschrift für Friedrich Delekat, pp. 219-39. Theologische Abhandlungen, vol. 26. Munich: Christian Kaiser, 1957.

Wolfinger, Franz. Der Glaube nach Johann Evangelist von Kuhn: Wesen, Formen, Herkunft, Entwicklung. Göttingen: Vandenhoeck and Ruprecht, 1972.

Yerkes, James. The Christology of Hegel. Albany: State University of New York Press, 1983.

Ziegler, Theobald. David Friedrich Strauß. 2 vols. Strasbourg: K. J. Trübner, 1908.

INDEX

98; use of historical criticism, 96, 99, 100

Marheineke, Philip, 7, 19

Michaelis, J. D., 125

Miracles, 10, 58-59, 94, 98, 104, 105, 129, 137, 138, 161, 162

Möhler, Johann Adam, 91, 153, 156, 160, 164, 169; assessment of Jesus, 160-161, 162; construal of faith, 160-161, 163; understanding of miracle, 161, 162

Myth, 6, 10, 11, 12, 47, 50-51, 53, 93, 96, 98, 107, 131, 167, 182

Mythical School, 11

Ogden, Schubert, 185, 186, 187

Old Testament: influence on gospels, 47, 96-97, 108, 132, 182

Pantheism, 8, 58, 104, 154, 158, 166, 169

Paulus, H. E. G., 53, 125, 138

Phillips, George, 156

Protestantism, 67, 70, 93, 153-158, 164, 168

Rationalism, 6, 92, 136, 157, 160, 169

Reimarus, H. S., 9, 154

Representation. See Vorstellung

Sailer, J. M., 92

Schelling, F. W. J., 14, 166

Schillebeeckx, Edward, 185, 186, 187

Schleiermacher, Friedrich, 7, 8-9, 59, 61, 102, 155

Schütz, A. von, 154, 155

Schweitzer, Albert, 1

Semler, J. S., 125

Sprissler, Joseph, 153, 166-168, 169; construal of faith, 168; use of historical criticism, 167, 168

Strauss, David Friedrich, 1, 5-26, 181, 186, 188; assessment of Jesus, 22-23, 24-27, 102, 139, 182; conception of religion, 12-13, 22, 93; construal of faith, 24-25, 65-66, 69, 101, 182; his Christian Faith, 18; intent of his Life of Jesus, 7-8, 15-16, 24, 69; mythical theory of, 10, 11-12, 22, 47, 50, 53, 93, 96-98, 132-133; on christology, 8, 21, 22, 23, 25, 69; presuppositions of, 57, 93, 94, 130; understanding of miracle, 9-10, 59, 94, 128; understanding of scientific scholarship, 9-10; use of Hegel, 7, 13, 17-19, 20; use of historical criticism, 21, 52, 57, 94-96, 130, 134

Supernaturalism, 6, 94, 104, 137, 139, 168

DATE DUE

HIGHSMITH   #LO-45220